THE CELT

PRAYER RHYTHMS
fourfold patterns for each day

RAY SIMPSON

kevin mayhew

The Celtic Prayer Book is published in four volumes:

Volume One
Prayer Rhythms: fourfold patterns for each day

Volume Two
Saints of the Isles: a year of feasts

Volume Three
Healing the Land: natural seasons, sacraments and special services

Volume Four
Great Celtic Christians: alternative worship

First published in 2003 by

KEVIN MAYHEW LTD
Buxhall, Stowmarket, Suffolk, IP14 3BW
E-mail: info@kevinmayhewltd.com

KINGSGATE PUBLISHING INC
1000 Pannell Street, Suite G, Columbia, MO 65201
E-mail: sales@kingsgatepublishing.com

9 8 7 6 5 4 3 2 1 0

ISBN 184417 077 2
Catalogue No 1500591

Front cover: St Matthew and his symbol, from *The Lindisfarne Gospels* by
Janet Backhouse. Reproduced by courtesy of the British Library
Cover design by Angela Selfe
Edited by Nick Fawcett
Typesetting by Richard Weaver

Printed and Bound in China

For the Churches and households of Britain,
Ireland and the English-speaking world
from The Community of Aidan and Hilda

Contents

Introduction

These patterns of worship draw deeply from the scriptures, the streets, the saints and the soil. They are inclusive of gender and types of people, and reflect the belief that as we reconnect prayer to the rhythms of our daily lives we will be drawn more fully into God's purposes. They represent the work of many years and fill a widely acknowledged vacuum.

Many people in the emerging Church look for patterns of worship that embrace but transcend the confines of one denomination, and that draw on spiritual roots that precede the Catholic/Protestant and the Orthodox/Catholic divides. Rigidly formal patterns of prayer are not, for many, a natural way to approach the Divine, yet God is worthy of the best and most hallowed devotions we can draw upon. *The Celtic Prayer Book*, Volumes One to Four, seeks to address these issues. It draws on diverse sources within, and occasionally beyond, the main Church traditions.

If many people find denominational liturgies too cerebral, others find 'alternative' liturgies too 'feely'. A book of common prayer needs to provide liturgies that people of all temperaments may benefit from.

Charismatic and non-liturgical worshippers increasingly see the need for a form of daily worship which is as natural as breathing, and which, because it does not need to be devised from scratch, is not energy-draining.

Prayer Rhythms, the first volume in *The Celtic Prayer Book* series, and the subsequent volumes, are offered by the Community of Aidan and Hilda to the wider Church, to households and to individuals as a framework for a renewal of peoples' worship.

Rhythms of the day and prayer stops

Christians in the first centuries after Christ prayed in harmony with the rhythms of the sun's rising, zenith and setting, as did Jews before and Muslims after them. This insight developed, until some communities punctured day and night with prayer and praise every three hours, that is eight times every twenty-four hours. The 'TwentyFourSeven' movement is restoring something of this today. Although such a pattern is not practical for any one individual today, our twenty-four-hour society lends itself to the restoration of the eight prayer periods, to be used according to the circumstances of different people. The fourfold patterns of worship provide for four of these eight prayer periods. The introductory section on prayer stops provides brief prayers for the other four.

Household and church candle-lightings

The material for most of the seasons begins with a choice of candle-lightings. These are suitable for households and cell groups and may precede a meal. In churches they should precede the normal patterns of worship.

Vigil prayers for the three Lents

In the Celtic tradition there are three seasons when Christians offload excess and create more time to contemplate God's will. These are the three forty-day Lents: before Easter, before the Nativity and after Pentecost. Each of these seasons is introduced by vigil prayers for personal use.

Creative activities

At the end of each day or season there is a list of suitable creative activities. Some worshipping communities will omit these, many will engage in them on special occasions, and others will include them in their normal worship patterns. As the text indicates, these are most often appropriate following the New Testament reading and any teaching, or before or after the printed patterns of worship.

The seasons

The Church seasons are included in this volume. Worship patterns for the natural seasons are included in Volume Three, *Healing the Land: natural seasons, sacraments and special services.*

Lament, music and movement

Some of the patterns of worship, especially during the three Lents, provide for Lament, rather than a perfunctory confession, and restores a biblical reality. Prophets (for example Micah) and priests sometimes publicly wept because of the peoples' sins (Micah 1:8). Celtic bards had laments for many occasions.

Recorded or live music for people to listen to can range from contemplative chanting to the sounds of nature.

Since preferred styles vary greatly, we make no reference to body movements in the text. Appropriate body movements may include: kneeling (confession or lament); sitting (listening, reading aloud or intercession); palms open (adoration); standing with raised arms (praise); prostration (silent vigil); walking in procession (festivals) or in circles (protecting prayers); marching in unified movements (proclamation) or dancing (informal celebration).

Bible readings and storytelling

Each Morning and Evening Prayer provides for a psalm, an Old Testament and a New Testament reading. Those who wish for a shorter form of Morning and Evening Prayer should omit one of the Bible readings and the Proclamation that follows. For the benefit of occasional users one or more suggested passages are indicated, but regular worshippers will use a lectionary. Unless another lectionary is used, we recommend the *Revised Common Lectionary,* published by the Consultation on Common Texts (a body representative of all major branches of the church in USA and Canada) in 1992. It was adopted by the English Language Liturgical

Consultation (ELLC) whose members come from ecumenical associations in English-speaking countries and continents. The Roman Catholic Church, the Anglican Church and most other churches have adopted it, in some cases with minor adaptations. The *Revised Common Lectionary* is truly therefore the lectionary of the world Church.

Storytelling is a vital part of the Celtic tradition. Bible readings may be told as stories, dramatised, projected on to a screen and read by everyone, or read by one or several readers. They may be enhanced with projections of scenes that illustrate the text.

Sights, scents, sounds and touch

Early Celtic Christians used the 'five-stringed harp' in their worship, meaning the five senses.

Water is a symbol of baptism – that is, immersion in the presence of God – and should be used regularly to remind us that this is to be a daily experience. Water can be sprinkled, using a sprig; worshippers may be invited to make the sign of the cross on their foreheads or palms with water. We encourage churches to have a well, baptistery or fountain in or near their worship building.

Incense need not be the preserve of any one liturgical tradition. Its sweet-smelling smoke lends itself for use in the late-autumn period when we focus on the eternal offering of praise and prayer (like incense) offered up by the saints and angels in heaven.

Recordings of birds or sea creatures, of the winds and the waves, or of human voices at worship in other lands and cultures, of panpipes or instrumental music have their place. At celebratory occasions there can be a place for rhythmic hand-clapping, drumming or festal shouts.

The laying on of hands for healing may be offered at any time. Anointing with oil also has its place in some traditions. Giving and receiving 'the Peace', through handshake, embrace or kiss, also varies according to culture. At informal gatherings it can be affirming to link hands in a circle and say a prayer together, perhaps at the close of the worship time.

Clergy and statutory public worship

The statutory public worship of the historic liturgical Churches is informed by canons or other regulations, which evolved over the years. *Prayer Rhythms (The Celtic Prayer Book,* Volume One*)* is intended to be compatible with these, in whole or in part. For example, under the Common Worship regulations introduced by the Church of England in 2000, the patterns of worship in this volume are legal, provided that the Lord's Prayer and a Collect are said.

The Celtic Christian tradition

Celtic spirituality can be seen as the inner dimension of Christianity. It draws its primary inspiration from the saints of the Church in Celtic lands of the fifth to tenth centuries, but it is a lived tradition, which has not fossilised and which has accrued universal dynamics that belong to the twenty-first century. It has a natural feel and a strong sense of God's presence in creation and in human life, celebrating God through all the senses, releasing creativity, respecting both women's and men's gifts and valuing contemplation. It weaves together the strands of Christianity, which have become separated.

The practices and literature of Christianity in Celtic cultures vary in each region and period, yet they are linked by a commitment to orthodox Christianity, a connectedness to the earth and ancient wellsprings of wisdom, and by a sense of pilgrimage and passion, penance and poetry.

Source documents are too fragmentary for us to piece together a comprehensive picture of worship in early churches in Celtic lands. Liturgical worship – including the chanting of psalms – centred on the monasteries, which formed the hub of church life.

The great liturgies of the first millennium come from five families within the Christian Church: the Syrian, Egyptian, Byzantine, Roman, and those from Gaul. The Gaul liturgies include the Gothic of Northern France, the Gallican of Southern France, and the Mozarabic in Spain. They are far more poetic, sometimes flowery and elaborate, but at their best are full of a warmth of devotion rarely found in other liturgies.

Churches in Britain and Ireland drew their liturgy from most of these families, but they shared with their fellow Celts in Gaul a similar warmth of devotion, a vivid imagination, a down-to-earthness, a sense of immediacy and poetic flow. Each faith community had its distinctive flavour, and new songs and prayers were written.

Worship in the early Celtic churches was twin track. The documents we have relate to worship in the monastic churches, but we know that worship also took place in the villages: it was informal, in the local dialect, and making use of wandering musicians. Columbanus' biographer, Jonas, for example, refers to clergy who carried their harps around.

The Celtic tradition has been likened to fire. It brings holy traditions to life in disaffected hearts. 'Tradition is the living faith of the dead. Traditionalism is the dead faith of the living.'

The Celtic dispersion

The beloved disciple John, so loved by the Celts, established faith communities among the Celtic peoples in the area now known as Turkey. Saint Paul ministered and wrote to the Celts of Galatia. But they were pushed out to the edges of the Roman Empire. During the sixteenth to nineteenth centuries, this process went into reverse. Many people from Ireland and Scotland emigrated to North America to escape afflictions such as the Penal Laws, the Irish famine and the Scottish land clearances. Others emigrated from throughout Britain to Australasia and Africa. They took with them certain Celtic instincts. The Aboriginal peoples often welcomed them as brothers and sisters and helped them to survive the harsh winters.

Disillusioned with centuries of compulsive acquisitiveness, many of these people increasingly came to realise that they carried in their gene pool a spirituality that makes for a wholeness that Western materialism lacks. First Nation peoples, learning now of Celtic spirituality, say, 'If you had brought this with you we could have shared your faith and journeyed together.'

Prayer Rhythms draws on certain Aboriginal as well as Celtic insights that seem to have been implanted by God. It appeals to the deepest aspirations of old world, new world and First Nation peoples alike.

The term 'Prayer Book' is used in the sense that prayers, worship material and phrases from many sources have been reworked and woven together, hopefully to be all of a piece.

RAY SIMPSON
Lindisfarne

How to use this book

Whenever you wish, instead of using the Pattern of Prayer for the day of the week, use the Pattern of Prayer for a special day or season. Since liturgical customs vary so greatly we leave the worshipper free to enrich these simple patterns as they wish.

This book may be used in many contexts: as the staple diet for ordered corporate or personal worship, as a framework for occasional celebrations, or as a resource to dip into. If it is used for personal devotion it is wise to intersperse spaces for silent reflection. If it is used for occasional celebrations, singing, dancing or prophesying may take place before the printed form of worship begins.

Psalm numbers

Psalm numbers follow those used in the Hebrew Bible since most English translations use these. The numbers used in the Greek Bible, which Orthodox and Roman Catholics often use in public liturgy, may be deduced from the following conversion list:

Hebrew Bible	Greek Bible
1-8	1-8
9 and 10	9
11-113	10-112
114 and 115	113
116:1-9	114
116:17 to end	115
117-146	116-145
147:1-16	146
147:17-150	147-150

Readers

First and Second, etc., may refer to individuals, men and women, people on right and left sides of the building, or adults and children, as is deemed appropriate.

Prayer stops for the
twenty-four hours

There is a reference in the Psalms (119:164) to a Jewish practice of punctuating each twenty-four-hour period with seven prayer points.

Early Christian faith communities punctuated each day seven or eight times. According to their system of telling the time, the first hour of the day was 7am, one hour after the average time of sunrise. These prayer stops became formalised as 'The Hours'.

Christians relate these prayer stops to key moments in Christ's life. Thus, Christ was placed on the cross at the third hour, 9am. At midday the sun eclipsed to mark his suffering. At 3pm (the ninth hour) they took Jesus' body down because this was the start of the Jewish sabbath.

The fourfold patterns of prayer may be taken by most people as prayer stops for roughly 9am, noon, 6pm and 9pm. We provide suggestions for marking each of the other three-hour periods. These prayer-stops are not a burdensome addition or requirement. They are, rather, a framework and an opportunity. They may be used as the Spirit moves according to the varied circumstances and constitutions of each person. Thus, most will be asleep at 3am, but perhaps someone will decide to keep a vigil and use the 3am prayers then. Or another may be on nightshift or unable to sleep and thus make use of it.

9am   use Morning Prayer

12noon   use Midday Prayer

3pm   use the prayer that follows

Remember that at this hour Jesus died on the cross.

As you died at this hour for me,
help me to put to death my destructive cravings
and to remain true to you.
I pray also for the people of the world
who suffer the heat and burden of the day.
Give them your peace.

6pm	use Evening Prayer
9pm	use Night Prayer
12midnight	use the prayer that follows

Remember that the Jewish people were led out of slavery in
Egypt at midnight (Exodus 12:29).

Jesus is expected to come again 'as a thief in the night'.

I remember before you all those who have died in you
and live with you, O Christ.
Shepherd of souls, you watch over those who cannot sleep.
I use this time to pray for those for whom I have a concern . . .

3am   use the prayer that follows

Jesus was raised from death 'very early in the morning while
it was still dark' (Matthew 28:1).

Risen Christ, be my light in the darkness
and shine on all who sleep but know you not.
Especially upon . . .

6am   or on waking, dressing or rising – use one or
                 more of the following

Thank you for the gift of sleep.
Thank you for the gift of a new day.

All that I am,
all that I do,
all whom I'll meet today,
I offer now to you.

Waken me, Lord,
to the wonder of this day,
to the pleasure of life,
to your voice in my heart.

I awake to the light of God.
I awake to the guiding of Christ.
I awake to the flow of the Spirit.

In the silence of my soul
I come to you
to guide me in the ways
I should walk this day.

Be with me today
in my meetings,
in my temptations,
in my loneliness.

Be with me today
in the humdrum,
in the heat,
in the opportunities.

Be with me through this day
in all I do and say.
Be with me through this day
and keep me in Christ's way.

I arise today
in the harmony of the Father,
in the beauty of the Son,
in the grace of the Spirit.

I arise today
in the glory of the Father,
in the splendour of the Son,
in the radiance of the Spirit.

I arise today
in the thinking of the Father,
in the feeling of the Son,
in the wisdom of the Spirit.

I arise today
in the knowing of the Father,
in the action of the Saviour,
in the seeing of the Spirit.

I arise today
in the confidence of the Father,
in the valour of the Son,
in the energy of the Spirit.

I arise today
in heaven's might,
sun's brightness,
earth's depths.

I arise today
in Trinity's love,
human friendship,
creation's joy.

I arise today
with the holy saints encouraging me.
I arise today
with the holy angels protecting me.
I arise today
with the Holy Trinity communing with me.

I arise today
with the Father who calls us,
the Saviour who gathers us,
the Spirit who binds us.

I arise today
with the saints who commune with us,
the creation that blesses us,
all people who neighbour us.

I arise today,
the sun to encircle us,
the earth to uphold us,
the air to enfold us.

I arise today,
God's laws to uphold us,
God's gifts to equip us,
God's love to inspire us.

DAYS OF THE WEEK

Sunday – New Life

In Jewish tradition Sunday is an image of the first day of creation. Jesus Christ, Son of God, rose from the dead on the first day of the week, so for Christians Sunday is a day to celebrate resurrection and new life.

Sunday Morning Prayer

Leader Rising from death, today Christ greets his people.
All Rising with all creation,
we greet him as our King.

or

Leader Shine on us, O God,
like the sun that lights up day.
Chase away the dark and all shadow of sin.

Thanksgiving

There may be singing

One of the following psalms, or the psalm of the day, may be read, sung or dramatised: Psalm 30; 33:1-12; 66; 81; 117; 118:1-19; 135:1-14; 146; 147:1-12; 147:13-21; 150. Or Psalm 24 may be read as follows

Leader The earth belongs to God,
as do all things and people who live on it.
Out of the fluid cosmos God created its firmness.

First Who may ascend to the high dwelling of God?

Second Whoever is clean of heart and whoever does not cling to what is false will receive the Almighty's blessing and the Saviour's embrace. Such are those who seek the face of our forebears' God.

All Open up the gates that the King of glory
may come in.

First	Who is the King of glory?
Second	The Immortal God, mighty and strong, is the King of glory.
All	Open up the gates that the King of glory may come in.
First	Who is the King of glory?
All	The Eternal and all-powerful God is the King of glory.
Leader	Let us recollect the presence of the Risen Christ with us now.

Short silence

The following or other words of confession and forgiveness may be used

Leader	Christ Jesus, in the light of your risen presence, and in union with your first frail apostles, we say sorry:
All	For not weighing your words, for not sharing your trials, for not believing your promises.
Leader	O loving Christ, hanged on a tree yet risen in the morning, scatter the sin from our souls as the mist from the hills. Begin what we do, inform what we say, redeem who we are.
All	In you we place our hope, now and for evermore.

God's Word

Reader	Isaiah 60:1-3, 19-22 *or the Old Testament reading of the day*

There may be singing
A Proclamation, or the following may be said

Leader	Jesus says: I am the resurrection and the life.
All	You break the power of sin and death.
Leader	I am the bread of life.
All	You feed and fill the hungry.
Leader	I am the true vine.
All	You bring us life everlasting.

Reader	Colossians 3:9-17 *or the New Testament reading of the day*

A Proclamation or the following may be said

Leader	We believe, O God of all gods, that you are the eternal Maker of life. We believe, O God of all gods, that you are the eternal Maker of love.
All	We believe, O Ruler and God of all people, that you are the Creator of the skies above, that you are the Creator of the oceans below, that you are the Creator of the eternal realms.
Leader	We believe, O Ruler and God of all people, that you are the One who created our souls and set their course; that you are the One who created our bodies from earth; that you gave to our bodies their breath and to our souls their possession.

The following is said, or sung

All   God, bless to us our bodies.
God, bless to us our souls.
God, bless to us our living.
God, bless to us our goals.

Silence, teaching, sharing or singing

Intercession

The following prayer may be expressed in movement

Leader   Thank you for bringing us
to the beginning of this week.
All   Keep us from falling into sin.
Leader   Through the resurrection of your Son
you overcame the hold of sin and death.
All   Transform us in all our ways.

Leader   Risen Christ, bring newness of life
All   Into our stale routines,
into our wearied spirits,
into our tarnished relationships.

There may be celebratory music, movement or singing

*If there is a Creative Activity, the following themes
may be used as headings for extended intercessions
either prepared or in informal groups*

Leader   We pray for believers.
All   May their lives be signs of joyful service.

Leader   May our churches bring honour to you,
and faith to the people.
All   May they be places of healing and welcome.

Leader   We pray for people in authority.
All   May they strive for justice and peace.

| **Leader** | May this be a day of refreshment for families and single people, traders and communities. |
| **All** | May our homes be places of hospitality and hope. |

There may be singing

| **Leader** | May we know your presence as we enjoy the company of others. |

The following blessing may be sung

| **All** | The God of life go with us, the Risen Christ beside us, the vibrant Spirit within us. Amen! |

Sunday Midday Prayer

This may be said before a meal and Alleluias may be sung

Reader   Psalm 103:1-5

Leader   You give us well-being in the midst of the day:
All   A day of renewal,
             a day of growth,
             a day of sharing food.

Leader   You were with us at the breaking of the day.
All   Be with us in the breaking of bread.

A candle may be lit
One of the following may be said

Leader   I would prepare a feast and be host
             to the great High King,
             with all the company of heaven.
             The nourishment of pure love be in my house,
             and the roots of repentance.
             May we have baskets of love to give,
             with cups of mercy for everybody.
             Sweet Jesus, be here with us,
             with all the company of heaven.
             May this meal be full of cheerfulness,
             for this is a feast of the great High King,
             who is our host for all eternity.

                                    Attributed to St Brigid

             May the freshness and the fragrance of the farms
             be with us as we eat.
             May the freshness and fragrance of Christ
             be with us as we meet.

The food that we are to eat
is earth, water and sun,
coming to us through pleasing plants.
The food that we are to eat
is the fruit of the labour of many creatures.
We are thankful for it.
May it give us health, strength and joy,
and may it increase our love.

Risen Christ of the miraculous catching of fish
and the perfect lakeside meal,
be with us as we share this meal.

Lord, as once you multiplied the five loaves
and two fishes,
multiply the gifts each of us brings,
so that from our sharing together
blessings may flow.

Sunday Evening Prayer

Leader Spirit of the Risen Christ,
as the lamps light up the evening
shine into our hearts and kindle in us
the fire of your love.

Candles may be lit
These words may be said or sung

Leader The light of Christ has come into the world.
All The light of Christ has come into the world.

A hymn is sung or the following is said or sung

All Light of the world, in grace and beauty,
mirror of God's eternal face,
transparent flame of love's free duty –
you bring salvation to our race.
Now, as we see the lights of evening,
we raise our voice in hymns of praise.
Worthy are you of endless blessing,
sun of our night, lamp of our days.

Reader Psalm 66 (key verses) *or the psalm of the day*
is read, or a psalm may be sung

This may be followed by a brief silence

Leader We offer to you, Lord, the troubles of this day.
We lay down our burdens at your feet.
Forgive us our sins,
give us your peace,
and help us to receive your Word.
All In the name of Christ.
Amen.

God's Word (1)

Reader   Let us attend. Hear the Word of God in Jeremiah
31:31-34 *or the Old Testament reading of the day*

(at close) This is the Word of the Lord.
All   Thanks be to God.

Thanksgiving

There may be singing or a Proclamation

Leader   We give you thanks, our Father,
that you are always present,
in all things,
each day and each night.
We give you thanks for your gifts of creation,
life and friendship.
We give you thanks for the particular blessings
of this day.

*There may be a brief pause, the naming of blessings,
singing in tongues, a creative activity and singing*

God's Word (2)

Reader   2 Timothy 2:8-13 *or the New Testament reading
of the day*

*There may be teaching, silent reflection, confession,
a creed, or singing*

Intercession

*In the following intercessions there may be prepared
or free prayer where indicated (. . .)*

*The people may say a response such as 'Lord,
graciously hear us' where indicated (R)*

Leader   Into your hands, O Lord,
we place our families,
our neighbours,
our brothers and sisters in Christ,
and all whom we have met today . . .
Enfold them in your will. (R)

Leader   Into your hands, O Lord,
we place all who are victims of prejudice,
oppression or neglect;
the frail,
the unwanted . . .
May everyone be cherished from conception to
the grave. (R)

Leader   Into your hands, O Lord,
we place all who are restless, sick,
or prey to the powers of evil . . .
Keep guard over them. (R)

Leader   Risen Christ,
bring renewal to the land and to the Church,
to ordained ministries
and to religious communities.
Raise up new callings and communities that meet
the need of our times.

There may be singing

Leader   Lord Jesus Christ, Light of the world,
by your cross you have overcome all darkness
that oppresses.
Come and shine on us here in . . .
that we may grow and live together in your love,
which makes us one with all humanity.

All   The grace of our Lord Jesus Christ,
the love of God,
and the fellowship of the Holy Spirit,
be with us all evermore.
Amen.

Leader   Bring us to our resurrection without end.

*There may be refreshments, sharing and prayer
ministry*

Sunday Night Prayer

An Easter candle is lit

Leader   Christ, rising in glory, scatters the darkness from our hearts.

All   Glory to you, Christ our King,
radiant with light,
the Sun who shines on all the world.
Earth exalt,
heaven rejoice,
morning and night give thanks and praise.

Reader   Psalm 136:1-3, 23-26 or Psalm 126

There may be singing

Leader   Lord Jesus Christ, who at this hour lay in the tomb
and so hallowed the grave to be a bed of hope,
may we lie down in hope and rise up with you.

Leader   We need no longer fear death,
All   For by your death you have destroyed death.
Leader   We need not lie down in anger,
All   For your love has triumphed over hate.
Leader   We need not sleep as those without hope,
All   For by your rising you bring hope
and life eternal.

Reader   Into our place of darkness,
into our place of strife,
into our fears and worries,
All   Come with your risen life.

Reader	Into those who are dying, into those weary of life, into those tired from exertions,
All	Come with your risen life.
Leader	Renew us this night, Lord, in body and soul, that waking or sleeping we may know your presence with us.
Reader	Luke 24:13-32; John 20:19-21 *or another reading*
Reader	Risen Lord, you burned in the hearts of two walkers who made room in their conversation for you.
All	Reveal yourself to us as we make room in our conversation for you.
Reader	Risen Lord, you revealed yourself to them as they welcomed you in their home.
All	Reveal yourself to us as we welcome you in our homes.
Men	This night, O Victor over death, raise me from the death of denial, raise me from the death of fear, raise me from the death of despair.
Women	This night, O Victor over death, wake me to the eternal 'Yes', wake me to the rays of Hope, wake me to the light of Dawn.
	There may be singing
Leader	The stone that sealed the tomb has been rolled away.
All	Christ is no longer among the dead, he is here with us.

Leader   Let us pray that the stones roll away from those
who are trapped in deathly places.

*In a time of prepared or free prayer examples may
be given*

Leader   Our loved ones bless and keep, O God,
wherever they are . . .

*Loved ones may be named aloud or in silence; there
may be other petitions followed by silent, prepared
or free prayer*

Leader   We lie down in peace, knowing our sins
are forgiven.

All   We lie down in peace, knowing death has no fear.

Leader   We lie down in peace, knowing no powers
can harm us.

All   We lie down in peace, knowing angels are near.

All   Deep peace of the setting sun,
deep peace of the forgiving heart,
deep peace of the risen Christ,
be ours, tonight, for ever.

Leader   You fell asleep in mortal flesh, O Lord and Leader,
but on the third day you rose again.
Now you watch over us as we sleep,
you restore our souls and preserve our life.
In love of you we will take our rest.

All   In love of you we will take our rest.

Leader   Great God,
as you brought Christ safely through the night
of sin and death to his rising at dawn,
so bring us through this night
that we may offer you our prayers at dawn
and walk in the light eternal.

Creative Activities

1. Music-making, feasting, prayer ministry, drama, walking.

2. Candle-lighting and eating.

3. Write on pieces of paper either the blessings of the past week or the burdens of the coming week and place these in a bowl.

Monday – Creation

Since Sunday, the first day of the week, was set aside as a day of rest as well as a celebration of Christ's resurrection, we use Monday, the first day of the working week in the lands of the Celtic dispersion, to focus on creation, the earth, and the creative activities of humans, who are co-creators with God.

Monday Morning Prayer

Leader   God of life, you summon the day to dawn
             and call us to create with you.

All   You are the Rock
             from which all earth is fashioned.
             You are the Food from which all souls are fed.
             You are the Force
             from which all power lines travel.
             You are the Source who is creation's head.

Thanksgiving

There may be singing

Reader(s) *The Psalm of the day or the following verses from
              Psalm 104 may be said*

First   Creator God, how great you are!
             You clothe yourself in light.
             You stretch out the skies like a tent.

Second   Winds are your messengers.
             Flames are your servants.
             You water the earth until it gives us food.

First   How abundant are your works, O God.
             In wisdom have you made them all.

Second   The creatures teeming the earth,
             the sea, vast and wide –
             innumerable things, small and great,
             live within it –
             all these look to you for their food in due season.
             When you send forth your Spirit they are created
             and you renew the face of the earth.

First   May your glory last for ever.
May you always have joy in what you have created.

Second   May our thoughts always give you pleasure.
May we always rejoice in you.

The Glory of Creation

Leader   For earth and sea and sky in the harmony
of colour,

All   We give you thanks, O God.

Leader   For the air of the eternal
seeping through the physical,

All   We give you thanks, O God.

Leader   For the everlasting glory dipping into time,

All   We give you thanks, O God.

Leader   For nature resplendent,
growing beasts,
emergent crops,
singing birds,
the energies of the city,

All   We give you thanks, O God.

Leader   For the Person you sent to restore us when we
fell away from the goodness of your creation,

All   We give you thanks, O God.

Leader   For harmony restored through your Spirit
moving upon the turbulent waters of our lives,

All   We give you thanks, O God.

Leader   For the honour you give us
of lives flowing in the rhythm of your tides,

All   We give you thanks, O God.

Leader   For setting each of us, like the stars upon their
courses, within the orbit of your love,

All   We give you thanks, O God.

God's Word

Reader   Genesis 1:1-5, 31; Job 38:1-18; Job 38:19-41;
Isaiah 55:6-13; *or the Old Testament reading for
the day*

Leader   Creator and Saviour,
we have exploited earth for our selfish ends,
turned our backs on the cycles of life
and forgotten we are your stewards.
Now soils become barren,
air and water become unclean,
species disappear,
and humans are diminished.
In penitence we come to you.

*There may be silence, free prayer, music of lament,
or the following confession*

Leader   God, have mercy.
All   Christ, have mercy.
Leader   God, have mercy.

Reader   John 6:28-34; Acts 14:8-17; Colossians 1:1-20;
or the New Testament reading for the day

All   I believe, O God of all gods,
that you are the eternal Creator of life.
I believe, O God of all gods,
that you are the eternal Father of love.
I believe, O Lord and God of the peoples,
that you are the Creator of the high heavens.
I believe, O Lord and God of the peoples,
that you created my soul and set its warp.

*This may be followed by meditation, teaching,
sharing, or free prayer*
There may be singing

Intercession

One or more of the following prayers may be said

Leader This we know: the earth does not belong to us.
All The earth is God's and so are all people.
Leader This we know: we did not weave the web of life.
All The earth is God's and so is all that breathes on it.
Leader Whatever befalls the earth
befalls the sons and daughters of the earth.
All The earth is God's and so we will serve it.

Reader Bless all work done today that enables
the human family to be clothed, fed and housed;
to travel and learn wisely,
to communicate and exchange,
to craft and celebrate,
in everything reflecting your glory.

Reader Caring Father God,
we offer to you the fuels and forests,
the seas and soil,
the air and animals,
the technology and the textiles of the world.
All May we steward your creation to your glory
and for the benefit of future generations.

Reader Worker Christ, as we enter our workplace
may we bring your presence with us.
Equip us to speak your peace and perfect order
into its atmosphere.
Remind us to acknowledge your authority
over all that will be thought, decided
and accomplished within it.
Give us a fresh supply of truth and beauty
on which to draw as we work.

Reader   In dependence on the God of life
may we cherish the precious earth:
the earth of the God of life,
the earth of the Christ of love,
the earth of the Spirit Holy.
In dependence on the God of Life
may our life this day have blessing:
the blessing of the God of life,
the blessing of the Christ of love,
the blessing of the Spirit holy.

There may be singing

Leader   God, bless the sky that is above us,
the earth that is beneath us,
your image deep within us,
the day that lies before us.

Monday Midday Prayer

Leader   Great Spirit,
whose breath is felt in the soft breeze,
and whose life surges through socket and screen,
we seek your strength in the midst of the day.
May we, and the peoples of the world,
work in dignity and walk in the beauty of the day.

All   Blessed be God the birther of life.
Blessed be God the giver of light.
Blessed be God the bestower of skills.

First   If God had not supported us,
evildoers would have swallowed us up,
the flood would have engulfed us,
the raging waters would have swept us away.
Praise God that we have escaped like a bird
freed from a trap.
Truly our help is in God,
maker of heaven and earth.

Psalm 124

Leader   O Son of God, change my heart.
Your spirit composes the songs of the birds
and the buzz of the bees.
Your creation is a million wondrous miracles,
beautiful to look upon.
I ask of you just one more miracle:
beautify my soul.

Second   O God, you called all life into being,
your presence is around us now,
your Spirit enlivens all who work.
May your kingdom come on earth.

47

Impart to us wisdom to understand your ways,
to manage well the tasks of this day.
Make us co-creators with you
so that when day fades we may come to you
without shame.

Third   You will labour, but God will bless your work.
         You will walk, but God will bless your footsteps.
         You will suffer, but God will bless your tears.
Fourth   Contained in the earth are the seeds of all.
         Contained in the soul is the Son of God.

Leader   Listen to the words of Christ:
         Happy you who are gentle –
         the earth belongs to you.

All   We pray for this world you have given us,
         for the planting of seeds and the propagation of
         stock in the soils and commerce of the world.

Leader   Encircle those who can neither sow nor reap
         because human ills have drained them.
         Give us wisdom to manage technology
         for the world's good.
         Sustain those who eke out the minerals,
         create textures, grow crops or rear cattle.

There may be singing or free prayer

Leader   Good God, be with us in every experience of life.
         When we neglect you
All   Remind us of your presence.
Leader   When we are frightened
All   Give us courage.

Leader   When we are tempted
All   Give us the power to resist.
Leader   When we are anxious and worried
All   Give us peace.
Leader   When we are weary in service
All   Renew our tired frame.

There may be singing

All   God who dances with creation,
       plants your likeness in the people
       and strikes the world with thunder,
       send us out to fill the world with love.

Monday Evening Prayer

Leader	We bless you, O God, and forget not all your benefits.
All	We bless you for your creation, which is alive with your glory.
Leader	You nod and beckon to us through every stone and star.
All	As the sun sets in the east so we settle down with you.

There may be singing
One of the Laments on page 57 may be used

God's Word

Reader	Psalm 50:1-15 *or the psalm of the day*
Leader	Lord, you are my island;
All	In your bosom I nest.
Leader	You are the calm of the sea;
All	In that peace I rest.
Leader	You are the waves on the shore's glistening stones;
All	Their sound is my hymn.
Leader	You are the song of the birds;
All	Their tune I sing.
Leader	You are the sea breaking on rock;
All	I praise you with the swell.
Leader	You are the ocean that laps my being;
All	In you I dwell.

Reader   Isaiah 24:4-5 *or the Old Testament reading*
              for the day

Leader   We bless you, Lord,
All   For the beauty of the trees,
              the softness of the air,
              the fragrance of the grass.

Leader   We bless you, Lord,
All   For the soaring of the skies,
              the rhythms of the earth,
              the stillness of the night.

Leader   We bless you, Lord,
All   For the twinkling of the stars,
              the freshness of the morning,
              the dewdrops on the flower.

Leader   We bless you, Lord,
All   For the taste of good food,
              the trail of the sun,
              and the life that never goes away.

                              Chief Dan George

Reader   Matthew 6:25-34 *or the New Testament reading*
              for the day

All   I believe, O God of all gods,
              that you are the eternal Creator of life.
              I believe, O God of all gods,
              that you are the eternal Father of love.
              I believe, O Ruler and God of the peoples,
              that you are the Creator of all that is.
              I believe, O Ruler and God of the peoples,
              that you created my soul and set its warp.

              There may be teaching, sharing, creative activity
              and singing

Thanksgiving

Leader	Creator Spirit,
All	May air and elements praise you,
	may flowers and fabrics praise you,
	may floor and desktop praise you.
Leader	Your people praise you at the dawn of the day.
All	May cars and buses praise you,
	may work and heat praise you,
	may grass and growth praise you.
Leader	Your people praise you in the midst of the day.
All	May eating and talking praise you,
	may thoughts and actions praise you,
	may male and female praise you.
Leader	Your people praise you at the end of the day.
All	May night and day praise you,
	may the seven days of the week praise you,
	may all the good that has been done praise you.
Leader	We give you thanks,
	because earth's life and fruitfulness flow from you,
	and all times and seasons reflect your laws.
	We give you thanks,
	because you created the world in love,
	you redeemed the world through love,
	you maintain the world by your love.
	Help us to give our love to you.

or

Men	We give thanks for moments of grace
	in the life of the cosmos:
	for the explosion of a star
	and the birth of our planet.

Women We give thanks for the moments of grace
in the life of a person:
the power of attraction and the wonder of a birth.

Intercession

Leader Generosity of God, spilling over into creation,
we bless you for flowers and their wealth of beauty,
for creatures and their glorious variety,
for seas and seasons and scents.
May we, too, reflect something of your glorious
generosity.

We pray for the well-being of the creation,
the healthfulness of the air,
the richness of the earth and its provisions,
and the beauty of the whole world.

Reader Creator, make us co-workers with you
so that the earth and all who live upon it
may reap a full harvest.
Show us how to reflect your rhythms in our life
and work,
and to conserve the world's rich resources.
Help us to give all creatures their due respect,
to tend cattle and crops with care.
Guide science along wise and considerate ways
that we may fashion agriculture that truly
enhances
and that we may sustain a vibrant environment.

There may be free or guided intercessions

Leader Creator God, hear us.
All Creator God, graciously hear us.

All   Peace to the land and all that grows on it.
Peace to the sea and all that swims in it.
Peace to the air and all that flies through it.
Peace with our God who calls us to serve.

Leader   The Creator who brought order out of chaos
give peace to you.
The Saviour who calmed the raging sea
give peace to you.
The Spirit who broods upon the deeps
give peace to you.

Monday Night Prayer

Leader   Let the light fade and the work be done.
Let the flowers and the desktops close.
Let the sun go down and the world become still,
and let the Son of God draw near.

Leader   Blessed be all creation,
All   And all that has life.
Leader   Blessed be the earth;
All   May it uplift our bed tonight.
Leader   Blessed be the fire;
All   May it glow in us tonight.
Leader   Blessed be the air;
All   May it make our night-breath sweet.

There may be singing

Reader   Psalm 104:1-4, 19-24 *or other verses from this psalm*

Leader   We give you thanks that you are always present,
in all things each day and each night.
We give you thanks for your gifts of creation,
life and friendship.
We give you thanks for the blessings of this day . . .

Blessings may be named in silence or aloud

Leader   When we are still we can sense you, our Maker,
we can feel your hand upon us.
All that has been made stirs within us
creation's song of praise.
Now we give you thanks for work completed.
All   We give you thanks for rest of night.

There may be silence or singing

Reader   Genesis 1:3-5, 31a *or words of Jesus*

Leader   Guardian of the planets,
kindler of the stars,
we pass into the darkness
encompassed by you.

We offer you our concerns and the needs
of your creation.

There may be prepared, silent or free prayer

Leader   Thank you for your love for us,
strong and nurturing.
All   We give back our lives to you.
Leader   Thank you for our minds and bodies.
All   We give back our lives to you.
Leader   Thank you for the past day.
All   We give back our lives to you.
Leader   After creation God rested.
All   We give back our lives to you.

Leader   Protect us through the hours of this night,
be they silent or stormy,
that we who are wearied by the changes
and chances of a restless world
may rest upon your eternal changelessness.

You created the world out of love.
All   Now we return to you in love.
Leader   Let us rest in God this night
All   And awake in newness of life.

Lament for Creation

Either of these may be used as an alternative to any of the Intercessions at Morning or Evening Prayer. Background music of lament may be played

Leader For polluting waste dumped by rich nations on lands of the poor,
All God, forgive.
Leader For the lust of the few to own and control life forms,
All God, forgive.
Leader For the new colonialism of women, plants and animals,
All God, forgive.
Leader For turning the world's farm-people into slaves of the gene giants,
All God, forgive.
Leader For turning your gifts of water and life itself into products for gain,
All God, forgive.
Leader For turning the sowing of seed from a sacred duty into a crime,
All God, forgive.
Leader For terminator technology that destroys biodiversity,
All God, forgive.

or

Leader Father, Creator, we have raped and spoiled your world.
All God, forgive.
Leader Jesus, Saviour, we have ignored your warnings.
All God, forgive.

Leader   Spirit, Sustainer, we have tried to live without you.
All   God, forgive.

*The following Prayer of Creation may be used as an alternative
to any of the Intercessions at Morning or Evening Prayer*

Reader   Creator of our land –
our earth,
the trees, the animals and humans –
all is for your honour.

All   Let the people say with joy that you are the Lord.

Reader   You pulled the continents out of the sea.
Out of wet mud you have fashioned
a wonderful world,
and what beautiful men and women!

All   Let the people say with joy that you are the Lord.

Reader   The grace of your creation is like a cool day
between rainy seasons.
We drink in your creation with our eyes
and with our ears.
How strong and good and sure your earth smells,
and everything that grows there.

All   Let the people say with joy that you are the Lord.

Reader   We drink in your creation
and cannot get enough of it,
but we forget the evil we have done.
Tear us away from our sins.
This wonderful world fades
and one day our eyes snap shut.
Then all that is not from you is over and dead.

All   Let the people say with joy that you are the Lord.

                                    Echoes a prayer from Ashanti, Ghana

Creative Activities

1. Display samples of creation and bless them.

2. Cut out or bring photographs that portray the wonder of life.

3. Listen to sounds of water flowing, either on a recording or by plugging in a water fountain.

4. Hold a stone, nut, leaf and so forth in the hand while praying.

Tuesday – Peace: God with us

The peace for which we pray today is not just the absence of war but is rooted in the fundamental peacemaking action of God, who has made peace with the hostile human race by becoming one with it, having been made present in our world in human form. The incarnation of God's Son is an act of peacemaking that initiates a ceaseless peace process on earth.

At his birth, angels proclaimed Jesus to be the Prince of Peace, and in the Celtic tradition Jesus is pictured as bounding down mountains towards human beings holding out a hand of reconciliation. Jesus calls us, in turn, to become peacemakers.

Tuesday Morning Prayer

Leader Glory to the most High God who has come
to live among us.

All You have come to make peace in a hostile world.

Leader Christ, born of the loveliest Mary,
All You are with us in our birth.
Leader Christ, brought up as a carpenter,
All You are with us in our work.
Leader Christ, friend of seeker and outcast,
All You are with us in our friendships.
Leader Christ, noble in suffering and death,
All You are with us in our trials.
Leader Christ, eternal Son of God,
All You are with us evermore.

There may be singing

Reader Psalm 1; 8; 19; 20; 82; 89:5-18; 96; 98; 112;
113; 117; 146; *or* 147:13-20

Leader Dear Son of Mary,
you took flesh to redeem us;
change our hearts.
All Dear Son of God,
you came to us with sacrificial love;
change our hearts.

*There may be silence, spontaneous words of
confession, or the following words of forgiveness*

Leader The Son of God bounds towards us,
reaching out a hand of reconciliation.
Let us take it, and listen to God's Word.

God's Word

Reader Micah 4:1-4 *or the Old Testament reading*
of the day

Leader We bless you great God of Israel,
All For you have set your people free.

Leader You have raised up for us a mighty Saviour,
All Born of your servant David's family.

Leader Through your holy prophets you promised of old
All That you would save us from all who hate us.

Leader You promised to show mercy to our forebears
All And to remember your holy covenant.

Leader You vowed to our ancestor Abraham
All To set us free to worship you without fear.

Leader The dawn from on high shall break upon us,
All To shine on those in darkness and to guide us
into peace.
Luke 1:68-79

Reader John 14:27 *or the New Testament reading*
of the day

There may be singing, teaching, sharing or a
creative activity

Intercession

Leader Babe of heaven, defenceless Love,
you had to travel far from your home.
All Strengthen us on our pilgrimage of trust
on earth.
Leader King of glory, you accepted such humbling;
All Clothe us with the garments of humility.

Leader	Your birth shows us the simplicity of the Father's love;
All	Keep us in the simplicity of that love.
Leader	Your coming shows us the wonder of being human;
All	Help to cherish every human life.

Reader Child of Glory, Child of Mary,
at your birth you were proclaimed
the Prince of Peace.
You came to remove the wall that divides
one people from another.
May walls of hostility and fear
come tumbling down; especially . . .

Suggestions may be made

Reader You call the peacemakers blessed.
Strengthen peacemakers in places torn apart
by the ravages of sin, especially . . .

Suggestions may be made

Christ who comes with justice and peace,
we pray for the peace and well-being
of the whole world
and of all the churches.
We pray for victims of oppression and violence;
especially . . .

*There may be prepared or spontaneous intercessions,
silence, singing or the Lord's Prayer*

Leader God direct your hours,
protect your assets,
still your hearts.
May you see the face of Christ in everyone
you meet.
May everyone you meet see the face of Christ
in you.

All Deep peace of the quiet earth to you.
Deep peace of the still air to you.
Deep peace of the forgiving heart to you.
Deep peace of the Son of peace.

Tuesday Midday Prayer

Leader In the whirling wheels of the world,
All You are with us.
Leader When the day takes its toll,
All You are with us.
Leader In the clamour of strife,
All You are with us.
Leader When the world turns sour,
All You are with us.

Leader Make me aware, dear God,
of the eye that beholds me,
the hand that holds me,
the heart that loves me,
the Presence that enfolds me.

First You forgave the sins of your people
and restored your land, O God.

Second Restore us too, O God our Saviour.
Show us your unfailing love.
Revive us again that we may rejoice in you.

First I will listen to what the Eternal God,
who promises us divine peace, will say.

Second Your salvation is near those who reverence you
so that your glory may dwell in our land.

First Love and faithfulness meet together;
justice and peace embrace.

Second Faithfulness springs forth from the earth;
righteousness looks down from heaven.

First The Eternal God will give us
a harvest of goodness.

Second   Righteousness prepares the way for you
to move among us.

From Psalm 84

There may be singing

Reader   Jesus says:
Happy are you who are peacemakers;
you will be called God's children . . .

My peace I give to you,
not as the world gives do I give to you.

There may be silence

Leader   Lead us from fear to trust.
All   Lead us from despair to hope.
Leader   Lead us from hate to love.
All   Lead us from war to peace.
Leader   Deep peace of the Son of peace,
All   Fill our hearts, our workplace, our world.

There may be sharing or singing

All   Circle us, O God, for the rest of the day.
Keep strife without.
Keep peace within.

Any   Circle us, O God.
Keep . . .

Suggestions may be made

Leader   May the eternal Glory shine upon us,
may the Son of Mary stay beside us,
may the life-giving Spirit live within us,
now and always.

Tuesday Evening Prayer

Leader The peace of Christ has come into the world.
All The peace of Christ has come into the world.

There may be singing, such as Mary's Song in this or another version

All Magnificat! Magnificat!
Praise God my soul, praise God.
The proud are downed,
the poor raised up.
Magnificat, my soul!

To the tune Amazing Grace

Reader Psalm 2; 45; 46; 48; 61; 62; 84; 89:1-4, 19-29;
98; 99; 103; 110; *or* 115

Pause

Leader We offer you, Lord, the troubles of this day.
We lay down our burdens at your feet.
Forgive us our sins,
give us your peace,
and help us to receive your Word.

All In the name of Christ.
Amen.

God's Word

Reader Isaiah 11:1-9 *or the Old Testament reading of the day*

Singing may follow

Leader When the day takes its toll,

All	Christ bounds down the mountains towards us.
Leader	When we cry out in pain,
All	Christ bounds down the mountains towards us.
Leader	When all's well with the world,
All	Christ bounds down the mountains towards us.
Leader	When we need strength to do right,
All	Christ bounds down the mountains towards us.

Reader   Hebrews 1:1-6 *or the New Testament reading of the day*

Thanksgiving

Leader   We give you thanks, our God,
that you are always present,
in all things,
each day and each night.
We give you thanks for your gifts of creation, life
and friendship.
We give you thanks for the particular blessings
of this day . . .

There may be a brief pause, the naming of blessings, singing in tongues or a song

Intercession

Any of the following prayers may be used

Leader   Christ,
the peace of things above
and the rest of those below,
establish in your peace the five continents,
and especially your universal Church.
Destroy wars from the ends of the earth
and disperse those who delight in terror.

69

Reader   Child of glory,
Child of Mary,
born in the stable,
King of all,
you came to our wasteland,
in our place suffered.
By choosing to be born as a child
you teach us to reverence every human life.
May we never despise, degrade or destroy life.
Rather, help us sustain and preserve it.

We offer to you lone parents, children
and families;
our schools;
those who care for frail loved ones.

Leader   Child of Humanity,
Trinity's only Son,
gentle and strong,
from whose line we were born,
bring your peace to your warring children:
All   Peace between rich and poor,
peace between believers and unbelievers,
peace between parents and children.
Leader   Bring your peace to those we name before you
now . . .

Persons may be named, aloud or silently

Leader   Help us, Lord,
to guard our words,
to overcome hostility with love,
to make peace,
in love of the King of Life.

All   Deep peace of the running wave be ours,
deep peace of the flowing air,
deep peace of the quiet earth,
deep peace of the shining stars,
deep peace of the Son of peace.

Tuesday Night Prayer

Leader Peace to you and to all who seek good.

All The peace of the Spirit be mine this night;
the peace of the Son be mine this night;
the peace of the Father be mine this night;
the peace of all peace be mine this night;
each morning and evening of my life.

There may be singing

Leader We offer you, Lord, the troubles of this day;
we lay down our burdens at your feet.
Forgive us our sins,
give us your peace,
and help us to receive your Word.

Reader Psalm 46 *or another psalm*

Leader May fears of day recede.
All May treasures of night draw near.

Leader O Christ, Son of the living God,
may your holy angels guard our sleep;
may they watch over us as we rest
and hover around our beds.
Let them reveal to us in our dreams
visions of your glorious truth.
May no fears or worries
delay our willing, prompt repose.

Reader *The following or other words of Christ are read*

Come to me, all you who are weary
and burdened,
and I will give you rest.

Take my yoke upon you and learn from me,
for I am gentle and humble of heart,
and you will find rest for your souls.

Matthew 11:28-29

*Thoughts on the reading may be shared, there may
be silence, or other words from God may be spoken
spontaneously*

Leader   Our dear ones bless, O God, and keep in every
place where they are.

Dear ones may be named

All   May heaven's peacekeepers encircle us all
with their outstretched arms,
to protect us from the hostile powers,
to put balm into our dreams,
to give us contented, sweet repose.

Leader   We lie down in peace
knowing our sins are forgiven.
All   We lie down in peace
knowing death has no fear.
Leader   We lie down in peace
knowing no powers can harm us.
All   We lie down in peace
knowing Jesus is near.

Leader   Deep peace of the Spirit to you.

The following may be said or sung

All   Peace to you: peace of the air flowing out to you.
Peace to you: peace of the stars shining out to you.
Peace to you.
Peace to you.
Peace to you.

Creative Activities

1. Make or bring white peace ribbons, pin them to clothing and wear them throughout the day.

2. Form a circle in silence and hold the hands of the persons next to you. Stay in peaceful silence for one minute.

3. All stand and face the direction of the exit; raise the right hand in blessing of the world with peace. Stand like this for half a minute, mirroring Christ's peace to the world.

Wednesday –
The Healing, Sending Spirit

In the middle of the week the focus is the God who sends
and whose Spirit heals us and gives gifts for mission.

Wednesday Morning Prayer

Leader	Come, Creator Spirit, fresh as the morning dew,
All	Revive us and make us new.

Leader	Let us arise today in the Spirit's power:

Leader	In the place of fear,
All	God's strength to uphold me;
Leader	In the place of emptiness,
All	God's wisdom to guide me;
Leader	In the place of confusion,
All	God's eye for my seeing;
Leader	In the place of discord,
All	God's ear for my hearing;
Leader	In the place of froth,
All	God's word for my speaking;
	to save me from false agendas
	that harm my body or soul.

There may be singing

God's Word

First	Happy are those who heed neither the words
	nor the ways of the godless,
	whose delight is in God's law
	on which they meditate day and night.

Second	They are like trees planted by streams,
	which yield their fruit every season.
	Their leaves do not wither;
	they flourish in all they do.

First	The godless are not so. They are like refuse
	blown about by the wind.

They are like wrongdoers who fail to fool
a court of justice;
even if they sidle in with those who do right
they are exposed for what they are.

Second   The way of the godless will come to nothing,
but God looks after the path of those who do right.

Psalm 1

All   Glory to God,
Creator, Redeemer, Sustainer for ever.
Amen.

*Or one of the following may be read: Psalm 8; 29;
46; 47; 65; 93; 111; 117; 145; 146; or 150*

Leader   From false desires and selfish deeds,
All   All-knowing God, deliver us.
Leader   From unworthy thoughts and prideful claims,
All   All-seeing God, deliver us.
Leader   From unclean hearts and petty ways,
All   All-cleansing God, deliver us.

Reader   Isaiah 49:1-8 *or the Old Testament reading
followed by a Proclamation or song*

Matthew 28:16-20 *or the New Testament reading
of the day*

*There may be meditation, silence, teaching, sharing
or singing*

Intercession

Leader   Come like fire and warm our hearts.
Come like wind and refresh our frames.
Come like water and revive our souls.
Come like the earth and nourish our being.

Reader	Holy Spirit, release us,
	that we may be strong and free.
	Sending Spirit, empower us to touch lives for you;
	may your Church grow in holiness
	and in numbers.
	Disturbing Spirit, stir us up to be just and true.

The following prayer may be sung or said

Leader	On those whose day is drab,
All	Come Holy Spirit.
Leader	On those who harbour fear,
All	Come, Holy Spirit.
Leader	On a parched land,
All	Come, Holy Spirit.

There may be free or prepared intercessions

Leader	Eternal God and Father,
	you create us by your power
	and redeem us by your love:
	guide and strengthen us by your Spirit
	that we may give ourselves in love and service
	to one another and to you.

Daily Office, revised

There may be singing

	May your Church grow in holiness
	and in numbers.
All	Peace and blessing from the Spirit,
	and from the Three who are ever One.

Wednesday Midday Prayer

Leader   Holy Spirit,
come as a gentle breeze that cools in the heat
of the day;
come as the calming Presence that restores
stillness to our being.

All   Wind of Heaven,
blow away dross and deceits.
Refresh our battered souls.
Brace us for what is to come.

There may be silence or singing

Reader   Psalm 61:1-4 *or* Psalm 23

Leader   Perfect Comforter! Wonderful Refreshment!
You make peace to dwell in our soul.
In our labour, you offer rest;
in temptation, strength.
From heaven, shine forth with your glorious light.

From the Taizé Prayer Book

The following may be read by readers or singers

When my life seems all duty and dust
in the midst of the day when we droop;
when routine things turn into rust
and people from valour do stoop;
then the Wild Goose comes to my aid:
her wings pass o'er and give shade,
make the day's scorching heat soon fade,
and I know in God's image I'm made
and that nothing of this world can degrade;
nothing of this world can degrade.

Andrew Dick

Reader	Happy are you when you are defamed
	or excluded.
	Leap for joy, your reward in heaven is great.
Reader	The Spirit will show you what to say.
Reader	The Holy Spirit joins with our spirit to affirm
	that we are children of God.
All	Alleluia!

*There may be singing, sharing, free prayer or the
Lord's Prayer*

Leader	Holy Spirit,
	for the rest of the day renew in us:
All	Joy in our work,
	life in our being,
	love in our relationships.

Wednesday Evening Prayer

Leader   Kindling Spirit, come;
            inflame our waiting hearts.
All   Consoling Spirit, come;
            you know our every need.

There may be singing

Reader   Psalm 74:1-17; 139:1-12 *or another psalm*

There may be a pause

*The following may be sung by all to the tune Veni,
Creator Spiritus, or read by a reader or together*

Come, Holy Spirit, our souls inspire,
and lighten with eternal fire.
Implant in us your grace from above.
Enter our minds and hearts with love.

O come, anointing Spirit of peace,
Well-spring of life and gentleness.
Past ages called you the Paraclete.
To us you bring your sevenfold gifts.

You are the Power of God's right hand,
promise of God to the waiting Church,
words of true life on human lips.
Illumine now our hearts anew.

Come pour your love into our souls,
refresh our weak frame with incoming strength.
Give grace and courage to endure.
Cast away our deadly foe.

Grant us your peace for evermore.
With you as Guide upon the way,
evil shall no more harm our souls.
We shall know as we are known.

Teach us the Trinity to know,
Father, Son and Spirit, One:
The Three in One and One in Three
Now and ever, eternally.

Adapted from Veni, Creator Spiritus,
ascribed to Rabanus Maurus,
a ninth-century Solitary in Gaul

God's Word

Reader   Isaiah 49:1-6 *or the Old Testament reading*
of the day

There may be silence

John 14:15-17; Romans 8:15-17; 8:26-27;
1 Corinthians 12:1-11; Galatians 5:22-25;
or the New Testament reading of the day

There may be meditation, teaching, sharing,
creative activity or singing

Intercession

Leader   Spirit of Truth, look down upon a world
in thrall to lies and illusions.

All   Work in the darkness to bring all things
into light.

Leader   Anointing Spirit, distribute among us your gifts:

All   Wisdom, understanding and strength;
knowledge, reverence and insight.

There may be silence, the use of spiritual gifts or singing

Leader   Great Creator of the blood red moon
and falling stars,
Great Saviour of the miraculous birth
and rising from death,
Great Spirit of the seers and sacred words,

All   Come into our minds,
come into our dreams,
come into our mouths,
until we become your presence and sign.

Leader   Comforting Spirit,
come to all who pass through trial
and to those we love.

Names may be mentioned aloud or in silence
There may be singing

Leader   Into the life of the Three I immerse you.
May their breath be yours to live.
May their love be yours to give.

Wednesday Night Prayer

Leader In the name of the God of wholeness,
in the name of Compassion's Son,
in the name of the healing Spirit,
tonight may we be one.

Christ is always present when we gather
in his name.
Tonight we welcome him as healer.

All Healer, we come to you with our wounds
and our hurts.
Release among us your power to heal.

*There may be singing, and a reading from a psalm
that builds faith, such as Psalm 23; 27; 30; 34;
42; 43; 51; 86; 103; or 121*

Leader To prepare ourselves to receive God's healing,
let us forsake those things that impede it.
All Father, for the ways we have marred your image
in us, forgive us.
Leader For resentment, rush or lack of trust,
All Forgive us.
Leader Let us open ourselves in love and faith to the
healing presence of Christ.

Pause

There may be readings about healing, such as,
Isaiah 35:3-6; 53:1-5; Mark 1:29-45; 2:1-12;
11:5-13; Acts 3:1-16; 28:7-10; 2 Corinthians
3:4-6; James 5:13-16

Leader   May the Divine Father make us instruments
of healing.
May the Complete Christ take from us all that
hinders healing.
May the Holy Spirit give us power for healing.

Christ always walks the world
with those who suffer.
Tonight we pray for people, unknown to us,
who suffer in broken places of the world.

*There is a pause, or any may mention the names of
places*

Leader   Strong God of life, come to the people
in all these places.
All   Reach into their bodies, minds and souls
with your healing love.

Leader   Tonight we circle in healing prayer
those we now name.
All   Spirit of the living God, present with us now,
circle these we name.
Enter their body, mind and spirit,
and heal them of all that harms.

*Any may mention names; afterwards, the above
words are repeated*

*If there is laying on of hands, use the form in the
Service of Healing in Volume Four of this series*

There may be singing

Leader	Great Spirit, who broods over the sleeping world, as we sleep this night,
All	Restore the garment of our self-respect, and remake us in your beauty.
Leader	Renew in us, as we sleep,
All	The stillness of our being, the soundness of our bodies, and bring to dawn our wholeness.

Creative Activities

1. Imitate Christ's last commission to his followers to make disciples of all peoples: one person stands on a platform or chair, holding out a globe of the world; the others stand in front of that person, holding out their arms in blessing.

2. Choose a saying of Christ and turn it into a teletext message.

3. Several people wave or dance with streamers, each of a different colour.

Thursday – God in Community

It was on a Thursday that Jesus prayed for unity, spoke of himself, the Father and the Spirit as a Co-unity in God, and instituted Holy Communion.

So on Thursdays we pray for unity, community and sacrament at the heart of the world.

Thursday Morning Prayer

Leader Birther of the human race,
you summon the day to dawn
and call us to live in communion.

All Thrice holy God, eternal Three in One,
make your people holy, make your people one.
Stir up in us the flame that burns out pride
and power.
Restore in us the trust that brings the servant
heart to flower.
Thrice holy God, come as the morning dew.
Inflame in us your love that draws all lesser loves
to you.

Thanksgiving

There may be singing

First God be gracious to us and bless us.
May your face shine upon us.

Second Make known your ways on earth,
your saving health among all nations.

All May all the peoples praise you, O God.
May all the peoples praise you.

First May the nations be glad and sing for joy,

Second For you rule the peoples justly
and guide the nations upon earth.

All May all the peoples praise you, O God.
May all the peoples praise you.

First   Then the land will yield its produce
and our God will bless us.

Second   You will bless us
and the ends of the earth will honour you.

Psalm 67

All   Glory to the Father,
to the Son
and to the Spirit,
one God who mothers us all.

or

Reader   Psalm 2; 12; 33; 46; 48; 68:4-10; 76; 78:1-8;
80; *or* 81:1-10

Lament

Leader   We confess to God in the company of this people
All   That our lives and the world are fragmented
by sin.

There may be a pause

Leader   Source of all,
All   Have mercy on us.
Leader   Saviour of all,
All   Have mercy on us.
Leader   Sustainer of all,
All   Have mercy on us.
Leader   The Saviour reaches out his hand to announce
a loving reconciliation.
All   Thanks be to God.

God's Word

Reader	Isaiah 56:1-8 *or the Old Testament reading of the day*
Men	May our sons be like plants that grow up strong.
All	Happy the people whose God is the Eternal Source.
Women	May our daughters be like pillars that grace a palace.
All	Happy the people whose God is the Eternal Source.
Leader	May our stores be filled with worthy goods.
All	Happy the people whose God is the Eternal Source.
Leader	May creatures and crops grow into well-being.
All	Happy the people whose God is the Eternal Source.
Leader	May our streets be free from clamour and crime.
All	Happy the people whose God is the Eternal Source.

From Psalm 144

Reader	Ephesians 2:11-18 *or the New Testament reading of the day*
	There may be meditation, sharing, teaching or singing

Intercession

After any of the following responses, examples of current concerns may be given

Leader	Ground of all being, all peoples come from you.
All	May we honour one another and seek the common good.

Leader Reconciler of all people –
employers, employees and shareholders
are like fingers on your hands.

All May the wealth and work of the world
be available to all and for the exploitation of none.

Leader Unity of the world, from you all peace,
all justice flow.

All May we cherish the web of life and respect
the rule of law.

There may be creative activity or singing

Leader Eternal God and Father,
you create us by your power
and redeem us by your love:
guide and strengthen us by your Spirit
that we may give ourselves in love and service
to one another and to you.

Daily Office, revised

All Amen.

Leader Into the Sacred Three I immerse you.
Into their power and peace I place you.

All May their breath be ours to live.
May their love be ours to give.

Thursday Midday Prayer

Leader   God of justice, God of peace,
in the heat of the day
we take refuge in you.

Leader   Glory to you, Father.
All   Glory to you.
Leader   Glory to you, Saviour.
All   Glory to you.
Leader   Glory to you, Spirit.
All   Glory to you.

Reader   How good it is, how pleasing,
for God's people to live together in harmony.
It is like precious ointment running down a face.
It is like dew falling on the hills.

From Psalm 133

Leader   We weave this day,
All   Silence of knowing,
clearness of seeing,
grace of speaking.
Leader   We weave this day,
All   Humility of listening,
depth of understanding,
joy of serving.
Leader   We weave this day,
All   Peace of being,
gift of loving,
power of meeting.

Reader   Jesus said: 'Where two or three come together
in my name I am there.'

Matthew 18:20

'Do for others what you want them to do for you.'

Matthew 7:12

There may be silent meditation
All may say, or sing to the tune Bunessan

All   Christ be within me,
Christ be beside me,
Christ in the stranger,
Christ in the friend,
Christ in my speaking,
Christ in my thinking,
Christ in my working,
Christ at my end.

Leader   God of community,
Spirit of energy and change,
pour on us, without reserve or distinction,
that we may have strength
to plant your justice on earth.

Your kingdom come,
your will be done,
on earth, as it is in heaven.

All   Your kingdom come.

Leader   Your kingdom come in the people or situations
we now name.

Any   Your kingdom come in . . .

People or situations may be named aloud or silently

All   The Three who are over our head,
the Three who provide our bread,
be with us wherever we tread.

Thursday Evening Prayer

Leader Holy, holy, holy is the eternal Flame undying,
burning here among us in sacrificial love.

Candles or spotlights may be lit

Thanksgiving

Leader We give you thanks, Kindling Light,
that you led our forebears in the Faith
through a cloud by day and a fire by night,
and that you ever lead your people on.
We give you thanks that you have led us
to this place.
Pour forth your kindness on your people,
Father, Saviour, and radiant Spirit.

There may be singing

Reader Psalm 80; 81; 82; 85; 87; 105:1-15, 16-45;
106:1-5; 122; *or* 125

God's Word

Leader We offer to you, Lord, the troubles of this day;
we lay down our burdens at your feet.
Forgive us our sins, give us your peace,
and help us to receive your Word.

All In the name of Christ.
Amen.

Reader Isaiah 51:4-6 *or the Old Testament reading
of the day*

Leader	Triune God who mothers us all, nurture the people through your Church. Through her pastors,
All	Nourish us.
Leader	Through her teachers,
All	Establish us.
Leader	Through her prophets,
All	Envision us.
Leader	Through her musicians,
All	Inspire us.
Leader	Through her saints,
All	Sanctify us.
Leader	Through her givers,
All	Bless us.

Reader Revelation 5:1-10 *or the New Testament reading of the day*

Teaching or silent reflection on the Word; occasionally this may lead to confession

There may be singing

Intercession

Leader Lord Christ,
you prayed for the unity of all who believe.
May your churches, rejoicing in the communion of heaven,
attain communion round one table on earth.
Lord Christ,
you call us to love our neighbours.
May our local communities seek
the common good.
Lord Christ,
through bread and wine you give us signs
of your Presence
transforming all creation.

Leader   May artists and those in the media
glimpse this vision,
and reflect it to the world.

The leader says one or more of the following,
or other prayers

O God, grant us unity.
Bless the oppressed,
bless the oppressor.
Draw all people home to you.

Deliver the oppressed,
pity the unnoticed,
raise the fallen,
show yourself to the needy,
heal the sick,
bring back those who have strayed,
feed the hungry,
lift up the weak,
remove the prisoners' chains.
May every people come to know
that you are God,
that Jesus Christ is your Child,
that we are your people.

Clement of Rome, c. 200

May petty ways drop from us like scales
until we seek the greatness of others,
we rejoice in being givers,
and heaven delights in our pleasure.

May our nation find your will as her destiny,
and God-guided representatives at home
and abroad.

Leader   May she find peace within herself
and become a peacemaker
in the international family.

Lord Jesus Christ, Light of the world,
by your cross you have overcome
all darkness that oppresses.

All   Come and shine on us in our communities
that we may grow and live together in your love
which makes us one with all humanity.

There may be singing

All   The grace of our Lord Jesus Christ,
the love of God,
and the fellowship of the Holy Spirit
be with us all evermore.
Amen.

Thursday Night Prayer

Three candles may be lit as a reader says (or readers say)
the following

Reader(s) I light a light in the name of the Father
who fosters us.
I light a light in the name of the Saviour
who embraces us.
I light a light in the name of the Spirit
who encircles us.

All One is the God from whom all people come.
One earth is the bed on which we make
our home.
One is the air that all creatures breathe.

Leader On your world, Lord,
All Your love descend this night.
Leader On your Church, Lord,
All Your love descend this night.
Leader On all who work, Lord,
All Your love descend this night.
Leader Where there is strife, Lord,
All Your love descend this night.
Leader Where there is neglect, Lord,
All Your love descend this night.
Leader On all who sleep, Lord,
All Your love descend this night.

Reader Psalm 111 *or another psalm*

There may be singing

Leader   We thank you for your presence through the day
and for friends who have helped us on our way.
As shadows fall
and the wheels of the world grow still,
forgive us for our failures in love.
Visit this house and drive away
all that would harm.
May holy angels preserve us in peace.

Reader   Romans 12:15-18 *or* 1 Peter 2:9-10

Leader   Circle the world, Lord.
All   Keep grudges without.
Keep friendship within.
Leader   Circle the world, Lord.
All   Keep wrangling without.
Keep trust within.
Leader   Circle those we bring before you now.

*Names may be mentioned aloud or silently
and there may be singing*

Support us, Lord,
through life's troubled day,
until the shadows lengthen
and evening comes,
the fever of life is over
and our work is done.
Then, Lord, in your mercy,
give us a holy rest,
and peace at the last.

*After a prayer of
Cardinal Newman*

There may be silence or singing

Leader	Kindle in our hearts, O God,
	the flame of that love which never ceases;
	that it may burn in us this night,
	till we shine for ever in your presence.

Leader	God with us lying down,
All	God with us rising up,
Leader	Christ with us sleeping,
All	Christ with us waking,
Leader	Spirit with us now,
All	Spirit with us evermore.

Creative Activities

1. Using the image of the world's work being like fingers on God's hand, form a circle, hold out the right arm with the five fingers extended, so that pairs of hands with outstretched fingers converge at the centre of the circle.

2. Form a circle and hold hands, silently praying for the unity of that for which you have prayed.

3. Using a bowl of water and a sponge, wash an object, picture or person symbolising an area of the world or an area of need that needs to be served, as Christ washed his disciples' feet.

4. Place a globe in the front or centre of the worship area.

Creative Activities

...

Friday – The Cross

On a Friday, Jesus the Christ, Son of God, was put to death on a cross. In common with the universal Church, Christians in the Celtic tradition make themselves one with Christ's suffering on Fridays, and also with the suffering and broken people of the world.

Aidan's disciples ate no food until 3pm on Fridays in order to develop empathy with Christ and time for meditation.

Friday Morning Prayer

Leader On this day of Christ's suffering and death,
let us be one with him in his wounds.

All We seek to tread in the steps of Christ,
who has shown us the way, when strong,
when weak.

Either

Reader Psalm 3; 6; 13; 25; 26; 32; 39; 56; 74:1-12; 77;
116; *or* 142

All Glory to the Supreme God,
the Maker, the Saviour, and the Spirit,
who pour out their life for us,
always and for ever.

or

Leader Who has believed what we heard foretold about
the arm of God?

First He grew up before God like a tender shoot;
like a root out of dry ground.

Second He had no beauty or majesty to attract us to him;
nothing in his appearance to make us desire him.

First People despised and rejected him.
He was a man of sorrows, steeped in grief.
Like someone from whom people avert their gaze,
he was looked down upon and given no esteem.

Second Yet even though we thought God had afflicted him
and cast him down,
there is no doubt he took our frailties
and carried our sorrows.

First   He was pierced for our sins,
             he was crushed for our wrongdoing.
             His punishment brought peace to us;
             we are healed by his wounds.

Second   Like sheep we have all gone astray,
             we have each followed our own way
             and God has pinned our failings on to him.

First   After his soul-suffering he will see the light of joy.
             This righteous servant will put right many people.

Second   He will be ranked with the greatest
             because he poured out his life and his prayers
             for us.
                                                    Isaiah 53:2-5

All   Glory to the Maker,
             glory to the Son,
             glory to the Spirit,
             ever Three and ever One.

Lament

Leader   Jesus, you were driven to the sands
             by the searching Spirit.
All   Strip from us what is not of you.

Confession is made in silence, or as follows

Leader   Forgive us for our selfish deeds,
             our empty speech
             and the words with which we have wounded.

Pause

All   Forgive us for our false desires,
             our vengeful attitudes
             and for what we have left untended.

107

There may be a pause or music of lament

Leader Holy Jesus, hanged on a tree, victorious over death,
forgive us for these sins,
free us from these evils
and power us into new ways.

There may be singing

God's Word

Reader Genesis 22:1-14 *or the Old Testament reading of the day*

Leader Jesus, Saviour of the world,
come to us in your mercy.
All We look to you to save and help us.
Leader By your cross and life laid down, you set your people free.
All We look to you to save and help us.
Leader When your disciples were about to perish, you reached down and saved them
All We look to you to come to our help.
Leader In the greatness of your mercy, free us from our chains.
All Forgive the sins of all your people.
Leader Come now, and dwell with us, Lord Christ Jesus.
All Hear our prayer and be with us always.
Leader And when you come in your glory,
All Make us to be one with you and to share the life of your kingdom.

Leader John 19:31-37 *or the New Testament reading of the day*

There may be silence, a Proclamation, creative activity, sharing or singing

Intercession

Leader   Jesus, broken on the cross,
we bring to you those suffering
from broken dreams,
broken relationships
and broken promises.

There may be silence or any may mention names

Leader   Jesus,
All   Have mercy on them.

Leader   Jesus, who lost everything,
we bring to you those who have suffered
loss of work, mobility and well-being.

There may be silence or any may mention names

Leader   Jesus,
All   Have mercy on them.

Leader   Jesus, Defenceless victim,
we bring to you those who are victims
of violence, abuse and false accusation.

There may be silence or any may mention names

Leader   Jesus,
All   Have mercy on them.

Leader   Jesus, alone and destitute,
we bring to you those who are lonely,
homeless and hungry.

There may be silence or any may mention names

Leader   Jesus,
All   Have mercy on them.

Leader	Saviour, you died that we may be brought back to you. Save and raise up those who have none but you to turn to.
Leader **All**	Jesus, Have mercy on them.

The Lord's Prayer may be said.
There may be singing

Leader	May the Christ who walks with wounded feet walk with you on the road. May the Christ who serves with wounded hands stretch out your hands to serve. May the Christ who loves with wounded heart open your hearts to love.

Friday Midday Prayer

Leader   Jesus, Master Carpenter of Nazareth,
who, through wood and nails,
won our full salvation,
wield well your tools in this your workshop
that we who come to you rough hewn
may here be fashioned into a truer beauty
by your hand.

Traditional

Reader   Psalm 31:1-5; 42:1-5; 43; 86:1-13; *or* 90

There may be silence or singing

Leader   We draw aside in the midst of the day.
We weep for the hungry and poor;
the children mistreated; those broken by force;
and the maimed who can't finish their course.

All   We plead for your justice to fill all the lands
as the waters cover the sands.

Leader   We pray against cruelty, hatred and pain;
against pride and greed for gain.
We pray for the homeless and victims of war;
the strangers to love at the door.

All   We plead for your justice to fill all the lands
as the waters cover the sands.

Andrew Dick

Leader   Lord Jesus,
at this hour you hung on the cross,
stretching out your arms in love to all.
May the peoples of the world be drawn to your
uplifted love,
especially those we shall work with or meet today.

111

All	Give us the will to share our bread with the hungry, to give shelter to those who feel rejected, and to reach out to those in need.
Leader	We pray for those whose tasks are backbreaking, whose bodies are mutilated or whose spirits are crushed.

During a silence, think of the hungry, the poor and the oppressed, and of Jesus on the cross in solidarity with them

There may be free prayer

Reader	Hear these words of Jesus – Happy you who hunger for justice:
All	You will be filled.
Reader	Happy you who show mercy:
All	You will receive mercy.
Leader	Happy you who weep for the world:
All	You will laugh.

There may be singing

Leader	Lord Jesus, in the midst of mockery and madness, you found peace to remain in your Father's will.
All	In the midst of fretful day, give us peace to remain in our Father's will.
Leader	Our Father in heaven, honoured be your name. Your kingdom come, your will be done on earth, as in heaven. Give us this day our daily supplies, and forgive us our sins as we forgive those who sin against us.

Leader   Lead us not into time of trial,
but deliver us from evil.

All   For yours is the kingdom,
the power and the glory,
for ever and ever.
Amen.

Friday Evening Prayer

Leader	Sacrificial Love lingers still among us,
All	Calling us to wait and to watch.
Leader	Eternal Light,
All	Shine into our hearts.
Leader	Eternal Goodness,
All	Deliver us from evil.
Leader	Eternal Power,
All	Strengthen us.
Leader	Eternal Wisdom,
All	Scatter the darkness of our ignorance.
Leader	Eternal Pity,
All	Have mercy on us.
Leader	With our whole being we shall seek your face,
All	Until we are brought to your holy Presence.

After Alcuin

There may be a chant, meditative singing or a Kyrie

Reader	Psalm 139:1-13, 23-34 *or the psalm of the day*

Lament

Leader	Lord, you were tested by the evil one.
All	Break in us the hold of power and pride.
Leader	You knew deep tears and weaknesses.
All	Help us to be vulnerable for you.
Leader	You followed to the end the Way of the Cross.
All	Help us to be faithful to you to the end of our days.
Reader	Lamentations 3:25-40 *or the Old Testament reading of the day*

There may be silence or a Proclamation

God's Word

Reader   John 10:11-18 *or the New Testament reading of the day*

There may be teaching, creative activity, sharing or singing

Intercession

Leader   Lord, teach us to understand that your Son died to save us,
not from suffering, but from ourselves;
not from injustice, but from being unjust.
He died that we might live as he did,
who died to himself.

George MacDonald

All   In union with witnesses and martyrs of Christ,
in communion with all who have died
in the faith of Christ,
we commit ourselves to our living God.

Leader   As we struggle to be faithful to you and to establish justice,
we bring to you those who are in chains.

There may be a pause, prepared or free prayer

We bring to you those who are persecuted
or oppressed,
the homeless, the hungry
and those in grinding poverty.

There may be a pause, prepared or free prayer

We bring to you those who are in pain
behind closed doors.

All   Lord Jesus, you were released from the pain
of the cross.
In you may the suffering find release.

Leader   We bring to you those who are locked into hatred.
All   Calm their hatred.
Fill their hearts and ours with generous love.

There may be singing

Leader   We go in the sign of the cross of Christ *(make sign)*:
the cross before us to keep us true,
the cross behind us to shield us from ill,
the cross above us to lead us through.

Friday Night Prayer

There may be singing

Leader	Shadows darken this day:
All	The day Christ was laid in a grave.
Leader	The darkness shall not engulf us,
All	For with you the darkness is light.

Leader	Lord, by your Cross and precious death,
All	Save us from the powers of evil,
	save us from another's harm,
	save us from our selfish failings.
	Come this night and give us calm.

Reader	Psalm 88:1-9; 90:1-12; 130; 139:1-12; *or* Isaiah 53:2-5

Leader	Give us sorrow for our violations
	of human dignity
	and our sins against hospitality.
	Give us sorrow for the sins of the day:
All	That when our bodies become but ashes
	we may live with you for ever.
Leader	Let us reflect on the things that drive Christ
	from us.

There may be a silent examination of conscience

Leader	Forgive us our sins.
All	Lord, forgive.

Words such as Lord have mercy, or Kyrie eleison may be sung

117

Reader	As he was dying a martyr's death Jesus said:
	'My God, my God, why have you forsaken me?'
Leader	Christ forsaken,
All	Have mercy on all who are forsaken.
Leader	Christ afraid,
All	Have mercy on all who are afraid.
Leader	Christ betrayed,
All	Have mercy on all who are betrayed.
Leader	Christ unnoticed,
All	Have mercy on all who are unnoticed.

Leader   In silence or aloud, let us name those who need our prayers.

People may mention names

Leader   Great God who mothers us all,
gather the sufferings of all
into the communion of the crucified Christ.

All   Shield and deliver them
and look on them with your merciful gaze.

There may be singing, a creative activity, sharing, or one of these readings: Zechariah 12:8, 10; Song of Songs 8:6-7 *or* 1 Thessalonians 5:9-10

Leader   Jesus said:
Father into your hands I commit my life.

All   Father, into your hands we commit our lives.

Leader   Father, at the foot of your Son's cross,
help us to see and know your love for us.

All   Father, into your hands we commit our lives.

All   At last, all-powerful Master,
you give leave to your servant
to go in peace according to your promise.
For my eyes have seen your salvation,

which you have prepared for all nations –
a light to illumine the world
and give glory to your people.

Nunc dimittis

Or all sing or say

Faithful vigil ended,
Watching, waiting, cease:
Master, grant your servant
his discharge in peace.

All your Spirit promised,
all the Father willed,
now these eyes behold it
perfectly fulfilled.

This your great deliverance
sets your people free;
Christ their light uplifted
all the nations see.

Christ, your people's glory!
Watching, doubting cease;
grant to us your servants
our discharge in peace.

Timothy Dudley Smith

Leader O Christ,
who at this evening hour rested in the tomb
and made it become a bed of hope,
visit this house tonight,
that we may pass through the death of sleep
and rise from our beds in hope of life eternal.
All Then, Lord, give us a peaceful night
and a good ending to life.

Leader I make the sign of the cross of Christ *(make sign)*:
All My Christ,
    my Shield,
    my Saviour;
    each day, each night,
    in light, in dark;
    my Treasure,
    my dear One,
    my eternal home.

Creative Activities

1. Provide a container of sand placed on a cloth over the floor. Each person may place a bare foot in the sand and then leave a footprint on a sheet of white paper, praying inwardly to Christ, 'Lead me into the desert with you.'

2. Go without lunch and visualise people who are malnourished in another part of the world and Christ who was without food on the Friday of his crucifixion.

3. Display recent newspaper cuttings of broken, hungry or homeless people.

4. Lay a large wooden cross on the floor or ground where you pray together.

Devotion before the cross
An Alternative Friday-night Vigil Service

People gather in silence to kneel or sit around a cross or crucifix before which lights are burning. On the cross, the Saviour offered himself for the whole world, so at the foot of the cross we make ourselves one with him and join our prayers with his. Crosses of prostration were common throughout the Celtic highlands and islands up to the last century, and the custom in the Eastern Church of expressing devotion to Christ without words, by touching the cross with the forehead, fits well with the Celtic emphasis on using all five senses in devotions. Meditative singing may precede the Prayer.

> *This or another prayer of adoration is used, with a sung response (R) after each sentence, such as the chant O Adoramus Te, Domine*

Leader	Lord Jesus Christ, you gave up everything to restore our lost innocence.
All	(R)
Leader	You made your home on this earth, you overthrew the strongholds of Satan, and you freed those in prisons of sin.
All	(R)
Leader	Strong yet gentle, you take the burdens of all who are broken or bruised.
All	(R)
Leader	Suffering and victorious Champion of the poor, you open the gates of heaven's kingdom to all who call upon you.
All	(R)

The following words of Christ, spoken from the cross, may be said, with a sung response (R) such as O Christe, Domine Jesu after each

Reader Father forgive them,
for they know not what they do.

All (R)

Reader Truly I say to you,
today you will be with me in paradise.

All (R)

Reader He is your son; she is your mother.

All (R)

Reader My God, my God, why have you forsaken me?

All (R)

Reader I am thirsty . . . It is finished.

All (R)

Reader Father, into your hands I commit my spirit.

All (R)

Or the Reproaches in the Good Friday service may be used with a sung response; or there may be a Bible reading that records, presages or reflects Christ's passion, followed by a sung response

Leader In silence at the foot of Christ's cross,
we commune with Christ and Christ communes
with us.

Silence

Leader We bring to you the concerns of our heart.

Concerns or people may be named; there may be prepared intercessions

The leader invites any who wish, to kneel by the cross and touch it with their forehead or lips

This may be accompanied by quiet, meditative music, or by singing in the Spirit, which may continue longer

Leader   Hail! life-giving cross,
invincible banner of pure religion,
gate of paradise,
strength of believers,
defence of the Church.
By you the curse has been undone, destroyed,
the power of death devoured,
and we have been raised from earth to heaven.
Unbeatable weapon,
demonic powers' foe,
martyrs' glory,
boast of holy monks,
salvation's harbour,
from you the world receives great mercy.

When all creation saw you,
all things' Maker and Creator,
hang naked on the cross,
it was changed by fear and wailed.
The sun's light failed and the earth quaked.
The rocks were rent and the temple's veil
was rent in two.
The dead were raised from their tombs,
and the powers of heaven cried out
in astonishment:
How amazing this is!
The Judge is judged,
he wills to suffer death,
to heal and renew the world.

From an Orthodox Vespers

Leader O Christ, you were put to death by cruel people
who nailed your arms to a cross.
Yet, long before, you stretched out your arms
in love to all.
May your way be our way.
May we, too, stretch out our arms in love to all.

All Christ of the tears, of the wounds,
of the piercings,
may your cross this night be our shield:
your cross between us and all enemies without;
your cross between us and all enemies within;
your cross our sure way from earth to heaven.

Saturday –
God's Rule on Earth
and in Heaven

For many people Saturday is a time for leisure, shopping, or converse with the world. Morning and Midday Prayer reflect these pursuits.

The week is drawing to a close, and we prepare to move into a higher plane. Evening and Night Prayer introduce the theme of converse with the saints.

Saturday Morning Prayer

Leader   Life-giving God, the world lies open before you,
All   And you summon the day to dawn.
Leader   Open our being
All   And we shall show life.
Leader   Open our hearts
All   And we shall show love.
Leader   Open our mouths
All   And we shall show praise.

There may be singing

God's Word

Reader   God is my shepherd,
who refreshes me in green pastures,
restores me by quiet waters
and leads me to the right ways.

All   With God I lack nothing I truly need.

Reader   Even though I walk through the valley
of the shadow of death
I will fear no evil,
for you are with me,
your protecting staff comforts me.

All   With God I lack nothing I truly need.

Reader   You prepare a feast for me
even when hostile people surround me.
You anoint me with oil and my life overflows.

All   With God I lack nothing I truly need.

Reader   Surely goodness and mercy shall follow me all
the days of my life,
and I will dwell in your presence for ever.

Psalm 23, adapted

or

Reader   Psalm 33; 92; 97; 113; 117; 119:129-136; 125;
145; 147:1-14; *or* 149

Reader   Isaiah 66:7-14a *or the Old Testament reading
of the day may be read*

Leader	All that moves on the earth,
All	Bless your God.
Leader	All that swims in the water,
All	Bless your God.
Leader	All that flies in the air,
All	Give glory to God who nurtures us all.

Leader	Parents and children,
All	Bless your God.
Leader	Friends and lovers,
All	Bless your God.
Leader	Musicians and sportsfolk,
All	Give glory to God who nurtures us all.

Leader	Parks and play areas,
All	Bless your God.
Leader	Streets and shops,
All	Bless your God.
Leader	Homes and gardens,
All	Give glory to God who nurtures us all.

Reader   Matthew 7:7-12 *or the New Testament reading
of the day*

There may be meditation, teaching, singing or the following Proclamation

Men	We believe, O God of all gods, that you are the eternal God of life.
Women	We believe, O God of all peoples, that you are the eternal God of love.
Men	We believe that you create earth and seas and skies.
Women	We believe that you create us in your image and give us eternal worth.
All	We honour you with our whole being snd consecrate this day to you.

Intercession

Leader Let us pray.
Make whole the leisure and activity of this day.
Restrain its hostile impulses.
Fill its moments.

There may be silent reflection

Our Father in heaven,
hallowed be your name.
Your kingdom come,
your will be done,
on earth, as in heaven.

Leader	In our pleasures,
All	Your kingdom come.
Leader	In our leaders,
All	Your kingdom come.
Leader	In our gatherings,
All	Your kingdom come.
Leader	On the roads,
All	Your kingdom come.

Leader	On the networks,
All	Your kingdom come.
Leader	In each thing we do this day,
All	Your kingdom come.
Any	In . . . *(may mention examples)*
All	Your kingdom come.

Leader	Give us this day our daily supplies, and forgive us our sins as we forgive those who sin against us. Lead us not into temptation, but deliver us from evil.
All	For the kingdom, the power and the glory are yours, now and for ever. Amen.

There may be singing

Leader	May we do this day on earth
All	As the saints do in heaven.
Leader	May we live this day in your light,
All	And walk in the hope of your kingdom.

Saturday Midday

Leader	O Being of life,
	O Being of peace,
	O Being of time,
All	Be with us in the middle of the day.

Pause

Leader	O Being of truth,
	O Being of sight,
	O Being of wisdom,
All	Give us discernment in our choices.

There may be singing

| Reader | Psalm 119:1-8, 8-16, 33-40 *or* Psalm 119:169-176 |

Leader	Christ who stilled the storm,
All	Still the turmoil within.
Leader	Christ who overcame evil,
All	Overcome the evil without.

There may be a creative activity

Leader	Listen to Jesus' words:
	Happy you who are poor in heart;
	yours is the kingdom of God.
	Happy you who are clear in heart;
	you will see God.

There may be singing

First	Spirit,
	kindle in my heart a flame of love
	to my foe,
	to my friend,
	to all.

Second   In God is my strength;
God alone is sufficient.

Leader   Guardian,
be over the restless people a covering
of truth and peace.

There may be silent or free prayer

May the saints and the Saviour watch over us
and keep us true in all we do.

All   May we live the rest of this day
in the joy of the Saviour's will.

Saturday Evening Prayer

Leader Let us go for a while to the courts of heaven
and join with the saints in praise.

Thanksgiving

There may be singing or a short silence

Reader Psalm 84 *or the psalm of the day*

Leader If our mouths were full of song as the sea,
our tongues with joyful sounds
like the roar of its waves,
our lips with praise like the outspread sky,

All We still could not thank you enough, Yahweh.
for the good you have done to us
and our forebears.

Leader If our eyes were shining like the sun and the moon,
our hands stretched out like eagles' wings
in the air,
our feet as swift as the wild deer,

All We still could not thank you enough, Yahweh,
for the good you have done to us
and our forebears.

Leader You rescued us from the tyrant.
You freed us from slavery.

All In times of famine you fed us.
In times of plenty you built us up.

Leader From violence you delivered us.
From plagues you saved us.

All Therefore to you who breathed life into us
we shall give praise with all our breath,
honour with all our memory,
worship with all our being.

God's Word

Reader Ecclesiasticus 44:1-15 *or a reading from the Old Testament or from the Life of a saint*

Leader We bless you with all our being.
All Glory to our Maker,
glory to Christ,
glory to the Spirit,
one God who mothers us all.

Reader Hebrews 12:22-23 *or the New Testament reading of the day*

There may be meditation, creative activity or singing

Intercession

Leader God of the call, as we give thanks for the saints,
we pray for those who feel thwarted in their
vocation.
All May they do on earth as the saints do in heaven.

Leader God from whom all truth and justice flow,
we pray for the rule of law to prevail.
All May we do on earth as the saints do in heaven.

Leader God of resurrection,
in their worship, may our churches
bring honour to you,
joy to the people,
and healing to the land.
All May they do on earth as the saints do in heaven.

There may be free prayer and singing

Leader Let us bless the Lord,
All For yours, Lord, is the glory,
the power and the majesty,
for ever and ever.
Amen.

Saturday Night Prayer

On occasions when Saturday Night Prayer is extended into a night vigil, the reading for Sunday's main worship may be read and pondered, there may be creative activities, or there may be the slow, thoughtful repetition (say fifty times) of the Jesus Prayer: Lord Jesus Christ, Son of God, have mercy.

Leader	Eternal Creator of the weeks and years, as this week draws to a close, draw close to us,
All	And we will draw close to you.
Leader	Eternal Creator of the days and nights, as darkness deepens, draw near to us,
All	And we will draw near to you.

Most merciful God,
we confess to you,
before the company of heaven and one another,
that we have sinned in thought, word and deed,
and in what we have failed to do.
Forgive us our sins,
heal us by your Spirit,
and raise us to new life in Jesus Christ.

Reader   Psalm 119:52-62 *or* Psalm 130:1-6

The following or another hymn may be sung

Before the ending of the day,
Creator of the world, we pray
that you, with steadfast love, would keep
your watch around us while we sleep.

From evil dreams defend our sight;
from fears and terror of the night.
Tread underfoot our deadly foe
that we no sinful thought may know.

O Father, this we ask be done
through Jesus Christ, your only Son,
and Holy Spirit, by whose breath
our souls are raised to life from death.
Amen.

Reader   Hebrews 3:12–4:1

Leader   In our tiredness be our Rest.
All   In our stumbling be our Shield.

Reader   Into our place of darkness,
into our place of strife,
into our fears and worries,
All   Come with eternal life.

Reader   Into those who are dying,
into those weary of life,
into those tired from exertions,
All   Come with eternal life.

Leader   Let us bring before God the concerns of this day.

These may be mentioned aloud or in silence

There may be singing

Jesus,
master of apostles,
teacher of evangelists,
strength of martyrs,
friend of the poor,
crown of saints,
lead us through the night into a day of renewal.

May we rest secure in your love
All   And rise up to serve you with joy.
Leader   Come with the breaking of day
All   And meet us in the breaking of bread.

Creative Activities

1. Create a collage, pictures for projection on to a screen, or a mime of scenes of weekend life.

2. One person holds up an intercession banner or stick of a symbolic colour chosen for that week. The rest gather around and indicate, with paint, clay, spoken or written words, aspects of the restless world that they wish to bring under the banner of intercession.

3. Provide reminders of 'the great cloud of witnesses'; for example, by displaying their names, icons, or by using incense or smoke machines to symbolise the prayers they offer.

CHRISTIAN SEASONS

Advent –
A Second Lent Season
Before the Nativity

In the Celtic tradition the celebration of the Nativity of God's Son is preceded by a lesser Lent, a period of reflection, repentance, fasting from indulgent habits, and contemplation of the first and second comings of Christ. During this time, songs of celebration tend to recede, and vigil becomes more central.

In the Eastern Orthodox Church the first day of the fast begins forty days before Christmas, on 15 November. In the Western Church this was shortened and became synonymous with Advent, which seems to have been introduced from Rome in the late sixth century, Advent beginning on the fourth Sunday before Christmas Day and marking the beginning of the Church Year.

We are called to contemplate the coming among us of the Divine-Human King; also the four final realities of death, judgement, heaven and hell, and the fact that all people have to give account to God who comes as the light that exposes darkness. During this season, the Christian Church seeks to identify with countless people before Christ's birth who had intimations of his coming, and with the witnesses who prepared his way.

In Jewish tradition the religious year begins on the ninth day of Tishrei with Rosh Hashanah, the Day of Judgement.

As a sign of the common heritage that Christians share with Jewish people, a seven-branched candelabrum, or Menorah, may be used. A special Advent celebration that draws on Jewish tradition might include the blowing of a trumpet up to nine times and the use of drums to build up a sense of anticipation.

The Church also seeks to identify with those in today's world who look for the fulfilment of their aspirations.

In parts of Wales the tradition of The Plygain still flourishes. This is an early service held before dawn during Advent and Christmas when groups sing carols at length, full of wonder, of the birth, life and death of the one long prophesied.

In the Celtic imagination the drama of the incarnation can take place again in our own hearts and homes. But in order for something divine to be cradled and born in us, we have, during Advent, to be as Mary was before the birth: believing, waiting, praying; inviting the Holy Spirit to work within us.

In homes, echoing a Jewish custom, an apple may be dipped in honey before a meal, followed by prayers such as these:

Renew us to do what is true and right
that we may prepare a way for you to come anew, O God.

We bless you, O God, that you call us
to live clean and righteous lives.

Today may you mark us, O God,
to live this coming season a life of goodness.

The keeping of Advent as a time of preparation runs counter to the twenty-first-century secularised version of Advent, which is dominated by pressure to buy and party to excess. There is, however, a meeting point in the feast of

Saint Nicklaus, or Nicholas (Santa Claus) on 6 December (this will be developed in Volume Two). This monk and bishop used his inherited wealth to prevent poor people falling into bad ways. From 6 December households and churches may turn their fasting into almsgiving. Some churches call at homes with gifts for children or needy people, dressed as St Nicholas or with a card telling the story of Nicholas. Others collect gifts or money for the homeless and hungry, or arrange a Christmas meal for them.

Advent Candle-lightings

Variations of the following are traditional: four purple candles are placed on a circular base or wreath and a fifth, white candle is placed in the centre. Each candle may represent one or more persons who prepared the way for Christ's first coming, or who prepare the way for his coming now or in the future, or they may represent an aspiration. One candle is lit during the first week of Advent, two on the second and so on. The central candle, which represents Christ, is lit from Christmas night onwards.

Week 1 – The candle of people's longings

Reader We light the first candle of Advent:
the candle of longing,
the candle of solidarity with the yearnings
of the people
and with the hopes of our forebears in faith.

Reader If we walk by the divine light
we shall not go astray,
either to the right or to the left.
We shall always keep on the straight way,
chanting with the conquering Psalmist:
'O my God, light up my darkness,
for through you I shall be delivered.'

Columbanus

Reader	Creator of light,
All	Enter our darkness.
Reader	Saviour, who is the Light,
All	Enter our darkness.
Reader	Spirit, bringer of light,
All	Enter our darkness.

One candle is lit

Reader The candle of longing for Christ,
the Light of the world.

Reader Where people long for an end to injustice,
All Shine into their hearts.
Reader Where people long for conflict to cease,
All Shine into their hearts.
Reader Where people long to right inhuman working
conditions,
All Shine into their hearts.
Reader Where people long to restore the scarred places
of earth,
All Shine into their hearts.
Reader Where people long for dignity in human
relationships,
All Shine into their hearts.

Reader Come, God of justice.
Come, Prince of Peace.
Come, Liberator of the people.
Come, Saviour of the earth.
Come, Friend of all.

All Eternal Light, shine into our hearts.
Eternal Goodness, deliver us from evil.
Eternal Power, strengthen us.
Eternal Pity, have mercy upon us.
Eternal Wisdom, scatter the darkness
of our ignorance.
Amen.

Alcuin

145

Week 2 – The candle of the prophets' urgings

Reader   We light the second candle of Advent:
the candle of prophets calling for justice,
struggling for right to replace wrong,
for dignity to replace oppression;
the candle of prophets calling for waste places
to be renewed,
pointing to light emerging from the darkness.

Two candles are lit

Reader   The Lord will bring to light
the things now hidden in darkness
and will disclose the purposes of the heart.

1 Corinthians 4:5

Reader   Father, who sends the light,
Jesus, who is the light,
Spirit, who radiates the light,
we bring to you those in darkness.

Reader   Tend your sick ones.
All   Come to them, O Christ.
Reader   Rest your weary ones.
All   Come to them, O Christ.
Reader   Bless your dying ones.
All   Come to them, O Christ.
Reader   Soothe your suffering ones.
All   Come to them, O Christ.
Reader   Pity your afflicted ones.
All   Come to them, O Christ.
Reader   Shield your joyous ones.
All   Come to them, O Christ.
    All for love's sake.

After a prayer of St Augustine

Reader Send out your light and your truth.
Let them lead me,
let them bring me to where you make
your home.

All Amen.

Psalm 43:3

Week 3 – The candle of the Preparer

Reader We light the third candle of Advent:
the candle of the Preparer,
clearing away human resistance to God,
humbling the monuments to human pride,
giving voice to those who have no voice;
a sign of those who point the way to Christ,
who overturn false ways,
who live by the values of God.

Three candles are lit

Reader These point to the Light of Christ:

All a light that no darkness can quench.

Reader As the prophet foresaw:
The people who walked in darkness
have seen a great light.
The light has shined on those who lived
in a place of great darkness.
You have increased their joy.

Isaiah 9:2-3a

Reader To turn away from you, Lord,
is to turn to darkness.

All Come to us in our darkness.

Reader In the darkness, we lose our way.

All Come to us in our lostness.

Reader	In the dark, longings for love and birth arise.
All	Come to us in our longings.
Reader	In the dark, anger at injustice and neglect rises up.
All	Come to us in our anger.

Reader	Send us, O Lord, the light of your truth.
	Burn away evil desire.
	Dispel from our path the darkness of sin
	and ignorance.
All	Amen.

Week 4 – The candle of the God-bearer

Reader	We light the fourth candle of Advent:
	the candle of Mary who bears the Divine Glory,
	the candle of purity,
	the candle of all midwives of faith
	who bring the Divine to birth.

Four candles are lit

Reader	The angel comes to greet the God-bearing virgin.
All	Blessed be the coming Lord.
Reader	Envisioning the Child as the Lord embodied,
	the angel was rapt in wonder.
All	Blessed be the coming Lord.
Reader	You, O virgin, are the throne of the King.
All	Blessed be the coming Lord.
Reader	Through you the Joy of the world shall shine.
All	Blessed be the coming Lord.
Reader	To you through whom the Creator is to be born,
	creation will be reborn.
All	Blessed be the coming Lord.
Reader	Lord, out of the silent darkness at the beginning
	of time, you created light.
All	Blessed be the coming Lord.

Reader   We watch for the light that will gleam through
      the waiting earth.

All   Blessed be the coming Lord.

Reader   God is light, in whom there is no darkness at all.

                              1 John 1:5

      Blessed be God who has called us out of darkness
      into his glorious light.

All   Amen.

Shorter Advent Candle-lightings

Advent Candle-lighting 1

First   I light a candle for spiritual parents
who picture and pattern God's ways.

Second   I light a candle for prophets
who shine like candles in the dark.

Third   I light a candle for front-runners
who clear obstacles from God's way.

Fourth   I light a candle for virgins who give their all
to be bearers of God's life.

Fifth   I light this candle for Jesus Christ,
Light of the world,
Saviour of us all,
who has come to live among us.

Advent Candle-lighting 2

First   I light a candle to remind us of the darkness
before Jesus came,
All   And we remember the greater light that will
dawn when he returns.

Second   I light a candle to remind us of God's Word
spoken through prophets long ago,
All   And we remember that God still speaks through
faithful messengers today.

Third   I light a candle to remind us of the divine
kingdom which is among us now,
All   And we remember to prepare ourselves
for the greater kingdom which is still to come.

Fourth	I light a candle to remind us that a young woman saying 'yes' initiated the birth of God on earth,
All	And we remember that God is coming to birth in us at this time.

Fifth	I light a candle to remind us that Christ has been born and has become one of us,
All	And we remember that we are to live as his brothers and sisters.

Advent Candle-lighting 3

First	We bless you, our God, for Abraham and the spiritual forebears who laid foundations without which the world would never have been ready for you to come.

Second	We bless you, our God, for Isaiah and the prophets who pinpointed what humans had got wrong and what you wanted to accomplish.

Third	We bless you, our God, for John the Forerunner who prepared your way by turning many away from dishonest and proud ways.

Fourth	We bless you, our God, for the Blessed Virgin Mary who believed the angel and conceived you in the power of the Holy Spirit.

Fifth	We bless you, our God, for our Lord Jesus Christ, King of kings, Lord of lords, Emmanuel – God who became incarnate in human flesh.
All	Alleluia!

Advent Candle-lighting 4

Use may be made of drama or story to tell of the Celtic saint(s) referred to after each of the four candle-lightings

First   The candle of longing.
Patriarchs and Psalmists fostered a longing for you
in the people among whom you were born.
Forebears of the Faith in our land, such as Aidan
and Hilda (*or . . .*)
have fostered a longing for you in our land.

Second   The candle of prophecy.
Prophets in the Bible pointed to your coming.
Prophets of our land, such as Fursey (*or . . .*)
that point to your presence among us.

Third   The candle of the Preparer.
John the Baptist cleared a road for you.
Preparers such as Columba (*or . . .*)
cleared blocks of human resistance to you.

Fourth   The candle of the Christ-bearer.
You were brought to birth
through the most pure devotion of Mary.
Midwives of the Faith such as Brigid (*or . . .*)
brought you to birth in our lands.

Advent Candle-lighting 5

First   One candle for the founders of a people
called of God;
Abraham and Moses and others they begot.

Second   And two for all the prophets
who exposed the things that harm,
each pointed to a world of good
that surely was to come.

Third And three for John the Baptist,
who calls on us to sing:
'Prepare the way for Jesus Christ. He's coming,
he is King.'

Fourth And four for Mary, saying 'I cannot see the way,
but you promised me a baby; I believe you
and obey.'

Fifth The fifth and final candle is for Christ
on Christmas Day.
He's the light right at the centre. He is with us
through life's way.

Advent Candle-lighting 6

First I light this candle as a reminder of the darkness
before Jesus came,

All And we remember the greater light
which will dawn when he returns.

Second I light this candle as a reminder of prophets
who pointed to one greater than they,

All And we remember that God still speaks
and points us to a greater day.

Third I light this candle as a reminder of God's
kingdom that is among us,

All And we remember to prepare ourselves
for the kingdom that is yet to come.

All Eternal Light, shine into our hearts.
Eternal Goodness, deliver us from evil.
Eternal Power, be our support.
Eternal Wisdom, scatter the darkness
of ignorance.

All   Eternal Pity, have mercy on us
               that with all our heart, mind and strength
               we may be brought by your mercy
               into your holy presence,
               through Jesus Christ our Saviour.
               Amen.

               There may be singing

Leader   Jesus, revealed in glory,
               worshipped by angels,
               proclaimed among the peoples,
               radiant in the heavens,
               shine into our hearts and give us peace,
               now and always.
All   Amen.

Advent Morning Prayer

Either the Advent Candle-lighting or the following

Leader   In the wasteland may the Glory shine.
In the land of the lost may the King make his
home.

or

Leader   Let us wake to Christ's summons,
urgent in our midst.

All   Let us wake to the truth that his power alone
will last.

Leader   The worlds that scorn him will vanish
like a dream.

All   When he comes to his own
he will bring to fruition a world of good.

Echoes words of George McLeod

*There may be singing or, at larger gatherings,
trumpets or music*

Reader   Psalm 50; 75; 76; 94; 139:1-6; *or* 139:19-24

Reflection

Week 1

Leader   All-knowing God,
poets and parents-in-God picture and pattern
your ways.

All   Forgive us for following idols and illusions.

A moment of silence

Week 2

Leader	All-seeing God, prophets shine like candles in the night.
All	Forgive us for staying in the dark.

A moment of silence

Week 3

Leader	All-holy God, forerunners like John clear obstacles from your path.
All	Forgive us for blocking your way.

A moment of silence

Week 4

Leader	All-giving God, the Virgin Mary offered her all as the bearer of your Life.
All	Forgive us for holding ourselves back.

Leader	Lord of creation, King of the last judgement, Immortal, Holy and Mighty, you sit with the Book of Life and Death open before you.
All	All mortals pass before you, one by one, like sheep.
Leader	In your Book of Life all our deeds are written.
All	You see our hearts. You know our every thought.

There may be silence or a song of confession such as Kyrie eleison, and a declaration of forgiveness such as the following

Leader	The all-merciful God forgive us for past sins and free us to do good.

God's Word

Reader   Let us attend; the Word of God comes to us.
Illumine our hearts, O Lord.
Implant in us a desire for your truth.
May all that is false within us flee.

Reader   Isaiah 40:1-11 *or the Old Testament reading
of the day*

    There may be a pause, singing, or the following

A Song of the Wilderness

First   The wilderness and the dry land shall rejoice;
the desert shall blossom and burst into song.

Second   They shall see the glory of the Lord,
the majesty of our God.

First   Strengthen the weary hands
and make firm the feeble knees.

Second   Say to the anxious, 'Be strong, fear not,
your God is coming with judgement,
coming with judgement to save you.'

First   Then shall the eyes of the blind be opened
and the ears of the deaf be unstopped.

Second   Then shall the lame leap like a hart
and the tongue of the dumb sing for joy.

First   For waters shall break forth in the wilderness
and streams in the desert.

Second   The ransomed of the Lord shall return
with singing,
with everlasting joy on their heads.

First   Joy and gladness shall be theirs,
and sorrow and sighing shall flee away.

Isaiah 35:1, 2b-4a, 4c-6, 10

All	Glory to the Father
	and to the Son
	and to the Holy Spirit;
	the God who was,
	and is,
	and is to come.

Reader	Let us attend; Christ the living Word comes to us.
	Hear the Word of Christ in Matthew 24:36-44
	or the New Testament reading of the day

| **Reader** | *(at the close)* This is the Word of Christ. |
| **All** | Praise to the coming King. |

Reader	I wait for the Lord;
	my soul waits and in God's Word I put my hope.
All	Saviour of the world, come to us.
Reader	My soul waits for the Lord more than those
	who watch for the morning.
All	Saviour of the world, come to us.
Reader	O people, hope in the Lord!
	For with the Lord there is steadfast love and full
	redemption.
All	Saviour of the world, come to us.
Reader	In our darkness there is no darkness with you,
	Lord.
	With you, the deepest dark is as clear as the day.
All	Saviour of the world, come to us.

or

The song of Zechariah, the father of John the Forerunner

We bless you, Lord God of Israel,
coming to ransom your people;

Raising up saving power
in the family of your servant David,
as you said by the mouth of your prophets
in days of old.

You set us free from oppression,
free from the hands of our foes.
This is your bond of love with our forebears,
your covenant binding for ever,

Your oath to our father Abraham
assuring us that, freed from fear,
delivered from all oppression,
we will serve you in goodness and love
to the end of our days.

This child will be called your prophet.
He will walk in your presence
and prepare the way you will come,
announcing your people's salvation,
with pardon for all their sins.

Through the love in the heart of our God
the Rising Sun will come to us,
shining on those in the dark
who lie in the shadow of death
and guiding our steps into peace.

Luke 1:68-79

*There may be singing and creative activity or
teaching*

Intercession

Any of the following prayers may be said

Leader Calm us to wait for the gift of Christ.
Cleanse us to prepare the way for Christ.
Teach us to contemplate the wonder of Christ.
Anoint us to bear the life of Christ.

Reader	Help us to prepare a way for you,
All	By our thoughtfulness towards others,
	by our care in little things,
	by our upholding of the oppressed.

Reader	Help us to prepare a way for you,
All	By our thoughtful use of things,
	by our care of crops and kitchens,
	by our upholding of creation.

Leader	The earth is becoming a wasteland:
All	Breath of the Most High, come and renew it.
Leader	Humanity is becoming a battleground:
All	Child of Peace, come and unite it.
Leader	Society is becoming a playground:
All	Key of Destiny, open doors to our true path.
Leader	The world is becoming a no-man's land:
All	God with us, come and make your home here.

There may be free prayer

From 17 December

Leader	Come Wisdom, Breath of the Most High,
	Bough of creation,
	permeating all that live with the birth pangs
	of suffering love.
	Come and teach us your ways.
All	Maranatha, come redeeming Lord.

Leader	Come, head of the family of Israel.
	You revealed yourself to Moses in the fire
	of the burning bush
	and gave him laws to guide his people.
	Come and dispel our confusion.
All	Maranatha, come redeeming Lord.

Leader Come, descendant of King David's father Jesse.
You are a sign to the nations:
the world's rulers will give way to you,
the world's people will summon your aid.
Come and free us from oppression.

All Maranatha, come redeeming Lord.

Leader Come, heir of King David,
the Majesty of every people,
the key to their destiny.
You open doors that none can shut.
You close doors that none can open.
Come and lead us to our destiny.

All Maranatha, come redeeming Lord.

Leader Come, Morning Star, bright Sun of Justice,
bring light to all who are in the darkness
of ignorance or self-will.
Come and bring us eternal light.

All Maranatha, come redeeming Lord.

Leader Come, Cornerstone of the new world to be built.
You formed us of the one earth.
You make opposing peoples one.
Come and save us from destruction.

All Maranatha, come redeeming Lord.

Leader Come, Emmanuel, God with us,
Wonderful Counsellor.
You understand all people.
You are the Hope of all nations.
Come to live among us.

All Maranatha, come redeeming Lord.

There may be silence, free prayer, the Lord's Prayer
or singing

Leader   The King of life appear to you.
The Son of life shed light on you.
The Spirit of life flow into you.
The Holy Three come near to you.

All   Amen.

Advent Midday Prayer

Leader	Christ, Light of the world,
All	Meet us in our place of darkness.
Leader	Christ, Light of the world,
All	Meet us in our place of longing.
Leader	Christ, Light of the world,
All	Meet us in our place of working.

A candle may be lit

Leader	I light this candle, as a sign of the King who comes to rule.
Leader	Jesus our health, rule in our bodies.
All	Come, Lord Jesus, come.
Leader	Jesus our worth, rule in our work.
All	Come, Lord Jesus, come.
Leader	Jesus our love, rule in our households.
All	Come, Lord Jesus, come.
Leader	Jesus our life, rule in our dying.
All	Come, Lord Jesus, come.
Reader	God says, 'Establish justice and do what is right, for soon my salvation will come and my deliverance will be revealed.'

Isaiah 56:1

Leader	Among the hungry, among the homeless, among the friendless,
All	Come to make things new.
Leader	Among the powerful, among the spoilt, among the crooked,
All	Come to make things new.

Leader	In halls of fame, in corridors of power, in forgotten places,
All	Come to make things new.

Leader	With piercing eyes, with tender touch, with cleansing love,
All	Come to make things new.

Reader	Just as Jesus has left you for heaven, so he will come again.

Acts 1:11

All	Restore to us, Lord, what has been eaten away. Bring into being what is yet to be.

There may be silence, singing, free prayer or the following prayer

First	All-wise God, sourcing and permeating creation, source and permeate me. Civilising God, who revealed laws that brought good order out of cruel anarchy, civilise me. Redeeming God, who through your regents rescued your people from hell and destruction, rescue me.

Second	God of Destiny, the Key that unlocked the greatness of great David's kingdom, unlock the greatness of our lives and our land.

164

Third   Morning Star,
              who dispersed the gloom
              of your oppressed people,
              cheer our spirits and put sin and neglect to flight.

Fourth   Emmanuel, God with us,
              who came to live in a lost and lonely world,
              make your home in us today.

Leader   You call your people,
              you gather those who have strayed –
              you the One who is coming.
              Gather us to you in the midst of the day
              and keep us faithful until your appearing.

All   May we be a hand to the weak,
              an anchor in the storm,
              and a light in the dark.

Advent Evening Prayer

On special occasions this may be preceded by a candle-lit vigil of silence or drumbeats that build up a sense of anticipation. An Advent Wreath may be placed on a table. If there is a Candle-lighting, the service starts with the psalm

Leader Heaven, shed your dew.
Clouds, rain down salvation.
Earth, bring forth the Saviour.

There may be singing

Reader Psalm 50:1-6; 52; 75; 85; 89:46-52; 94:1-15;
or 102:1-16

or

First O God, I long for you from early morning;
my whole being desires you.
Like a dry, worn-out and waterless land
my soul is thirsty for you.

Second Let me see you in the place of prayer;
let me see how glorious you are.
Your constant love is better than life itself,
and so I will praise you.

First I will give thanks as long as I live.
I will raise my hands to you in prayer.
My soul will feast and be satisfied,
and I will sing glad songs of praise to you.

Psalm 63

All Praise the One who comes.
Praise the One who came.
Praise the One who calls us now
to greet the highest Name.

God's Word

Leader   Where times are dark,
where wrong parades as right,
where faith grows dim,

All   We pray for light.

Leader   Christ, Light of the world,
meet us in our place of darkness,
journey with us
and bring us to your new dawning.

Reader   Isaiah 44:1-8 *or the Old Testament reading
for the day*

Mary's Song may be said or sung

Reader   1 Thessalonians 5:1-11 *or the New Testament
reading for the day*

The following or a creed may be said

All   You are holy; you are whole.
Let earth give praise from pole to pole.
You are coming, coming here,
to bring your hard-pressed people cheer;
bringing to them heavenly birth,
born of heaven, born of earth;
bringing to them bread and wine,
giving hope of life divine.
You are coming; you are whole.
Let earth give praise from pole to pole.

*There may be meditation, teaching, sharing,
creative activity or singing*

Intercessions

Any of the following may be said

Leader	Desire of every nation, we bring to you those who are empty and who long to find meaning.
All	Come to them, Lord Jesus.
Leader	Desire of every nation, we being to you those who are overlooked and who long to know their worth.
All	Come to them, Lord Jesus.
Leader	Desire of every nation, we bring to you those who are exploring but who do not know what they search for.
All	Come to them, Lord Jesus.

Leader Lord, you keep us waiting for signs of hope.
You keep us looking for ways in which you come.
The pain of the world,
the anguish of the people,
cry out to you, O Lord.

All Come, Lord Jesus, come.

Leader We pray for blighted areas:
make them bloom.

Examples may be given

In your mercy,
All Come, Lord Jesus, come.

Leader We pray for those who are shut out
from your Presence:
bring them in.

Examples may be given

In your mercy,
All Come, Lord Jesus, come.

Leader   We pray for our homes:
make them places of peace and light.

Examples may be given

In your mercy,
All   Come, Lord Jesus, come.

Leader   We pray for those who govern:
may peace and justice mark their rule.

Examples may be given

In your mercy,
All   Come, Lord Jesus, come.

Leader   We pray for our places of learning:
make them sources of truth and wholeness.

Examples may be given

In your mercy,
All   Come, Lord Jesus, come.

Leader   We pray for those who are dying:
may perpetual light shine upon them.

Examples may be given

In your mercy,
All   Come, Lord Jesus, come.

From 17 December

Leader   Wisdom,
Breath of the Most High,
permeating and restoring creation,
come and unite us to our Source.

Especially we pray for . . .

Suggestions may be offered

Come, Lord Jesus, come.
All   Come, Lord Jesus, come.

Leader Leader of God's people of old,
you revealed yourself to Moses in the burning
bush and gave him laws to guide your people.
Come and dispel our confusion.

Especially we pray for . . .

Suggestions may be offered

Come, Lord Jesus, come.
All Come, Lord Jesus, come.

Leader King David's descendant,
you are the key that opens the door
to the destiny of each nation.
Come and release all that is good and creative
in our people.

Especially we pray for . . .

Suggestions may be offered

Come, Lord Jesus, come.
All Come, Lord Jesus, come.

There may be free prayer, silence or singing

Leader God be with us on our journey
towards Christmas.
Help us to go deeper into what is real,
until we are brought to the wonder of your birth
and know your incarnate love afresh.

Advent Night Prayer

Leader   In darkest night, we pray,
              may the Light of Lights come to us.
All   We wait for the Lord more than those
              who watch for the morning.

*Silence, confession, or meditative singing
followed by one of the readings below or another*

Reader   Psalm 4; 17:1-8; 139:7-12; Isaiah 45:2-8;
              55:6-11 *or* (4th week) Psalm 119:113-20

Leader   We wait in the darkness, expectantly, longingly.
All   Come, O God Most High.
Leader   In the darkness we can see the splendour
              of the universe –
              blankets of stars,
              the solitary glowings of the planets.
All   Come, O God Most High.
Leader   In the darkness of the womb,
              mortals are nurtured
              and the Christ-child was made ready for the
              journey into light.
All   Come, O God Most High.
Leader   In the darkness the wise three found the star
              that led them to you.
All   Come, O God Most High.
Leader   In the darkness of dreams you spoke to Joseph
              and the wise ones
              and you speak still to us.
All   Come, O God Most High.
Leader   In the darkness of despair and distress we watch
              for a sign of hope from the Light of Lights.
All   Come, O God Most High.

Women	O God of life, darken not to us your light.
Men	O God of life, close not to us your joy.
Women	O God of life, soften to us your anger.
Men	O God of life, crown to us your goodness.

A candle is lit

Leader	Christ is the light that comes into the world:
All	A light that no darkness will quench.

There may be singing, such as the following, to the tune Bunessan

Christ, as a light, illumine and guide us.
Christ, as a shield, protect us from harm.
This night draw near us and be within us,
guarding our sleep and lighting our dawn.

Christ in the lonely, Christ in the hungry,
Christ in the sleepless, Christ in the worn,
Christ, as a light, illumine and guide them,
Christ, as a shield, protect them from harm.

The following or another reading may be said

Reader	Jesus said, 'I am the light of the world.
	Whoever follows me will not walk in darkness,
	but will have the light of life.'

John 8:12

Leader	Son of the prophets,
	on our longings
All	Let your light shine.
Leader	Son of Mary,
	on our littleness
All	Let your light shine.
Leader	Son of Eternity,
	on our lying down

All   Let your light shine.

Leader Let us ask that the Light shine also
on those in darkness
and on those we love.
Let us name these now in silence or aloud.

Names may be mentioned

Leader For the darkness of night enfolding the day's
labour,

All   We bless you, dear God.

Leader For the sweetness of sleep restoring the tired
frame,

All   We bless you, dear God.

Leader Call forth this night, bearers of your presence
that we may rest in the undying flame of your
love,

All   And wake to the light of your dawning.

Advent Prayers for use from 17 December

Reader	Come to us, Wisdom, moving in the flux and flow of the cosmos to bring worlds into being.
All	Come to us, O Christ.
Reader	Come to us, Wisdom, permeating all creation: the life of soil and seed and seasons.
All	Come to us, O Christ.
Reader	Come to us, Wisdom, shaping nations and ensouling peoples.
All	Come to us, O Christ.
Reader	Come to us, Wisdom, encompassing the mysteries of the unseen world and the mysteries of the soul.
All	Come to us, O Christ.
Reader	Come to us, Wisdom, the seeing eye of art and science; the ear of all that breathes.
All	Come to us, O Christ.
Reader	Come to us, Wisdom, the light of our darkness; the reconciler of that which is divided.
All	Come to us, O Christ.
Reader	Come to us, Wisdom, the weaver of earth's destiny, the completer of our call.
All	Come to us, O Christ.

Advent Daily Antiphons*

17 December

Leader Wisdom,
permeating creation and informing all peoples,
come and bring us the mind of God.

18 December

Leader Shaper of peoples,
who through Moses gave guidance
that would make a people great,
guide us into the ways of true greatness.

19 December

Leader Bedrock,
Sign of community,
come to places of instability and root them
in realities that nothing can destroy.

20 December

Leader Key to Destiny,
unlock our potential: our capacity to be
soul-friends and to serve others,
that we may be mentors and companions
amid a needy people.

21 December

Leader Light-bringer,
illumine places of darkness, despair and disease.

---

* An antiphon is a sentence repeated before or after a reading.

22 December

Leader   True Fulfiller of Desire,
           harness our deepest longings to your infinite
           purpose of love.

23 December

Leader   God with us –
           the Presence that cannot be taken from us –
           may we live with you and you live in us.

Vigil Crib Prayers

Prayers to be said before a crib on Christmas Eve
(see page 188) are also suitable for use the week before.

Creative Activities

1. Make an Advent Prayer Tree. Place a small tree or branch in a container. Each day tie a white prayer ribbon to it. The prayer may represent something you long for. If desired, the request may be written on or pinned to the ribbon. From 17 December the prayer may consist of the Advent Antiphon for that day.

2. Make or use an Advent Wreath.

3. Make or use an Advent Calendar.

4. Precede the worship or the prayers by building up a sense of mounting anticipation through live or recorded use of drums, trumpets or other music.

5. Turn off artificial light until candles have been lit.

6. Figures of Mary and Joseph are taken to local homes. By the first day of Advent a list of hosts is made. Each host takes the figures to the next house on the list. On Christmas Eve the figures are placed in a central crib in a church or place of prayer.

The Nativity or Christmas

In the Celtic Christian tradition Christmas is known as the Nativity. In common with the rest of the universal Church in the West, 25 December was chosen as the official date when Jesus' birth would be celebrated. The actual date of Jesus' birth is not known. Orthodox Churches in Celtic lands who use the new-style revised Julian Calendar also now celebrate the Nativity on 25 December; other Orthodox Churches celebrate it on 6 January.

Christmas worship begins on Christmas Eve, 24 December, and continues for twelve days from 25 December until Epiphany (6 January in the Western Church).

Epiphany is itself a particular expression of Christmas, so although we provide a pattern of worship for Epiphany, it is appropriate to use Christmas material at any time until 1 February, the start of the Celtic spring, which Christians turned into a celebration of the dedication of the infant Christ in the Jewish temple.

We may be sure that the Celtic Church celebrated the Nativity of God's Son with wonder, simplicity, and with a flare for making Bethlehem 'present' in each locality. In the Celtic imagination, Bethlehem becomes as near as our own town, and our own hearts and homes can become like the stable where Christ was born.

Candle Lightings

Christmas Candle-lighting 1

Reader Jesus, born of Mary *(light first candle)*,
All Light up our darkness.
Reader Jesus, proclaimed by angels *(light second candle)*,
All Light up our darkness.
Reader Jesus, worshipped by shepherds *(light third candle)*,
All Light up our darkness.
Reader Jesus, adored by wise men *(light fourth candle)*,
All Light up our darkness.
Reader Jesus, God who is with us now *(light the fifth and central candle)*,
All Light up our darkness.

All Eternal Light, shine into our hearts.
Eternal Goodness, deliver us from evil.
Eternal Power, strengthen us.
Eternal Pity, have mercy upon us.
Eternal Wisdom, scatter the darkness
of our ignorance.
Amen.
Alcuin

Reader Jesus Christ is the Light of the world:
All A light that no darkness can quench.

Reader Blessed are you, Giver of light.
Blessed are you, Being of light.
Blessed are you, Transmitter of light.
May your light shine in us for ever.
Amen.

Christmas Candle-lighting 2

Reader   We light the candles of Christmas:
the candle of grace *(light first candle)*;
the candle of truth *(light second candle)*;
the candle of light *(light third candle)*;
the candle of life *(light fourth candle)*;
the candle of God with us *(light fifth candle)*.

Reader   Jesus Christ is the Light of the world.
The Light has come to us and shines among us.

All   Glory to the Lord.

Reader   The power from on high encompassed
the Virgin.

All   Glory to the Lord.

Reader   Shepherds heard angels extolling the birth.

All   Glory to the Lord.

Reader   Heaven joined earth in songs of rejoicing.

All   Glory to the Lord.

Reader   The curse of sin was usurped by God's gift.

All   Glory to the Lord.

Reader   The Blessed Trinity danced in a stable.

All   Glory to the Lord.

Reader   Light of the world,
bathing the world in bright sheen,
illuming our way,
restoring our lost innocence,
you bring us into the light of a new day,
scattering darkness from our path.

Reader   God is light;
the one in whom there is no darkness.
Therefore let us walk in the light.
If we walk in the light we will have fellowship
with one another
and the shadows of sin will depart.

Christmas Candle-lighting 3

Reader   In the beginning was the Word,
and the Word was with God,
and the Word was God.
He was with God in the beginning.
Through him all things were made;
without him nothing was made
that has been made.
In him was life,
and that life was the light of all people.
The light shines in the darkness,
but the darkness has not overcome it.

John 1:1-5

The Christmas candle is lit

Leader   Jesus Christ is the light of the world:
All   A light no darkness can quench.

Reader   Light has come into the world:
All   A light no darkness can quench.

Leader   The light exposes the deeds of evil:
All   A light no darkness can quench.

Leader   The light reveals to us the way we should go:
All   A light no darkness can quench.

Leader   The light shines that we might live
by its goodness:
All   A light no darkness can quench.

The following may be sung instead of read

Reader   Christ, as a light, illumine and guide me.
Christ, as a shield, o'ershadow and cover me.
Christ under me, Christ over me.
Christ beside me, on left and on right,
Christ behind me, Christ before me,
Christ this day within, without me.
Christ, as a light, illumine and guide me.

St Patrick's Breastplate,
adapted by John Michael Talbot

All   Light of the world, in grace and beauty,
mirror of God's eternal face,
transparent flame of love's free duty –
you bring salvation to our race.
Now, as we see this light of evening,
we raise our hearts in songs of praise.
Worthy are you of endless blessing,
sun of our night, lamp of our days.

Midday Candle-lighting between Christmas Eve and Epiphany

This may take place before the main meal any day between Christmas Eve and Epiphany or before the giving of presents. Different people may read for each candle

Reader   This is the candle of longing:
may our hopes for all that is good come to pass.

Each person may say or think of some good thing they long for

Reader   This is the candle of expecting:
may all that prophets foretold come to pass.

Each person may say or think of a promise in the Bible of something God will do

Reader   This is the candle of preparing:
        may all that gets in the way of God be cleared
        from our lives.

        *Each person may say or think of something they
        wish to be rid of*

Reader   This is the candle of bringing:
        as Mary let Jesus be born in her,
        may we let his presence come amongst us.

        *In silence, each person invites Jesus to be born anew
        in their hearts*

        *Now one person lights the central candle, with these
        words:*

Reader   This is the candle of Christ,
        the Light of the world,
        who has come to live among us.

        *All may sing the chorus of 'The light of Christ
        has come into the world' or a carol*

Reader   Hail King, blessed are you. Let there be joy!
        Bless the King, without beginning,
        without ending.
        Let this house and all generations cry:
        He is everlasting, let there be joy!

        This is the Gift to us who live here:
        Son of the dawn; Sun of the planets;
        Son of the sky; Sun of the earth;
        Son of the elements; Sun of the heavens;
        Son of Mary of the mind of God;
        Son of God, firstborn of all creation.

Leader   Bless this house and all it contains.
Deliver this house from all that stains.
Be health to us all and cure our pains.
Today is joy that Christ is born.
Today is joy that his Presence does dawn.
Hail King! Blessed are you!
Let there be joy!
Let the feasting and giving begin!

A Candle-lighting for the days after Christmas

Reader   The candle of Mary, the Mother of God.
(light first candle)

The candle of Stephen, the first martyr for Christ.
(light second candle)

The candle of John, the Evangelist of Christ.
(light third candle)

The candle of the slaughtered infants, silent witnesses to Christ.
(light the fourth candle)

The candle of Christ, Light in the darkness, shining still among us.
(light the fifth, middle candle)

This is followed by prayers from other candle-lightings

A Candle-lighting between 2 and 5 January

The central candle in the Advent Wreath is lit

Reader   I light this candle as a sign of the holy family
in whom God has become incarnate in human
flesh.
Jesus Christ is the Light of the world:

All   A light that no darkness can quench.

*Each of the four candles is lit in turn as each of the
following sentences are spoken*

Reader   I light this candle as a sign of Stephen,
the first martyr in Jesus' wider family.
I light this candle as a sign of John,
the foster-brother of Christ.
I light this candle as a sign of Basil and Gregory
who proclaimed in eastern lands that God
became incarnate in Christ.
I light this candle as a sign of Seraphim of
Russia, flame in the snow,
who spread the light of Christ among his people.

We bless you for your holy family
which has come to embrace people of all nations
and times;
and we bless you for all who have reflected the
light of Christ in their age.

May we be a holy people, dedicated to you,
shining as lights in the world.

Glory to the Father
and to the Son
and to the Holy Spirit.

All   As it was in the beginning,
is now and ever shall be.
Amen.

A Candle-lighting before Epiphany

Reader   We light the candle of Stephen, the first martyr for Jesus. *(light the first candle)*

We light the candle of John, the foster-brother of Jesus. *(light the second candle)*

We light the candle of Basil, the teacher of the Divine Glory of Christ. *(light the third candle)*
We light the candle of Seraphim, Christ's flame in the snow. *(light the fourth candle)*

We light the candle of Christ, eternal Son of God. *(light the fifth and middle candle)*

Reader   Jesus Christ is the Light of the world:
All   A light that no darkness can quench.

Reader   In the darkness of this passing age,
your saints proclaim the glory of your Word
made flesh.
Chosen as lights in the world,
they beckon us on
as we journey towards the place of eternal light.

We do not proclaim ourselves.
We proclaim the light of the Gospel
of the glory of Christ,
who is the image of God.

All   Glory to Christ,
Son of God,
Light of God,
present with us now,
dwelling with us for ever.

Prayers for use at a Vigil before a Crib

*For use on Christmas Eve and during the last week of Advent.
A candle may be lit in front of the crib. Silences for
contemplation may be kept between each prayer*

Reader   Jesus, you are the glory of eternity shining now
among us,
the tenderness of God here with us now.

All   God who is with us, we adore you.

Reader   Jesus, you are the Healing Person,
the pattern of goodness,
the fulfilment of the highest human hopes.

All   God who is with us, we adore you.

Reader   Jesus, you are the champion of the weak,
the counsellor of the despairing,
the brother of us all.

All   God who is with us, we adore you.

Reader   Jesus, you are the splendour of the Father,
the Son of Mary,
our Bridge between heaven and earth.

All   God who is with us, we adore you.

Reader   Jesus, you are the source of life,
the goal of the universe
the people's friend,
the world-pervading God.

All   God who is with us, we adore you.

Reader Jesus, you are one of the human family,
Prince of peace,
joy of angels.

All God who is with us, we adore you.

There may be extended silence

Reader As we look into the face of the babe
of Bethlehem,
the face of Defenceless love,
in your mercy look upon your troubled world.
Fear and violence,
homelessness and pollution,
grief and anxiety stalk it.

Move the hearts of governments and peoples
to use your gifts of wealth and skill
to build your kingdom of love,
where we shall live free from cruelty, neglect
and fear;
free to look into the face of every person
with welcome.
You are among us, Lord, as you were in the
homeless babe in the stable.
As we come face to face with eternal Goodness,
may the human spirit be renewed.

Christmas Eve Morning Prayer

*This may begin with the winter candle-lighting
for the fourth week in Advent*

Leader   Mary, chosen gateway:
through you there came to earth
the Bridge of life to aid us,
to give us eternal worth.

All   Glory to the Most High God who comes
to live among us.

There may be singing

Leader   Today is the Eve of the Great Nativity,
All   When to Virgin Mary will be born a son.
Leader   He will be Star Child and Earth Child,
All   Triumph of Life, and our Saviour.
Leader   Glory to our Maker,
glory to the Son,
glory to the Spirit
All   Glory to the triune God
who will make earth and heaven one.

Reader   Psalm 98

Leader   Dear Son of Mary,
you took flesh to redeem us.
Change our hearts.
All   Dear Son of God,
you came to us with sacrificial love.
Change our hearts.

*There may be silence, spontaneous words of
confession or these words of forgiveness*

Leader   The Son of God bounds towards us,
reaching out a hand of reconciliation.
Let us take it, and listen to God's Word.

God's Word

Reader   Micah 5:2-5a

Reader   For nine months he who is angels' Lord
was hidden, love's furnace, in a little room
humbler than all, whom all adored.
A pure lamb, he stole down to earth
to free us from our sin so blind.
No city home will shield his birth.
His mother a stable for bed must find.

Tadg Gaelach O Suilleabhain,
medieval Irish

Reader   Luke 1:26-45

There may be meditation, sharing, singing,
teaching or the following Proclamation may be said

All   Christ was revealed in human form,
shown to be right by the Spirit,
contemplated by angels,
proclaimed among the nations,
believed in throughout the world,
taken up into heaven.

A very early creed – 1 Timothy 3:18

Intercession

Leader   Lord of time and eternity,
prepare our minds to celebrate with faith
the commemoration of your birth on earth.
Fill our hearts with joy and wonder
as we recall the precious moment
when you were born as our brother.

Jesus, may we journey with you, Mary
and Joseph,
to your birthplace at Bethlehem,

and along the path that leads to life,
firm in the faith,
loyal to the truth
and obedient to your Father's will.

There may be other prayers, free prayer or singing

Leader   Let the troubles of life grow dim,
let the skies and our hearts grow clear,
until the Son of God comes striding towards us,
walking on this earth.

Christmas Eve, Midday or Later

For use at Midday, or later at a Crib. This may be used instead of or as well as the Midday Christmas Eve Candle-lighting

Leader   Be with us, Lord, in the middle of the day.
Keep us in the spirit of Bethlehem.

All   Keep us in the trust of Mary.
Keep us in the honouring of Joseph.
Keep us in the simplicity of the shepherds.

Reader   Jesus said: Blessed are the pure in heart, for they shall see God.

There may be a pause

Reader   In the midst of bustle, give us stillness.
In the midst of tinsel, fill us with awe.
In the midst of tensions, infuse us with peace.

Prayers for the Vigil before a Crib may be used

All   Lead us from fear to trust.
Lead us from despair to hope.
Lead us from hate to love.
Lead us from war to peace.
Deep peace of the Son of peace,
fill our hearts, our workplace, our world.

The Peace prayer, adapted

There may be silent meditation, singing, the Lord's Prayer or free prayer

Leader   Lord, keep us in your peace that we may be ready to welcome your coming among us.

Christmas Eve Evening Prayer

*There may be the winter candle-lighting for the fourth week
of Advent followed by singing*

Reader   Psalm 8

Leader   This night is the long night, the eve of the Great
Nativity.
This night is born Mary Virgin's Son.

Reader   This night is born Jesus, Son of the King of Glory.
This night is born to us the root of our joy.

Leader   This night gleamed the sun of the mountains high.
This night gleamed sea and shore together.

Reader   This night was born
Christ the King of greatness.

Leader   Before it was heard that the Glory was come,
heard was the wave upon the shore.

Reader   Before it was heard that his foot had reached earth,
heard was the song of the angels glorious.

Echoes Carmina Gadelica

There may be singing or creative activity

God's Word

Reader   Zechariah 2:10-13

Reader   By the Son of God, saviour of souls,
the archangel of heaven appeared to Mary
and said that the heavenly Spirit would fill her
with radiance.

All   Glory to the King who comes.

Reader   That she should bear the Triumph of Life,
the Bright Son,
the mighty child of God,
the glorious Creator.

All   Glory to the King who comes.

Echoes Advent Lyrics, ninth century Mercian

Leader   This night is the long night.

All   Glow to him, wood and tree,
glow to him, mount and sea,
glow to him, land and plain,
when his foot touches earth's terrain.

Echoes Carmina Gadelica

Reader   Acts 13:16-23

*There may be teaching, sharing, silence, singing
or creative activity*

Intercession

Leader   Babe of Heaven, Defenceless Love,
in order to come to us
you have to travel far from your home.
Come to strengthen us
on our pilgrimage of trust on earth.
Your birth will show us
the simplicity of the Father's love,
the wonder of being human.
Help us to live fully human lives for you.

Jesus, may we journey with you, Mary
and Joseph,
to your birthplace at Bethlehem
and along the path that leads to life,
firm in the faith,
loyal to the truth,
and obedient to your Father's will.

There may be other prayers, free prayer or singing

Leader   Let the cares of the past grow dim,
let the skies and our hearts grow clear,
until the Son of God comes to meet us,
striding on this earth.

Christmas Eve Night Prayer

Leader   Eternal God,
who made this most holy night to shine
with the brightness of your one true light,
may that light now shine brightly in our hearts
and minds.

Reader   Out of the deep silence of night
your Almighty Word leapt down from heaven.
All   Glory, glory to God in the highest.

Reader   Isaiah 9:2, 6, 7

Reader   Great Spirit, swirling in the elements,
you brought to birth a world.
Mighty Father, swirling in the elements,
you brought to birth a Son.
Eternal Christ, swirling in the elements,
you stride towards us now.
All   Glory, glory to God in the highest.

Reader   John 1:1-14

Leader   Now is born Christ the King of greatness.
Now is the time of the great Nativity.
All   Glow to him, wood and tree,
glow to him, mount and sea,
glow to him, land and plain.
Come to him, people, and let him reign.

There may be singing

Leader   God is light
All   And in him is no darkness at all.
Leader   Christ is the light of the world:
All   A light that no darkness can quench.

Leader   Christ of glory, Christ of Mary,
come to us in our need.
You were shut out from the inn:
come to those who feel shut out from love.
You became a refugee:
come to the homeless and those who seek asylum.
Though ignored by the world, you were given
your own special name:
come to those we name before you now.

Names may be mentioned
There may be singing, sharing or feasting

Leader   Homemaker God,
come this night to all who are sleeping rough;
come to the cardboard huts
and the dampened squats;
come to the young who have lost their way;
come to the old who have been forgotten.
May the light of the Bethlehem stable
be a light to the homeless tonight.

Michael Mitton

Reader   Father of creation, on this holy night
your Son was born in human form.
May he make our humanness complete.
On this holy night Mary in pain of labour
brought your Son to birth.
May all who are in pain be held in your love.
On this holy night shepherds were drawn
to wonder at your presence.
May all your people be drawn in wonder to you.

Leader   May the trust of Mary be yours.
May the faithfulness of Joseph be yours.
May the peace of the Christ-child be yours.

All   The peace above all peace be yours tonight.

Christmas Morning Prayer

This may be preceded by the winter candle-lighting for Christmas

Leader   You whose cupped hand contains the sea
are born in a cave –
your glory fills the heavens,
and the manger is filled with your splendour.
Great is the amazement of this earth of ours
that the Lord of all has come down to it.
God has become a human being,
the Ancient has become a child,
the Master has become like his servants,
the King's Son as someone despised.

St Ephrem

All   Glory to God, who has come to live among us.

There may be singing

Leader   Christ, born of the loveliest Mary,
you are with us at this time/on this day* of joy.
(* *as appropriate*)
The eternal Son of God is with us evermore.

Reader   Psalm 46; 97; 98; 105:1-11; *or* 115

If a Confession is desired the following may be used

Leader   Jesus, God's Gift of Love, before you
I am so hard-hearted.
All   Forgive the hurts I have caused.

Leader   Jesus, God's goodness, before you I am so selfish.
All   Forgive me for filling my life with things
that do not satisfy.

199

Leader   Jesus, God's servant, before you I am so proud.
All   Forgive me for not being my true self.

There may be a creative activity or singing

God's Word

Reader   Isaiah 62:1-5 *or the Old Testament reading of the day*

All   Glory and honour to you, our God,
             for revealing your love in human flesh.
             Glory and honour to you, our God,
             for filling Mary with the life Divine.
             Glory and honour to you, our God,
             for sharing our life on earth.

Reader   Luke 2:1-14 *or the New Testament reading of the day*

Thanksgiving

All   The soles of his feet have reached the earth –
             the soles of the Son of Glory.
             All the world gives homage to him.
             The sun on the housetops shines for him.
             The voice of the winds with the song of the streets
             announce to us that Christ is born.
             God the Lord has opened a door –
             the Door of Hope, the Door of Joy.
             Golden Sun of earth and sky –
             all hail! Let there be joy!

There may be singing, meditation, teaching or creative activity

Intercession

Leader   Babe of heaven,
           you had to travel far from your home.

All   Strengthen us on our pilgrimage of trust on earth.

Leader   Defenceless Love,
           your birth shows us the wonder of being human.

All   Help us to live fully human lives for you.

Leader   King of glory,
           you come among the poor with justice and peace.

All   Help us to serve others as you serve us.

*There may be free prayer after each of the following
petitions followed by the response*

Leader   May every mother and child be cherished
           as Mary cherished you . . .
           Lord, in your mercy,

All   Hear our prayer.

Leader   May those who seek a room to live in
           not find the door shut in their face . . .
           Lord, in your mercy,

All   Hear our prayer.

Leader   May those who work on the land,
           and may creation itself,
           be as responsive to your presence
           as were the shepherds and stars . . .
           Lord, in your mercy,

All   Hear our prayer.

Leader   May those who are out in the cold
             find a stable place as warm as yours . . .
             Lord, in your mercy,
All   Hear our prayer.

There may be free prayer and singing

Leader   The eternal Glory shine upon you.
             The Son of Mary stay beside you.
             The life-giving Spirit grow within you.

Christmas Midday Prayer

A candle is lit

Leader Marvellous exchange! The Creator takes our flesh!
Truly human, yet owing us nothing.

Lord, what you give us is your being.
Your Being is your Goodness.
Your Goodness is your Love.

Eckhardt

There may be silence or singing
At larger gatherings a different person may read
each line of the prayer that follows

First Jesus, you are –
the tender holy Babe,
the Shepherd of your flock,
the Healing Person,
the Christ of the people,
the world-pervading God,
pattern of goodness,
brother of the poor,
champion of justice,
Emmanuel, God with us.

Second Jesus, you are –
the Glory of eternity shining now among us,
Son of the High King of the universe,
Splendour of the Father,
Source of life,
Prince of Peace,
Wonderful Counsellor,
Son of Mary,
joy of angels,
friend of all.

There may be silence

On Christmas Day the following prayers may be said before or after the main meal instead of Midday Prayer

Host The earth gave you a cave.
The skies gave you a star.
The angels gave you a song.
All In this feast we will give you our love.

Leader The love that Mary gave her Son,
All May we give to the world.
Leader The love that you give us through your Son,
All May we give back to you.

The service continues

Reader Glory to God in the highest,
and on earth peace, and goodwill among all.
Luke 2:14

Leader The love that Mary gave her Son,
All May we give to the world.
Leader The love that you give us through your Son,
All May we give back to you.

There may be free prayer, silence, the Lord's Prayer or singing

Leader The blessing of God be with us,
the Son of God beside us,
the angels of God around us,
the joy of God within us.

Christmas Evening Prayer

Leader   The Virgin gives birth to the Glory from God
and earth offers a cave
to the Son of the Most High.

All   Glory to the Most High God
who has come to live among us.

or

Leader   In the manger cold and lowly
is born the Shepherd of our flock;
born of Mary of lovely countenance
the Trinity eternal by her side.
We come to give the best we have
to the Healing Person,
the Lord of all without a home;
the tender baby driven forth;
Emmanuel.

Thanksgiving

There may be singing

Reader   Psalm 8 *or the psalm of the day*

Leader   Son of the dawn, Son of the clouds,
Son of the planet, Son of the star,
Son of the flame, Son of the light,
Son of the spheres, Son of the globe,
is dwelling now among us.

All   Alleluia!

God's Word

Reader Isaiah 52:1-5 *or the Old Testament reading of the day*

Leader Son of the elements, Son of the heavens,
Son of the moon, Son of the sun,
Son of Mary of the God-mind,
Son of God, firstborn of all creation,
you are dwelling now among us.

All Alleluia!

Reader Matthew 1:18-25 *or the New Testament reading of the day*

There may be teaching, creative activity, singing or the following Proclamation

Leader When the ride is bumpy
and the world passes us by,

All You are God with us.

Leader When we are edged aside
and doors are shut in our face,

All You are God with us.

Leader When our lives are but a flicker
in the encroaching dark,

All You are God with us.

Leader When others are out to get us
and our home is not secure,

All You are God with us.

Intercession

Reader Jesus, in you we see God's face smiling upon us –
gentle,
strong,
loving,
obedient.

Jesus, you radiate what the world so needs today.
In you, may we find
gentleness as the answer to violence,
tenderness as the answer to ill-will,
truth as the answer to lies,
hope as the answer to despair.

There may be other prayers, free prayer or singing

Leader May the long-reaching gladness of Christmas
stretch far down the days before you,
surrounding you with the goodness of Jesus Christ,
child of love,
teacher of truth,
man of sorrow, laughter and judgement;
sin-forgiver,
life-giver,
death-conqueror,
dwelling with you for ever.

Christmas Night Prayer

Leader   Night stars gleam o'er mountains high,
All   God almighty journeys nigh;
Leader   The soles of his feet have touched the earth;
All   The soles of the Son of glory.
Leader   The Lord has opened from heaven a door –
All   A door of hope, a door of joy.

*The following may be sung to the tune Tallis' Canon
or another song may be sung*

Glory to you our God this night
for all that's dawning on our sight.
Glory to you dear Mary's Son,
who scatters far our dark and gloom.

O Babe of Heaven, defenceless Love,
you left for us your home above.
You come to take us in your hand.
Let all give thanks throughout the land.

Reader   Psalm 110:1-4; 126:1-3; *or* Isaiah 11:1-5

Leader   Marvellous exchange! The Creator takes flesh!
    Truly human, God is now with us.
All   Alleluia!
Leader   Tonight we may rest in peace.
All   Alleluia!
Leader   You were born of the Virgin Mary.
All   Be born in us tonight.
Leader   In silence we bow before you.
All   In stillness we feel your love.
Leader   God with us, come, and gently enfold us,
All   As we rest in trustful calm.

In silence or aloud blessings are recalled

Reader   Luke 1:41-53 *or* Colossians 1:15-19a

Leader   Child of glory, Child of Mary,
born in a stable, King of all,
your greatness holds the universe.
Hold also those who are sleeping rough,
those who feel shut out of society,
those who are cold and hungry,
and those we name before you now.

Names may be mentioned

Leader   May the light of the Bethlehem stable
shine on these dear ones tonight.
All   Amen.

There may be singing

Leader   Child in the manger,
you are Creator of the galaxies,
your heavens shone with glory
before earth heard you were born.
All   May the skies and the souls of this place
glow with the glory of your birth.

Leader   Love's furnace was hidden in a little room.
All   Homemaker God, come to our homes this night.

Leader   As it was in the stillness of the morning,
All   So may it be in the silence of the night.
Leader   As it was in the hidden vitality of the womb,
All   So may it be in the hidden life of our sleep.

Leader   Jesus, lie down with us.
All   Spirit, lie down with us.
Leader   Father, lie down with us.

Leader Prince of Peace,
All Your peace be on us at the ending of this day.

Leader In the fellowship of Mary and Joseph,
in the joy of the shepherds, the angels
and the Lord,
All We shall lie down in peace.
Amen.

New Year

In the holistic spirit of the Celtic tradition, this book seeks to weave together the saints and holy days that follow Christmas Day so as to continue, broaden and deepen the Christmas celebration.

Thus we visualise the holy family as expanding to embrace Stephen, the first martyr, and John, the foster-father of Christ.

Following the New Testament reading, as a 'creative activity' a reader may say the following on the day indicated at morning or evening prayer.

The days following Christmas Day

26 December – St Stephen's Day

Reader   Today is the first day after the birth of Christ.
Today shepherds leave their flocks
and make time to wonder at the birth
of God's Son.
Today we leave our routines
and live in the wonder of this sacred birth.

Yesterday our King left heaven,
put on the robe of flesh,
and brought earth the gift of love.
Today a brother of Christ leaves his body of earth
and goes to heaven out of love of the King.

Today is the day of Stephen,
the first of the martyrs for Christ.
Today is the first day of Christmas,
when I shall give my all.

27 December – St John

Reader   Today is the second day after the birth of Christ.
Your beloved disciple taught us
that you became a human being
so that we might become children of God.
All   Lord, make us your family.
Reader   Your beloved disciple took your mother to himself.
All   Lord, make us your family.

28 December –
The slaughter of innocent infants in Bethlehem

Reader   Today is the third day after the birth of Christ.
By being born you made every birth sacred.
Yet tyrants resist this truth.
King Herod, seeking to kill all rivals,
ordered Bethlehem's infant boys to be killed.
Today we remember that you remain God with us.
In you truth is stronger than falsehood,
light is stronger than darkness,
love is stronger than hatred
and life is stronger than death.

The first Sunday after 28 December or
a nearby weekday – The Holy Family

Reader   Today is the . . . day *(enter as appropriate)* of
Christmas.
Today we remember the little family of Mary,
Joseph and Jesus –
how, in love, they embraced the wider family
of animals and angels.
Their forebears, springing from first human stock,
were God-guided folk.
This holy family carries in its heart
that vast family of all
who love Jesus as their brother.

30 December

Reader   Today is the fifth day after the birth of Christ.
Brigid was a nursemaid of Christ.
May we, in turn, assist in bringing Christ to
birth in human hearts.

May we be as Mary to those in whom Christ
is being born.
May we be as Joseph, giving faithful service,
to guard what God is doing.

31 December –
New Year's Eve (in Western Calendars)

Leader   Today is the sixth day after the birth of Christ.

God,
who took flesh from the blood of generations,
as we leave behind one year
and prepare to live another,
give us heartfelt forgiveness
towards all who have hurt us,
discernment to understand
what you have brought about,
and the will to step out from the springboard
that another year offers.

1 January – New Year's Day and the Naming
of Christ and Basil of Caesarea

Leader   Today is the seventh day after the birth of Christ:
the day when Jesus was given his name
in the temple
and a day on which we usher in a new year.
Eternal God,
as your servant Basil proclaimed how,
by your incarnation,
you gathered into one
things earthly and heavenly,
gather all that we are and do this coming year
into the divine glory,
that it may shine in us now and through the ages.

2 January – Seraphim of Sarov

Leader Today is the eighth day after the birth of Christ.
Out of the silence of eternity your Word
brought life to the world.
Out of the silence of years
your servant Seraphim spoke words
that brought life to a people,
and your divine warmth became incarnate
in the frozen snows of Russia.
Out of the stillness of our devotion
may your Word be made flesh in us.

Holy Families

For use the first Sunday that follows 28 December or on a nearby weekday instead of Morning or Evening Prayer. Any of the prayers may be used at services throughout the day. This may also be used for any celebration of family life.

There may be singing and an introduction

Leader   The Lord who was born into a human family
has called us to live in families.
The families of people who do what is right
live on
Proverbs 12:7
God invites us to be part of his holy family.

There may be singing

Reader   Jacob was the father of Joseph, the husband
of Mary.
Mary was the mother of Jesus who is called Christ.

We come into your presence, Virgin of the lowly.
We come into your presence,
Mother of Jesus Christ.

We come into your presence,
Dwelling of meekness.
We come into your presence, Home of peace.
Carmina Gadelica

God's Word

Reader   When Joseph and Mary had finished doing all
that they were required to do,
they returned to their home in Nazareth.

The child grew and became strong;
he was full of wisdom,
and God's blessings were upon him.

Luke 2:39-40

All   May our sons grow up strong and straight
like young trees.
May our daughters have the beauty
of inner serenity.
May our farms and industries overflow.
May the voice of complaining cease
from our streets.
Happy are the people,
from whom such blessings flow,
who put their trust in God.

From Psalm 144:12-15

Reader   Honour your father and mother
as the Lord your God has commanded you,
so that you may have long life
and prosper in the land that the Lord your God
gives you.

Deuteronomy 5:16

There may be music, singing or creative activity

Reader   I would prepare a feast and be host
to the great High King,
with all the company of heaven.
The nourishment of pure love be in my house,
and the roots of repentance.
May we have baskets of love to give,
with cups of mercy for everybody.
Sweet Jesus, be here with us,
with all the company of heaven.
May our meals be feasts of the great High King,
who is our host for all eternity.

Traditional, adapted

217

Reader Jesus went down with his parents to Nazareth
and lived under their authority.

Luke 2:51

Leader May our homes be gladdened
by the love of parents,
the laughter of children,
the wisdom of elders,
the memory of forebears:
no word or thought to darken the day,
no memory or hurt to trammel the night,
songs, smiles and stories to open the doors of joy.

There may be silence, teaching, sharing or singing
Any of the following prayers may be said

Intercession

Leader God our Father,
in the holy family of Nazareth you have given us
a model of Christian family.
Grant that by following Jesus, Mary and Joseph
in their love for each other,
and in the example of their family life,
we may reflect your life in ours.

Leader We adore the Son of the living God,
who became a child in a human family.
All Lord Jesus, bless our families.

Leader Jesus, eternal Son of the Father, you willingly
offered respect to your human parents.
Teach us the humility of respect.
All Lord Jesus, bless our families.

Leader Mary stored in her heart all you said and did.
Teach us the way of contemplation.
All Lord Jesus, bless our families.

Leader   Christ, yours was the strength that shaped
the universe,
yet you readily learned the tasks of a carpenter.
Help us to see our work as a sharing in yours.

All   Lord Jesus, bless our families.

Leader   You advanced in wisdom and in the esteem
of God and people.
Help us to live life to the full and to build up
your body, the Church, in love.

All   Lord Jesus, bless our families.

Leader   We pray for parents to keep their marriage vows
and to think deeply about their children's
character and calling.
We pray for those who provide foster-homes
and for people who have no decent house
to live in.
In particular we pray for . . .

*There may be prayer for our loved ones, followed by
singing*

Leader   Lord Jesus, by the love that filled your home
All   Give us the grace of harmony in our homes.
Leader   By your reunion with Mary and Joseph
in the joy of heaven,
All   Welcome our dead into the eternal family.

All   The love of God,
the grace of our Lord Jesus Christ,
and the fellowship of the Holy Spirit
be with us all, evermore.
Amen.

Christmas creative activities

1. Display a crib.

2. Provide a decorated Christmas tree.

3. Make a Jesse Tree and hang on it a different symbol of the Nativity each day. To make the 'tree', place a branch in a container, and hang various cards and objects on it (Jesse was an ancestor of Jesus).

4. Make mince pies in the shape of a crib and give them to neighbours or shoppers.

5. During evening worship project an image of a night sky on to a wall or screen.

6. At a night-time worship service give each person a candle instead of using artificial light.

7. Make a Christmas cake and cut it into twelve slices. Over the twelve days of Christmas, give a piece to a different person each day.

8. A real or 'sample' family with offspring of varying ages sit around a table. They make up their own dialogue, or say one of the Christmas prayers. The congregation may then circle them and pray for them.

9. Walk the streets imagining you are Mary and Joseph looking for a warm place to stay, praying that the people in each house you pass will open the doors of their heart to Jesus and his holy family this Christmas.

10. Place a marble or stone in the palm of your hand and move around gazing at it – a little thing, like a baby, in the hand of God.

Epiphany or Theophany of Christ

This season celebrates the showing forth of Christ's presence to the world. It is known as Epiphany in the Western Church and as Theophany in the Eastern Church. It is an extension of Christmas and begins twelve days after Christmas; that is, 6 January in the Western Church.

Its themes are: the wise men taking knowledge of the infant Christ back to their countries; the baptism (immersion) of Christ into the world and the world into Christ; the transformation of everyday life and creation, symbolised by the changing of water into wine; the unifying of the whole created world with Christ (ecumenism) and the light spreading across the world.

Candle-lighting for Epiphany Eve

Reader   Soon the tender shoot will burst into sight,
           the light will flood dark lands,
           drooping hearts will rejoice,
           and the people will say,

All   Amen.

A candle may be lit

Reader   Christ, who has been heralded by angels,
           born of Mary and adored by shepherds,
           will be found by wise seekers from diverse lands,
           and the people will say,

All   Amen.

Reader   The lame shall leap for joy,
           blind eyes, closed ears shall open,
           all shall see God's splendour,
           and the people will say,

All   Amen.

Echoes Isaiah 35:6a and 5

The central Christmas candle is lit

Reader   Light of the world,
All   May we see you in all your glory.

Reader   O star-like sun, O guiding light,
           O home of the planets,
           O fiery-maned and marvellous one,
All   May we see you in all your glory.

Reader   O holy scholar of holy strength,
           O overflowing, loving, silent one,
           O generous and thunderous giver of gifts,
           O rock-like warrior of a hundred hosts,

All   May we see you in all your glory.
            Attributed to St Ciaran, adapted

All   Glory to the Birther,
            glory to the Son,
            glory to the Spirit,
            ever Three in One.

Candle-lightings for Epiphany

*Use one large candle and three small candles
or night-lights*

First candle-lighting

The reader lights the large candle

Reader	Jesus, Word made flesh dwelling among us,
All	Light up our darkness.
Reader	Jesus, born of the Blessed Virgin Mary,
All	Light up our darkness.
Reader	Jesus, proclaimed by the angels,
All	Light up our darkness.
Reader	Jesus, worshipped by the shepherds,
All	Light up our darkness.

The reader lights the first small candle

Reader I light the candle of Gaspar, who offered gold.
May the riches of Christ be shown to the world.

The reader lights the second small candle

I light the candle of Melchior, who offered
incense.
May the wisdom of Christ be shown
to the world.

The reader lights the third small candle

I light the candle of Balthazar, who offered
myrrh.
May the sacrifice of Christ be shown
to the world.

Reader   Jesus, reveal your presence to seekers.
All   Where there is darkness, bring light.
             Where there is despair, bring hope.
             Where there is ignorance, bring truth.
             Where there is hatred, bring love.

Second candle-lighting

Reader   Jesus, adored by the wise men,
All   Light up our darkness.

Reader   Jesus, our hope and our joy,
All   Light up our darkness.

Reader   Jesus, here and with us now,
All   Light up our darkness.

Reader   Flame of love,
All   Light us up.
Reader   Flame of beauty,
All   Light us up.
Reader   Flame of wisdom,
All   Light us up.
Reader   Flame of peace,
All   Light us up.

Reader   Reveal your presence in our homes.
             Where there is despair,
             bring the light of hope.
             Where there is darkness,
             bring the light of Christ.

Epiphany Morning Prayer

Leader Arise, shine for the rays of God's glory
spread across the earth.
All The Sun of suns is rising.
Kings and peoples shall be drawn to the light.

There may be singing or creative activity
Candles may be lit

First I welcome the light that burns in the rising sun.
Second I welcome the light that dawns
through the Son of God.
Third I welcome the light that gleams
through the growing earth.
Fourth I welcome the light that you kindle in my soul.

There may be singing
Use the following, as appropriate

The first week of Epiphany – The light spreads

Reader Psalm 72:1-19 *or the psalm of the day*

Incense may be used

Leader As gold is purified in fire,
purify us that we may be royal priests to you.
All We offer ourselves to you as gold.

Leader As the rising incense speaks of your Presence,
may our hearts always rise to you in adoration.
All We offer ourselves to you as incense.

Leader As myrrh spreads the fragrance of perfume,
may our beautiful deeds be fragrant to you.
All We offer ourselves to you as myrrh.

The second week of Epiphany – The peoples' representative is immersed in the stream of life

Reader   Psalm 29 *or the psalm of the day*

Leader   The Immortal who bowed the heavens
          bows his head before a mortal.
All   Glory!
Leader   The Uncreated enters the stream of created life.
All   Glory!
Leader   God becomes one with us,
          and we are made one with God.
All   Glory!
Leader   Our lost innocence is restored
          and the world is charged
          with the grandeur of God.
All   Glory!
Leader   Father-love cascades over the Son;
          the Spirit pours upon him,
          God in Trinity is revealed.
All   Glory! Glory, ever and everywhere!

Water may be sprinkled

Leader   You transform water into sparkling wine.
          You transform our poverty with the riches
          of your grace.

All   Glory to you, Father, glory to you.
          Glory to you, Saviour, glory to you.
          Glory to you, Spirit, glory to you.

Glasses of water may be replaced with champagne-style drink

The third week of Epiphany – Christ unifies the whole created world

Reader   Psalm 122 *or* 133 *or the psalm of the day*

All   In Christ there is no longer Jew and foreigner,
there is no longer slave or free,
there is no longer male or female.
All are one in Jesus Christ.

God's Word

Reader   Ezekiel 37:15-28 *or the Old Testament reading of the day*

The following or another Proclamation may be said

All   From the womb of Mary light streams forth.
From the womb of earth light streams forth.
From the womb of the waters light streams forth.

Reader   Lord, flood the world with light.
Shine into the drab places
and fill with the glory of your Presence
those who wait for you.

Reader   Colossians 1:6-14; 1:15-23 *or the New Testament reading of the day*

Leader   You became poor to make many rich.
All   Transform our drabness with vibrant joy.
Leader   Transform our shallowness with Wisdom's deeps.
All   Transform our suffering with deepening trust.

There may be teaching, creative activity or singing

Intercession

Leader May the star of justice always shine in our world.
We pray for places where injustice holds sway.

Suggestions may be offered here

Pour into the empty cups of the world
the beauty and blessings of Christ.

Again, suggestions may be offered

May your Presence
draw people across the created world,
reveal your mother heart of compassion
and gather together your children.

There may be singing

Leader May God, who laboured in love to create all life,
continue creating within us new vision, new life.

May you be lit by the glory of God,
drawn by the light of God,
warmed by the fire of God.

Midday Prayer for Epiphany

Leader   Keep us aware of your presence in the middle
of the day.

A candle may be lit

Leader   Jesus,
truly God, truly human,
truly infinite, truly frail,
your greatness holds the universe,
your lovely countenance attracts our hearts,
your goodness beckons all that is good in us,
your wisdom searches us,
your truth sheds light on our darkness,
your generosity enriches our poverty,
your friendship consoles the unwanted,
your strength turns away all evils,
your justice deters wrongdoing,
your power conquers hell,
your love-enflamed heart kindles our cold hearts,
your miraculous hand fills us with all blessings,
your sweet and holy name brings joy
to all who love you,
your mercy brings forgiveness.
Have mercy on us,
bring us to true sorrow for our sins.
Give us eternal life,
for your glory fills eternity,
your glory fills the universe.

or

Leader   As Christ enters the stream of created life,
we are immersed in the stream of divine life.
As Christ comes up out of the water,
the world is charged with the glory of God.

All   O Saviour, who takes away the sins of the world,
immerse us in your waters:
the waters that cleanse and heal,
the waters that overwhelm evil,
the waters that renew our God-given nature,
the waters of creativity,
the waters of life everlasting.

Reader   2 Corinthians 3:18 *or* 4:5-6

Leader   Jesus, you became one with us so that we
may become one with you.
May your peace and your Presence
fill our hearts, our workplace and our world.

All   Where there was fear, may there be trust.
Where there was greed, may there be faith.
Where there was darkness, may there be light.
Where there was strife, may there be peace.

Leader   Deep peace of the Child of Peace be ours.

*There may be silence, free prayer, singing or the
Lord's Prayer*

Leader   May Mary's Son be beside us.
May his light shine through us.
May his Spirit renew us.

Evening Prayer for Epiphany

Leader   A star leads the wise three to the Christ.
All   Alleluia!
Leader   Jesus is revealed as Christ in the waters
    of baptism.
All   Alleluia!
Leader   Christ transforms water into festive wine.
All   Alleluia!
Leader   Let us worship the Lord whose Glory streams
    towards us.

There may be singing

Reader   Psalm 113 *or the psalm of the day*

All   Holy, holy, holy, is the Lord our God,
    Emmanuel, present with us now.

All may sing the following

Faithful vigil ended,
Watching, waiting, cease:
Master, grant your servant
his discharge in peace.

All your Spirit promised,
all the Father willed,
now these eyes behold it
perfectly fulfilled.

This your great deliverance
sets your people free;
Christ their light uplifted
all the nations see.

Christ, your people's glory!
Watching, doubting cease;
grant to us your servants
our discharge in peace.

Timothy Dudley Smith

God's Word

Reader Isaiah 60:1-6 *or the Old Testament reading
of the day*

All Christ was revealed in human form,
shown to be right by the Spirit,
contemplated by angels,
proclaimed among the nations,
believed in throughout the world,
taken up into heaven.

A very early creed – 1 Timothy 3:18

Reader Matthew 2:1-12; John 1:29-34; John 2:1-11
or the New Testament reading of the day

*There may be singing, teaching, sharing or creative
activity*

Proclamation

One of the two following Proclamations is said

Leader Christ,
Splendour of the Father's glory,
sustaining all the worlds by your Word of power,
renew your Presence in our lives.

Christ,
begotten of the Father before time,
born at Bethlehem in time,
may your Church be a sign of simplicity and joy.

233

Leader   Christ,
truly God, truly human,
fulfilling the desires of the peoples,
bring us to completeness in you.

Christ,
child of Mary, rich in wisdom,
Prince of Peace, God with us,
lead the world into justice and peace.

Christ,
our bright Morning Star,
when this world's darkness is past
bring us into your eternal light.

Sinless Saviour,
you enter the streams of life
and become one with all creation,
you move through the cleansing waters,
you immerse the world in the glory of God.

All   Glory to you, Father, glory to you.
Glory to you, Saviour, glory to you.
Glory to you, Spirit, glory to you.

Intercession

*A reader may prepare intercessions to follow any of
the headings below*

Reader   We pray for those who walk in darkness . . .
We pray for seekers . . .
We pray for those who research;
may they be sensitive, humble
and treat creation with care . . .

Reader   Reveal your presence
in our homes . . .
in our relationships . . .
in our work . . .
in government . . .
in trade . . .

There may be singing

Leader   The Lord bless you,
keep you
and be gracious to you.
The Lord's face shine upon you
and give you peace.

Epiphany Night Prayer

Leader The magi searched for an infant king.
All   Christ, lead us to your feet this night.
Leader They offered incense as their prayer.
All   We bow before you in awe this night.
Leader Myrrh they gave to mourn your death.
All   Our suffering love we pour out this night.
Leader The world is charged with the grandeur of God.
All   The stars rejoice, and so shall we.

or

Leader The earth has been made holy
by your holy birth.
The stars of heaven have proclaimed your glory.
Now our tarnished race has been restored
to innocence.
This night we give you praise.

There may be singing

Reader Psalm 8 *or* Psalm 19:1-4

First   We wait in the darkness expectantly, longingly.
The darkness is our friend.
Second In the darkness of the womb
we have all been nurtured and protected.
In the darkness of the womb the Christ-child
was made ready for the journey into light.
First   Only in the darkness may we see the splendour
of the universe and the glowing stars.
It was in the darkness that the wise three
saw the star that led them to the Christ-child.

Second In the darkness desert peoples find relief
from the searing heat of the sun.
In the blessed desert darkness Joseph and Mary
sought refuge for Jesus in Egypt.

First In the darkness of sleep dreams rise up.
In the darkness God gave dreams to Joseph
and the wise three.
Give to us dreams as and when you will.

Second In the aloneness of the darkness
our fears can rise to the surface;
we come to face ourselves and the road
that lies ahead.

Echoes a liturgy of the Presbyterian Church
of Aotearoa, New Zealand

Leader No more shall we languish in darkness or dread.
All The Lord will be our everlasting light.

All may sing the following

O star of wonder, star of night,
star of royal beauty bright,
onward leading, still proceeding,
guide us to thy perfect sight.

Leader We now name our loved ones . . .

Name loved ones aloud or in silence
All may sing, after or between petitions

O star of wonder, star of night,
star of royal beauty bright,
onward leading, still proceeding,
guide them to thy perfect sight.

Leader As his parents dedicate Jesus in the temple,
God's glory is revealed to Simeon the old.

237

All may sing or say the following

Faithful vigil ended,
watching, waiting, cease:
Master, grant your servant
his discharge in peace.

All your Spirit promised,
all the Father willed,
now these eyes behold it
perfectly fulfilled.

This your great deliverance
sets your people free;
Christ their light uplifted
all the nations see.

Christ, your people's glory!
Watching, doubting cease:
grant to us your servants
our discharge in peace.

Timothy Dudley Smith

Leader As once you changed water into wine,
All Change our drear day into sweet rest in you.
Leader Let us remember, too, the old and worn,
All And all for whom life's sparkle has gone.

Leader From the rising of the sun to its going down,
the Lord's name will be praised.
As the sun sets on us,
let us remember a people
on whom the sun is rising
that they may know the light of Christ.

Name a nation, aloud or in silence
There may be singing

Leader   Bring us to that place, the gates of which
are open night and day,
where there is no more sun or moon,
where the Lord our God
shall be the everlasting light,
shining in splendour for ever.

All   God, be gracious to us and bless us,
make your face to shine upon us,
and give us your peace.

Creative Activities for Epiphany

1. In the first week light a candle or night-light of prayer that the world's leaders might receive Christ's light as did 'the three kings'. In each of the four succeeding weeks light a candle or night light to represent that light spreading to the four corners of the world.

2. In the first week, figures of the wise kings may be added to a crib scene.

3. From the second week onwards, a picture of baptism by immersion may be displayed or projected.

4. People may be sprinkled with water from a sprig of greenery, such as rosemary dipped in a container of water, or dip a cross three times in a container of water, repeating words from the liturgy and then sprinkle the congregation.

5. From the third week onwards, visit or pray with another church.

6. Do a mime as follows: Four people stand back to back in pairs facing north, east, south and west. They each stand with feet astride and with both arms raised above their heads diagonally. In their hands they may hold a torch or lighted taper.

Festival of Lights – 2 February
Candle-lightings

Forty days after Jesus' birth he was dedicated to God in the temple according to Jewish law, as Luke 2:22-39 records. There, Mary dedicated the baby Jesus to God, and the holy man Simeon proclaimed him as the light to the countries of the world. The Eastern Church celebrated this from the sixth century and named this festival 'The Meeting', focusing on the meeting of Mary with the prophetic Simeon. Later, the Western Church also celebrated this day by the lighting of candles, and named it 'Candlemas'.

This day invites us to take a last look back to the joys of Christmas, and a first look towards the coming pains of Lent and the cross. Simeon's greeting of the Christ Child in the temple evokes rejoicing, but his prophecy about a sword piercing Mary's heart evokes suffering.

Since the Celtic world celebrated Imbolc, the return of light after the dark days of winter, from 1 February, it seems suitable, since St Brigid is celebrated on 1 February, to mark these two occasions with a Festival of Lights. This may replace or supplement the normal patterns of worship.

Creative activities may be borrowed from those given above for Epiphany.

At Morning Prayer

*Each reader in turn lights a candle from the large central
candle, using the following words, as appropriate*

First   I arise today in the presence
of the Bringer of Light.

Second   I arise today in the presence
of the Brightener of Seasons.

Third   I arise today in the presence
of the returning Glory.

Fourth   I arise today in the light of sun,
radiance of moon,
splendour of fire,
warmth of flame.

All   Shed light upon our brow,
light upon our cheek,
light upon our loved ones,
light on what we seek,
light upon the seeds,
light upon our deeds.

At Evening Prayer

Each reader in turn lights a candle from the large central candle, using the following words, as appropriate

Leader	One candle is already lit: the light of Jesus.
First	In our darkness we light a candle of truth.
Second	In our pain we light a candle of forgiveness.
Third	In our gratitude we light a candle of thanksgiving.
Fourth	In our wonder we light a candle of praise.
Fifth	In our poverty we light a candle of hope.
All	May all our lights together become one flame. May we all be heartened by its glow.

Echoes a Clonfert Diocesan Pilgrimage

Festival of Lights – Night Prayer

Candles or night-lights are lit

Leader Bride light lingers in the sky.
Thank you for this beautiful thing named 'light'.
In it we can observe, act and write, create
and feel good.
May our souls flame forth with the sun's
returning glory.

All As the lights shed their radiance upon us,
may they kindle in us the flame of faithfulness,
spur us to struggle more bravely for justice
and for truth,
and guide us towards you, the Everlasting Light.

Echoes Chanukah

The following or similar words may be chanted or said

All The Lord is my light, my light and salvation.
In God I trust, in God I trust.
Psalm 27

Reader Exodus 12:51; 13:2, 11-16; Leviticus 12:6-8;
or Isaiah 6:1-8

Reader From the fairest Mary shines forth Jesus,
Sun of suns –
All Christ, the true Sun, nothing can destroy.
Reader Created lights all perish –
All The Splendour of God, he shall reign for ever.
Reader In the temple Simeon embraces
the promised One –
All A light to his people, a light to the world.
Reader Anna foretells he will set people free –
All Free from dark prisons of fear and shame.

Reader   Glory to God the One in Three.
All   Glory to God eternally.

Reader   Luke 2:22-40 *or* Colossians 1:13-20

All may sing or say

Faithful vigil ended,
watching, waiting, cease:
Master, grant your servant
his discharge in peace.

All your Spirit promised,
all the Father willed,
now these eyes behold it
perfectly fulfilled.

This your great deliverance
sets your people free;
Christ their light uplifted
all the nations see.

Christ, your people's glory!
Watching, doubting cease:
grant to us your servants
our discharge in peace.

Timothy Dudley Smith

or

Light of the world, in grace and beauty;
mirror of God's eternal face;
transparent flame of love's free duty –
you bring salvation to our race.
Now, as we see the lights of evening,
we raise our voice in hymns of praise.
Worthy are you of endless blessing,
sun of our night, lamp of our days.

245

There may be teaching, activity, silence or singing

Reader   True and living God,
you have given us your Word to illumine
our journey.
Help us so to understand and live by it,
that it may shine more and more
until we reach the light of eternal day.

Reader   Great God,
in creation you commanded the light
to shine out of darkness.
As the season of darkness recedes,
may the incoming light be to us the true Light
in whose presence no unworthy thought,
no deed of shame,
may stubbornly remain.

Leader   Let us pray for Christ, the true Light,
to shine into the dark places of our hearts
and the world.

There may be silence or free prayer

All   Eternal Light, shine into our hearts.
Eternal Goodness, deliver us from evil.
Eternal Power, be our support.
Eternal Wisdom, scatter the darkness
of ignorance.
Eternal Pity, have mercy on us
that with all our heart, mind and strength
we may be brought by your mercy
into your holy presence,
through Jesus Christ our Saviour.
Amen.

There may be singing

Leader   Jesus, revealed in glory,
           worshipped by angels,
           proclaimed among the peoples,
           radiant in the heavens,
           shine in to our hearts and give us peace,
           now and always.

All   Amen.

A Prayer for the Days Between 2 February and Lent

All   We bless you, bounteous God of grace,
that your light now gleams through soil
and saint.
May it make our lives fruitful for you.

Creative activities for the **Festival of Lights** may be borrowed
from those given for Epiphany (page 240).

Lent

In the Celtic Christian tradition, Lent is an essential means to advancing in the Christian life, through fasting from foods and passions that hinder us from being what God intends.

It is a time for vigil and penitence. According to the earliest British and Irish penitentials, such as those of Gildas, David and Finnian, its aim is to 'destroy all evil deeds'; its motive is love, and its method is to replace negative with positive passions ('cure by contraries'). Although its specific prescriptions may not be appropriate to our mobile, multiform culture, something of this spirit is reflected in the following material.

We provide Vigil Prayers for use on any days throughout the three Lents – the forty-day periods preceding Easter and Christmas, and following Pentecost.

More material than usual is included in the fourfold patterns of worship for Lent, to cater for any extended times of worship. Bible readings, proclamations and prayers should be omitted as appropriate.

The fourfold patterns for ordinary days may at times be used during Lent.

Ash Wednesday

The patterns of worship for Lent may be used on this, the first day of Lent (forty days before Easter), but the following may be used instead of Morning or Evening Prayer, and on any days set aside for special spiritual discipline.

Singing may be interspersed with the prayers and readings

Leader In these forty days you lead us
into the desert of purging,
that through reflection and prayer
we may leave behind the things
that tie our spirits down
and learn again to be your pilgrim people.
Through fasting from the frenzied feeding
of false desires,
through study of your Word, meditation
and acts of service,
you open our eyes to your presence in the world
and free us to share your generous love.
By staying close to the Saving Victim
in his passion,
dying and passing from death to life,
we shall join with the saints and angels
in praising you
for the everlasting Easter joys.

There may be singing

Reader Psalm 6; 51:1-12 *or* 90:1-12.

Leader Creator God,
the world of innocence has been cursed by sin,
the land has been blighted,
the people blinded.

Saviour God, human champion,
you have become victim,
you have suffered betrayals,
not being listened to,
not being loved,
being used for money.
Spirit of God,
we long for innocence to be restored,
but we are caught between these conflicting ways.

Leader   Lord, have mercy on us.
All   Christ, have mercy on us.
Leader   Lord, have mercy on us.

Leader   Begin the fast with joy.
Prepare for spiritual battle.
Cleanse the soul.
Purify the body.
Abstain, as from food,
from every destructive habit,
indulging only in the Spirit's virtues.
Persevere in these with all passion.
So shall we be fit, rejoicing in spirit
to witness the passion and death
of Christ our God,
and his passing over from death to life.

There may be silence or singing

Reader   Isaiah 58:1-8; Joel 2:12-17 *or* Amos 5:6-15

Leader   We implore you, holy Jesus,
by your four Evangelists:
Matthew, Mark, Luke and John;
by your four prophets who foretold
your incarnation:

Daniel, Jeremiah, Isaiah and Ezekiel;
by the virgin Mary;
the holy Innocents;
angels;
apostles;
martyrs and saints of our lands:
take us under your defence and protect us.

All   Deliver us from the elements and all their pressings;
from the world and all its lusts and crimes;
from the dangers of this life
and the torments of the next;
from enemies, terror, and shame before your face;
from demons,
that they may have no hold over us now
or at our entry into the next world;
from every person under the stars
who has ill-will towards us.

Leader   O holy Jesus,
O gentle Friend,
O Morning Star,
O midday Sun,
preserve us from all sins,
establish in us all righteousness,
receive us at our lives' end into heaven,
in the unity of apostles and angels,
and in the unity that excels every unity –
the unity of the holy and exalted Trinity,
Father, Son and Holy Spirit.
Amen.

Reflects the early Irish prayer, Besom of Devotion,
of Colcu ua Duinechda, c. 796

Reader   1 Peter 5:6-11 *or* Matthew 12:22-29

Leader   Turn us from prejudice and pride.
Spur us to generous giving.
Aid us in creating space for you.
O one God, O true God, O chief God,
O God of one substance,
O God, only mighty, in three Persons,
full of pity,
forgive.

Attributed to St Ciaran

Leader   Let us love one another,
for love is of God.
The unloving know nothing of God,
for God is love.

Let us recall the divine laws of love.

Pause

Leader   Lord, you so loved the world
that you gave your only Son.
Friends, if God so loved us,
we ought to love one another.

Leader   The cross –
All   We shall take it.
Leader   The Bread –
All   We shall break it.
Leader   The pain –
All   We shall bear it.
Leader   The joy –
All   We shall share it.
Leader   The Gospel –
All   We shall live it.

Leader	The Love –
All	We shall give it.
Leader	The Light –
All	We shall cherish it.
Leader	The dark –
All	God shall perish it.

John Bell

Creative Activities
for Ash Wednesday

1. Bring a container of ashes (for example, from the burning of palm crosses used the previous year) and invite any who wish to have the sign of the cross made with the ashes on their forehead, to remind them of the Bible's advice to abstain from food and to put on ashes at times of repentance.

2. Place a cross, made of two branches of a tree, in a container. Place at its feet three large stones and three loaves, to symbolise Jesus' testings in the desert. (Matthew 4:1-11)

Prayers for Use During Days of Vigil

Any of the following may be used on Ash Wednesday and at any time

Waiting

Leader O God,
you meet us, not in the places that we control,
but in the deep heart's core.

Silence

After each response there may be silence

Leader With Abraham and Moses, waiting to be led
to a place of promise,
All We wait.

Leader With Amos and Hosea, Isaiah, Micah
and all the prophets,
believing that you are a God of justice,
All We wait.

Leader With Paul and Silas, and all God's people
imprisoned and persecuted for acting on their
faith,
All We wait.

Leader With Naaman and Jairus, Bartimaeus
and the Syro-Phoenician woman,
longing for an end to pain and rejection,
All We wait.

Leader	With Zacchaeus in his tree and the Samaritan widow at the well, yearning to be liberated from a half-life,
All	We wait.
Leader	With Sarah and Hannah, Elizabeth and Mary, looking forward to new life and new beginnings,
All	We wait.
Leader	With Jesus in the desert, and in the garden, because he asks us to,
All	We wait.

Echoes a prayer of The Wild Goose Resources Group

Devotion to Christ

All	Fountain of goodness, form of true humility, you bent your holy neck and let a cross be placed upon you. I thank you. I bend the neck of my heart low and ask you to forgive me.

You who are the arm of God
allowed your arms to be stretched out
on the wood of the cross.
Your tender hands were pierced through
with the marks of the nails.
I thank you.
Reach out your hands to me
and with the sharp point of fear and love
pierce my hardened heart
and guide and rule my way.

Intimate, merciful Saviour God,
you who lit up with all virtue
the pure and the strong,

257

you who keep in your heart the Spirit's
seven gifts and your eight blessings,
you who offer them without demanding a return,
I thank you.
Take from my heart the eight great sins,
cleanse my body and soul,
and light me up.

You who lift the lowly and strengthen the frail,
who in your weakness raised a fallen world,
and let sinners lift you on to a cross,
I thank you.
Lift me on to your shoulders,
like a shepherd who does not neglect
one lost sheep.
Lift me from earth to heaven.

Saviour all-merciful, all-powerful,
your passion affected the world,
your wounds shook the elements.
That day the world discovered shadows
and the light was seen to die with you.
The eyes of heaven were shut,
for those who killed you could not bear
to look at you.
I thank you.
I pray for those who violate you.
Protect me from those who desire
to destroy others.
Guard me and keep me fearless.
Lead me through the evil powers
to the shining seats of your kingdom.
I do not despair of reaching you,
Lord Jesus Christ,
Saviour, all-merciful, all-powerful.

All   Kind Father, faithful Saviour,
with head bowed your spirit passed across.
I thank you.
Receive me, at my end, into the hands
of the Father.
Breathe your last for me and hold me up.
Then raise me from the dead.
Cause the powers and principalities to fall back
that I may come swiftly to you.

*Echo prayers on the passion from the
Anglo-Saxon Convent of Nunnaminster,
Winchester, circa AD 900, combining Irish
and Roman elements*

A Self-examination

*This is based on the eight destructive passions which Celtic
Christians, in the tradition of the desert fathers and mothers,
constantly struggled to overcome*

Gluttony What do I excessively feed on? Food? Alcohol?
TV? The Internet? Talk? What else?
What will I give up in order to create spaces for
true nourishment?

Avarice What are the signs of this? Excessive hours of
work or shopping? Dishonest practices?
Accumulation of unnecessary possessions?
What will I give up in order to create spaces?
What alms or actions can I give to others?

Rage What are the signs of my over-controlling ego?
Temper? Abusive language or actions? Worry?
Violence? Abortion? Misrepresentation of
others? How will I let God meet my true
emotional needs? What acts of patience
and kindness will I perform?

Self-pity Am I complaining, inward-looking? Thoughtless towards others? What actions will I take to look to the needs of others or to promote justice?

Lust What cravings that do not bring wholeness to me and to others do I indulge in with my thoughts, eyes, or actions? How have I abused my bodily organs? What things that I crave for shall I abstain from in order to gain self-mastery?

Laziness What duties do I neglect, whether in the family or household, in work, in study or recreation, in friendships and society? What are the priorities I must take action on?

Vanity In what ways am I promoting myself at the expense of others? How am I failing to reflect the unity of the Trinity in the way I relate to others? What should I stop doing? What acts of apology and reconciliation can I make?

Pride Who do I envy, avoid or defame? Which rightful authorities do I disregard? What acts of service can I make?

Read Psalm 119

For the Beauty of Repentance

Grant my head the waters of lament
and the water of tears to my eyes.
The beautiful stones of the nature you have
given me have become defaced,
the precious robe of chastity has been torn,
devotions of love have been scattered,
creative inspirations have been squandered.

I plead to you from whom I hope to receive
the garment of immortality,
restore my soul,
wash away my stains,
receive me back with rejoicing.

Father,
I have sinned against heaven and before you.
Have mercy upon me and listen to me,
for I am not worthy to be called your son –
but your son I am.
So come to my aid, dear Father,
for you know how I long for you.
Show your favour to me:
snatch me from the wastelands,
raise me from degradation,
restore to me a place in your royal
commonwealth,
fill me once again with your Holy Spirit,
heal my wounds
and I will love you;
I will dwell under the shadow of your wings,
I will serve and enjoy you for ever.

Inspired by words of Moucan,
eighth century or earlier

Jesus, give me forgiveness of my sins.
Jesus, give me the grace of repentance.
Jesus, give me the grace of transparency
to make a freely offered confession at this time
as earnestly as if it were the moment of my death.

Carmina Gadelica

Lent Morning Prayer

Leader   Let us return to God who is all forgiveness.
All   With all our being we adore you.
    With all our mind we worship you.
    With all our senses we give you affection.

or

Leader   We seek to tread in the steps of Christ;
All   In the steps of Christ our Champion and King.
Leader   He has shown us the way when strong,
    when weak,
All   He is our Guide in everything.

Leader   We wait for the Lord
All   More than those who watch for the dawn.

Lament

Reader   Psalm 1; 25; 51:1-17; 78:1-8; 130; 131; *or*
    139:1-18, 23-24

    We have fallen short of what you desire, O God:
    wipe clean our sins and save us.
    Hear us, you who guided Noah
    upon the waves of the Flood,
    and who recalled Jonah from the abyss.
    Stir us up, O Christ, Son of God.
    You performed wonders among our forebears;
    reach out your hand to meet our needs.
    Free us, O Christ.
All   Free us, O Christ.
Reader   Hear us, O Christ.
All   Hear us, O Christ.

Reader	Through your cross, deliver us from all evil.
All	Hear us, and give us peace.
Reader	Saving Victim, who takes away the sins of the world,
All	Have mercy on us.

Echoes the Stowe Missal

There may be a Declaration of forgiveness, music of lament or the singing of words such as Lord have mercy

God's Word

Reader Exodus 34:1-10; Leviticus 19:1-18; Deuteronomy 26:1-15; Amos 5:6-15; *or* Hosea 8:11-14; 10:1-2

A Song of the Wilderness

Alternate verses may be read by two readers or by a reader and the people

First The wilderness and the dry land shall rejoice, the desert shall blossom and burst into song.

Second They shall see the glory of the Lord, the majesty of our God.

First Strengthen the weary hands, and make firm the feeble knees.

Second Say to the anxious, 'Be strong, fear not, your God is coming with judgement, coming with judgement to save you.'

First Then shall the eyes of the blind be opened, and the ears of the deaf unstopped;

Second Then shall the lame leap like a hart, and the tongue of the dumb sing for joy.

First	For waters shall break forth in the wilderness, and streams in the desert;
Second	The ransomed of the Lord shall return with singing, with everlasting joy on their heads.
First	Joy and gladness shall be theirs, and sorrow and sighing shall flee away.

Isaiah 35:1, 2b-4a, 4c-6, 10

All	Glory to the Father, glory to the Son, glory to the Spirit, eternal Three in One.
Reader	Luke 15:11-31 *or the New Testament reading of the day*
Leader	Christ, who was born in an outhouse,
All	You were with us in our birth.
Leader	Christ, who was thirty years at the carpenter's bench,
All	You are with us in our work.
Leader	You were driven to the sands by the searching Spirit.
All	Strip from us what is not of you.
Leader	You were alone, without comfort or food.
All	Help us to rely on you alone.
Leader	Though tested by the Evil One you clung to no falsehood.
All	Break in us the hold of power and pride.
Leader	You followed to the end the way of the cross.
All	Strengthen us to be true to you to the end.

There may be creative activity, teaching, singing or silence

Intercession

Leader   O Holy Fire,
            O Holy Grace,
            O Overflowing Silent One,
            By your birth,
All   Enable us;
Leader   By your overcoming of spirits,
All   Arm us;
Leader   By your integrity,
All   Make us true;
Leader   By your fortitude in trials,
All   Establish us;
Leader   By your self-giving in death,
All   Change us;
Leader   By your mission to unquiet spirits,
All   Raise us.

There may be singing, the Lord's Prayer, free prayer or a time of silent waiting.

Any of these or other prayers may be said

Reader   God of all seasons,
            in your pattern of things
            there is a time for keeping
            and a time for losing,
            a time for building up
            and a time for pulling down.
            In this holy season of Lent,
            as we journey with our Lord to the cross
            help us to discern in our lives
            what we must lay down
            and what we must take up,
            what we must end
            and what we must begin.

*The Book of Common Order
of the Church of Scotland*

Reader   Too long have I worried about so many things,
and yet, my Lord, so few are needed.
May I live more simply – like the bread.
May I see more clearly – like the water.
May I be more selfless – like the Christ.

From Russia

Reader   Great God,
as fish live in water, may we live in you,
as birds fly in air, may we fly in you,
as trees stand in earth, may we stand in you,
as flames blaze in fire, may we blaze for you.

I am giving you worship with my whole life.
I am giving you assent with my whole power.
I am giving you praise with my whole tongue.
I am giving you honour with my whole speech.

I am giving you reverence
with my whole understanding.
I am giving you dedication
with my whole thought.
I am giving you praise with my whole fervour.
I am giving you humility in the blood of the Lamb.

I am giving you love with my whole devotion.
I am giving you kneeling with my whole desire.
I am giving you love with my whole heart.
I am giving you affection with my whole sense.
I am giving you existence with my whole mind.
I am giving you my soul, O God of all gods.

My thought, my deed,
My word, my will,
My understanding, my intellect,
My way, my state,
I give my all to you.

Carmina Gadelica

Leader May the God of strength be with you,
holding you in strong-fingered hands.
May you be a sacrament of strength
to those whose hands you hold.
May the blessing of strength be on you.

Lent Midday Prayer

Leader   O God, create in me a clean heart.
Restore in me a true spirit.
Cast me not away from your presence.
Renew in me the joy of salvation.
Endow me with a generous spirit.
I will teach your ways
to those who have lost their way,
and they will return to you.

Reader   Psalm 119:9-16 *or* Psalm 119:33-40

There may be silence or singing

Leader   Christ, you are the refined molten metal
of our human forge.
Purge our desires,
strengthen our resolve,
sharpen our minds,
shape our wills.

Reader   Jesus said: Blessed are the poor,
for theirs is the kingdom of God.

Leader   In our time of need and in the midst of the day,
keep us thankful, true and faithful.

All   Let us pluck out by the roots
Adam's sinful greed in Eden
that proved deadly to the world.
Let us touch the tree of the cross
that pours out immortality on the world
like a new river from Paradise.
By it, all things are made alive.
O God of compassion, keep us close to you.

There may be silence, singing or free prayer

Leader Working and praying,
may we walk in the way of the cross
each hour of this day.

All Amen.

Lent Evening Prayer

Leader Holy God, you call us to throw off what clouds
your will.

All We will struggle with Christ against wrong.
We will share with Christ his trials.
We will embrace with him the suffering
of the world.

Reader Psalm 25; 26; 27; 32; 34; *or* 52

There may be singing

Lament

One of the following confessions may be said

Reader O great and glorious God, eternal and wonderful,
you keep covenant with those who love you
with their whole heart.
You are the life of all,
the help of those who flee to you,
the hope of those who cry to you.
Cleanse us from our sins,
and from every thought displeasing
to your goodness.
Cleanse our souls and bodies,
our hearts and consciences,
that with a pure heart and a clear mind,
with perfect love and calm hope,
we may venture confidently and fearlessly
to pray to you,
through Jesus Christ our Lord.
Amen.

St Basil

or

Reader	Father Creator,
	we have raped and spoiled your world.
All	Lord, forgive.
Reader	Jesus Saviour,
	we have ignored your teachings and warnings.
All	Lord, forgive.
Reader	Spirit Sustainer,
	we have tried to live without you.
All	Lord, forgive.

Leader	Every sin I have ever thought or done:
All	Forgive.
Leader	Everything I sought outside your love:
All	Forgive.
Leader	Every wasted moment:
All	Forgive.
Leader	Every ill-intent towards another:
All	Forgive.
Leader	Every failure of love towards your creation:
All	Forgive.

There may be silence, music of lament, sharing or acting out of sorrow for sins that spoil God's world

Leader	We will leave behind prejudice
	and meanness of spirit.
	We will play our part in the kingdom of your love.
All	All honour to you, our God who beckons us on.

271

God's Word

Reader   Exodus 17:1-7; 20:1-17; *or the Old Testament reading of the day*

Look and see that I am God
who once, for my people, rained down manna
and brought water from the rock
in the desert,
by my right hand alone and by my own might.

All   Let us hear you when you call,
give up our former sins
and revere you as Judge and God.

Reader   I have been wounded, I have been beaten.
Here are the nails which have pierced
my soul and body.
Here are the wounds and lashes inflicted
by those who indulged their uncleansed
passions.

All   Let us hear you when you call,
give up our former sins
and revere you as Judge and God.

Reader   Know and see that I am God.
I search hearts, reprove misdeeds, burn up sins.
I protect the powerless and care for the needy.

All   Let us hear you when you call,
give up our former sins
and revere you as Judge and God.
Echoes the Great Canon of St Andrew of Crete, 740

Reader   Luke 14:25-33; 15:1-7; 15:11-32; 17:1-4;
18:9-14; *or the New Testament reading of the day*

Reader	Come, let us return to the Lord who has torn us and will heal us.
All	God has stricken us and will bind up our wounds.
Reader	After two days you will revive us and on the third day will raise us up that we may live in your presence.
All	We will strive to know you, Lord; your appearing is as sure as the sunrise.
Reader	You will come to us like the showers, like the spring rains that water the earth.
All	O my people, how shall I deal with you? Your love for me is like the morning dew that goes early away.
Reader	That is why I have cut you down by the prophets and my judgement goes forth as the light.
All	Loyalty is my desire, not sacrifice, and the knowledge of God rather than burnt offerings.

Hosea 6:1-6

There may be teaching, silence, creative activity, sharing or singing
Any of the following or other prayers may be said

Intercession

Reader My Lord and my God,
take from me all that keeps me from you.
My Lord and my God,
give to me all that brings me nearer to you.
My Lord and my God,
take me away from myself and give me
completely to you.

Brother Klaus

273

Reader   Christ of the scars,
into your hands we place the broken,
the wounded,
the hungry and the homeless.

Specific situations of need may be mentioned

Christ of the scars,
into your hands we place those
who have been bereaved or betrayed;
those who have suffered loss of limb or esteem,
family or friends,
employment or home.

Specific situations of need may be mentioned

Christ of the scars,
into your hands we place unwanted babies,
children abused,
neighbours defamed,
lovers spurned,
spouses deserted.

Specific situations of need may be mentioned

Christ of the scars,
into your hands we place those
who are victims of violence or vandalism,
false accusation or sharp practice.

Specific situations of need may be mentioned

Leader   Lord and Master of my life,
keep far from me the spirit of futility,
discouragement,
the lust for power,
and empty speech.

All   O God, cleanse me, a sinner.

274

Leader	Grant to your servant the spirit of chastity, humility, patience and love.
All	O God, cleanse me, a sinner.
Leader	Yes, my Lord and King, grant me to see my own sins and not to judge my neighbour. For you are blessed for ever.
All	O God, cleanse me, a sinner.

St Ephraim of Syria, 373

Reader	Saving God, by your incarnation and birth in poverty,
All	Set us free.
Reader	By your prayers and self-discipline,
All	Set us free.
Reader	By your tender works of mercy,
All	Set us free.
Reader	By your struggle for truth and justice,
All	Set us free.
Reader	By your nobility in persecution,
All	Set us free.
Reader	By your self-giving even in death,
All	Set us free.

| Leader | Bearer of pain and Maker of love, steep our souls in your deeps. |
| All | May we walk in the steps of Christ through the pain to glory. |

There may be singing

| Leader | May the Christ who walks with wounded feet walk with you on the road. May the Christ who serves with wounded hands stretch out your hands to serve. May the Christ who loves with wounded heart open your hearts to love. |

275

Lent Night Prayer

Leader Tonight we seek your face
and forsake our empty hours.
Tonight we seek you above all things.

All Lord, let our memory provide no shelter
for grievance against another.
Lord, let our heart provide no harbour
for hatred of another.
Lord, let our tongue be no accomplice in the
judgement of a brother.

Northumbrian Office

Leader In the looming awfulness of your cross,
our sins stand out like great stones.

All Strip from us what is not true.
Give us well-being of the soul.

Reader Verses from Psalm 6; 38, 51; 90; 102;
or 119:145-152

Reader Loving Saviour,
show yourself to us that, knowing you,
we may love you as warmly in return –
may love you alone,
desire you alone,
contemplate you alone by day and night,
and keep you always in our thoughts.
May affection for you pervade our hearts.
May attachment to you take possession of us all.
May love of you fill all our senses.
May we know no other love except you
who are eternal;
a love so great that the many waters of land
and sea will fail to quench it.

Columbanus

Reader   Matthew 16:16-21 *or another Bible reading*

There may be silence or singing

Leader   Have mercy this night on a surfeited world,
which, through grasping, can't be grasped by you.

All   Have mercy this night on the weak and broken,
on the hungry and homeless, and on souls
without hope.

Leader   Have mercy on us and on those we name
before you now.

Concerns may be voiced

*The following or other words may be sung to the
tune Amazing Grace*

O Saviour God, forgive our sins,
have mercy on us all.
We seek your face, we leave behind
what blinds us to your grace.

Through many journeys you have been
your pilgrim children's strength.
Tonight we ask that nought we do
will cancel out your love.

We lay ourselves before you, Lord.
We rest in love divine.
We sleep in hope of glory years,
of being forever thine.

Leader   Great God,
in your goodness you protect us
from the snares of evil.
You who are the Creator of all,
bring us safely through the night
that we may offer you our prayers at dawn,
and, together with your gift of true light,

277

pour out in to our hearts
the treasure of knowing you
that enables us to do your will.
For you, dear God, are loving to all
and we give you the glory,
Father, Saviour and Holy Spirit,
now and ever, to the ages of ages.
Amen.

Orthodox

Leader	You have framed the warp of our souls;
All	At last we will rest in you.
Leader	We give thanks for the gift of sleep,
All	But also for the gift of struggle.
Leader	Awake, may we watch with you.
All	Asleep, may we rest in peace.

Creative Activities for Lent

1. A space is cleared with a cairn of stones in the centre. Each person chooses seven stones from a container of stones, letting these stand for seven sins or bad habits they wish to throw away. They stand in a circle around the cairn. When they are ready to discard these sins they throw the seven stones at the cairn, one at a time.

2. Provide a 'sin bin'. In this, any person may place an object or a piece of paper on which they have written something that they wish to strip from their lives because it is superfluous.

3. A large mirror is placed on the floor, and the words of Psalm 139:23-24 are attached to a corner. Any who wish can kneel in front of it, in silent reflection.

4. Fill a glass with water and add red food-colouring. Invite any who wish, to write down on a piece of dissolvable paper (available from confectioners) a sin they wish to leave behind. Then invite those who have done so to drop the folded paper into the water and watch it dissolve.

5. Stones are placed in a bowl next to indelible pencils or paintbrushes. Each person takes a stone and inscribes on it a virtue they wish to acquire.

6. Plant seeds of early-flowering plants in holes filled with sand. Place a flag to mark the name of the seed and of a person it represents who will be prayed for daily throughout Lent. After Easter, offer the flowers (assuming they grow!) to the persons named.

Holy Week – In the steps of the Suffering Christ

Holy Week is the week preceding Easter Day, when Christians throughout the world seek to follow in the steps of Christ through the last, momentous week of his earthbound life.

Fourfold patterns of worship are provided, as follows: for Sunday to Wednesday, for Thursday, for Good Friday, and for Saturday (Easter Eve).

The theme of Sunday is recognition by the crowds of Jesus' unique destiny. The theme of Monday is cleansing of the temple and of ourselves. The theme of Tuesday is teaching about the meaning of Jesus' mission. The theme of Wednesday is the stature of waiting and the beauty of service. The theme of Thursday is Jesus' farewell at the Last Supper, the foreboding and the betrayal. The theme of Friday is the trial, the beating, the crucifixion and the shudders of creation. The theme of Saturday is the grief and vigil by Jesus' tomb.

Morning Prayer for Holy Week

There may be singing

Lament

Leader	Children sing your praises,
All	But we have gone our own way.
Leader	Angels support and uphold you,
All	But we have gone our own way.
Leader	A donkey willingly bears your weight,
All	But we have gone our own way.
Leader	A thief will cry to you for mercy,
All	But we have gone our own way.

Leader   When you were crucified, O Word,
you offered your body and blood on behalf of all:
your body to refashion me,
your blood to wash me clean.
You gave up your spirit, O Christ,
to bring me to your Father.

From St Andrew of Crete

All sing or say

All   Jesus, Lamb of God, have mercy on us.
Jesus, Lamb of God, have mercy on us.
Jesus, Redeemer of the world, give us your peace.

Reader   Psalm 69:6-18 (Palm Sunday); 130 (Monday);
56 (Tuesday); 40 (Wednesday); 116:11-18
(Thursday)

God's Word

Reader   Isaiah 42:1-9; 49:1-7; 50:4-9a; Lamentations
1:1-12a; Zechariah 9:9-12; *or the Old Testament
reading of the day*

Reader	The leaders turned on you, the crowds turned from you.
All	But the children praised you, and the stones would have too.
Reader	You alone have the words of eternal life; who else could we go to?
All	The children and the stones and we, too, will praise you.

Pause

Reader	Sections of Matthew 26–27 *or the New Testament reading of the day*
	As his greatest trial drew near, Jesus looked upon the city and wept over it, because it did not recognise its salvation.
All	Open our eyes that we may weep with you. Open the eyes of our people that they may see you.

There may be teaching, creative activity or singing

Reader	When the ride is bumpy and the world passes us by,
All	You pour out your life for us, O God, right to the very end.
Reader	When we are edged aside and doors are shut in our face,
All	You pour out your life for us, O God, right to the very end.
Reader	When others are out to get us and our home is not secure,
All	You pour out your life for us, O God, right to the very end.

Reader   When our lives are but a flicker in the darkness
that encroaches,

All   You pour out your life for us, O God,
right to the very end.

There may be silent or free prayer and singing

Leader   Father,
in the life of Jesus you have shown us the way.
Give us his spirit of self-discipline;
lead us more deeply into the way of the cross.
Before his hands were stretched out on the cross,
they were stretched out in love to children,
women and men.
May your way of the cross be our way
that we, too, may stretch out our hands
in love to all.

Holy Week Midday Prayer

There may be chanting or singing

Leader	Lord, today you teach us.
	Your words hold the truth about this world
	and us.
	Yet even as you speak, some slip away from you
	in order to impose their agendas on this world.

Leader	Lord, have mercy on us.
All	Christ, have mercy on us.
Leader	Lord, have mercy on us.

Leader	Lord, some remain faithful to you.
	We too would be faithful,
	even when times seem bleak and hope grows dim.

Leader	Lord, have mercy on us.
All	Christ, have mercy on us.
Leader	Lord, have mercy on us.

Leader	Saviour of the world,
	by your cross and precious death
All	Save us and help us, we humbly beseech you,
	O Lord.

Leader	Lord, have mercy on us.
All	Christ, have mercy on us.
Leader	Lord, have mercy on us.

Reader	Jesus said: Unless you take up your cross
	and follow me you cannot be my disciples.

Leader	Lord, have mercy on us.
All	Christ, have mercy on us.
Leader	Lord, have mercy on us.

Reader	Unless a grain of wheat falls into the ground and dies it cannot bear fruit.
Leader	Lord, have mercy on us.
All	Christ, have mercy on us.
Leader	Lord, have mercy on us.

Leader	Jesus, master carpenter of Nazareth, who through wood and nails won our full salvation, wield well your tools in this your workshop that we who come to you rough hewn may here be fashioned to a truer beauty by your hand.

Traditional

Leader	In the middle of the day we offer our work and ourselves to you,
All	And all who are in our hearts.

There may be silence or names may be mentioned

Leader	May we carry your cross in our hearts through this day.
All	Your cross be in our eyes and in our looking. Your cross be in our minds and in our thinking. Your cross be in our mouths and in our speaking. Your cross be in our hands and in our working.

Evening Prayer in Holy Week

Leader   He who created us comes willingly to suffer for us.
All   Let us spread our resolves before him
             like palm leaves.
Leader   The Almighty comes to us as one gentle and
             lowly of heart.
All   Let us don clothes for him of humility and praise.

Leader   The spirit is willing but the flesh is weak.
All   Let us watch and wait with him.

             There may be singing

Reader   Psalm 26 (Monday); 35:11-16 (Tuesday);
             102:1-11 (Wednesday)

Lament

Leader   O Saviour of the human race,
             O true physician of every disease,
             O heart-pitier and assister in times of misery,
             O fount of true purity and true knowledge,
All   Forgive.

Leader   O star-like sun,
             O guiding light,
             O home of the planets,
             O fiery-maned and marvellous one,
All   Forgive.

Leader   O holy scholar of holy strength,
             O overflowing, loving, silent one,
             O generous and thunderous giver of gifts,
             O rock-like warrior of a hundred hosts,
All   Forgive.

                              Attributed to St Ciaran, adapted

God's Word

Reader Lamentations 3:19-33 (Monday); Isaiah 42:1-7
(Tuesday); Jeremiah 7:21-28 (Wednesday)

*There may be silence, singing, or the Proclamation,
Jesus, Saviour of the world*

Reader Luke 11:41-48 or 22:1-38 (Monday);
Mark 11:27-13:2 (Tuesday); Mark 14:1-11
(Wednesday)

*There may be teaching, creative activity, silence or
singing*

Intercession

Leader Jesus wept over the city and said:
'How often I would have gathered you
as a hen gathers her chicks,
but you would not heed me.'
'Come to me, my people.'

All We come to you, Lord. To whom else can we go?

Leader Jesus said:
Can you be baptised with the baptism I must be
baptised with?

All Lord, we seek to feel your sadness,
we seek to share your tears.

Leader O Christ, help us to become one with you.
In your defenceless love, teach us the grace
of self-offering.
In your weakness, teach us the grace of acceptance.
In your betrayal, teach us the grace of forgiveness.
In your testings, teach us the grace of believing.

There may be free prayer and singing

Leader May the Christ who walked on wounded feet
walk with us on the road.
May the Christ who serves with wounded hands
stretch out our hands to serve.
May the Christ who loves with wounded heart
open our hearts to love.

Holy Week Night Prayer

Leader	Our desire is to do your will, O God,
	our desire is to do your will.
All	Our frames are tired and our souls are bowed,
	yet still we desire your will.

Leader	In the dark night of the soul we cry out to you.
All	Our strength and our friends may fall away,
	yet still we cry out to you.

Reader	Psalm 3 *or* Psalm 10:1-11

Leader	You are our Saviour and Lord,
All	In our stumbling be our Shield,
Leader	In our tiredness be our Rest,
All	In our darkness be our Light.

Reader	Jesus prayed for the people:
	How I have longed to gather you to me
	as a mother hen gathers her chicks.

Leader	We pray, Lord, for your dear ones and ours,
	whom you long to gather to you in every place
	where they are.

Names may be mentioned

Leader	Christ forsaken,
All	Have mercy on all who are forsaken.
Leader	Christ afraid,
All	Have mercy on all who are afraid.
Leader	Christ betrayed,
All	Have mercy on all who are betrayed.
Leader	Christ unnoticed,
All	Have mercy on all who are unnoticed.

Leader   I place my soul and body under your guiding
this night, O Christ,

All   O Son of the journey through darkness,
may your cross this night be my shield.

There may be silence and singing

Leader   We make the sign of the cross of Christ
(make sign).
O Christ of the dying and of deathless love,

All   Be your cross between us and all things fearful,
your cross between us and all things
coming darkly towards us,
your cross our sure way from earth to heaven.

Morning Prayer for Thursday of Holy Week

Leader Let us wake to the day of covenant:
the day of your last supper with your disciples,
the day you washed their feet,
the day you prayed for us all to be one.

All Glory to the Father,
glory to the Son,
glory to the Spirit,
one God, who mothers us all.

God's Word

Reader Psalm 116:12-18

There may be singing

Reader Exodus 12:1-8, 11-14 *or* Jeremiah 31:31-34

Today the shadow of greed
fell upon the ungodly Judas
and he handed over, you, the just judge of all,
to unjust judges intent on their own ends.

See how love of money destroys what is good.
See how, because of money,
the betrayer hangs himself
and the Creator is led captive to the slaughter.

Leader Lord, have mercy.
All Christ, have mercy.
Leader Lord, have mercy.

Reader　We will stay close to you.
We will not draw back through fear.
We will commune with you at the mystical table
and in our hearts.
We will watch you wash your disciples' feet.
We will wash one another's feet.
We will have your bearing towards one another,
serving and honouring fellow members
of the Body of Christ.

All　Glory to the Father,
glory to the Son,
glory to the Spirit,
one God, who mothers us all.

Reader　Mark 14:12-26 *or* 1 Corinthians 11:23-32

There may be teaching, silence or singing

Intercession

Reader　Lord Jesus,
you taught us that what we do
for the least of our brothers or sisters
we do for you.
Give us the will to be the servant of others,
as you, who gave up your life and died for us,
were the servant of all.

We pray for those who have been betrayed,
those who are undergoing torture,
those who are in mental torment,
those who are unjustly punished,
those who are prisoners of conscience.

Additional suggestions for prayer may be added
There may be creative activity or singing

Leader   Father, look upon your family,
for whom our Lord Jesus Christ
was willing to undergo betrayal and torture.
Forgive our unfaithfulness.
Cure us of our sins.
Restore our unity.
Strengthen us to walk the way of the cross.
Bring us to the place of resurrection.

There may be singing

Leader   God give you grace to stay close to Christ
and to walk the way of the cross,
that you may bring forth the fruit of eternal life.

Midday Prayer for Thursday of Holy Week

Reader   Jesus says to his friends:
My heart is breaking with grief.
Stay with me,
watch with me
and pray with me.

All   Lord, we will stay with you,
we will watch with you,
we will pray with you.

Reader   Anguish and dismay came over Jesus.
He fell prostrate to the ground, and he prayed:
My heart is breaking with grief.
Stay with me,
watch with me
and pray with me.

All   Lord, we will stay with you,
we will watch with you,
we will pray with you.

Reader   Later Jesus said:
Now my hour has come.
The Son of humankind is betrayed
into the hands of sinful people.
My heart is breaking with grief.
Stay with me,
watch with me
and pray with me.

All   Lord, we will stay with you,
we will watch with you,
we will pray with you.

*A candle may be lit; there may be silent vigil
or singing*

Reader Psalm 103:6-18

Leader Saviour, you became obedient even to death;
teach us to do our Maker's will.
All Save us and help us, O Lord.
Leader Jesus, you were humiliated,
yet you had no self-pity or revengeful spirit.
All Save us and help us, O Lord.
Leader Brother, you gave yourself and your life
for love of God's family.
All Save us and help us, O Lord.

*The Jesus Prayer below may be repeated
(say ten, twenty or fifty times)*

Lord Jesus Christ,
truly God,
truly human,
have mercy upon me,
a sinner.

There may be silence or singing

Leader Let us go, always holding the cross of Christ
in our hearts.
All We will be true to him to the end of our days.

Thursday Evening of Holy Week

A variety of customs are followed on the Thursday evening of Holy Week. These mark, in one way or another, Jesus' last meal with his disciples, the Jewish Passover that provided the context for this, his washing of their feet and his final prayers for the Church.

There may be an informal meal, or a Passover meal according to Jewish practice, at which the story of the first Passover is told and the words and actions of Jesus instituting the Lord's Supper are repeated.

There may be a washing of feet or hands. A bowl of warm water for one or more groups of twelve is placed in the centre of the group. One person washes the feet or the hands of another; that person does the same for the next person and so on. This may be in the context of an informal gathering, a Holy Communion Service, or Evening Prayer.

In churches there may be a service of Holy Communion at which each item on and around the Holy Table is stripped away. Each person present carries one item away until the chancel is totally bare. The purpose of this is that those for whom the familiar church adornments are a precious part of their devotion to Jesus feel violated, stripped naked, as was their Lord at this time.

Or there may be the following brief Evening Prayer

Leader	The angel passed over the homes of the God-followers. The fleeing people passed over the sea. In their extremity you reached down to them, Lord.
All	Blessed be the God of eternal covenant.

Leader	Lord, have mercy upon us.
All	Christ, have mercy upon us.

Leader	Christ walked the land doing works of justice and mercy.
	Tyrants pinned him down and brought him to the gate of death.
	In his extremity he called out to you and you heard him.
All	Blessed be the God of eternal covenant.

There may be singing

God's Word

Reader	Psalm 39

Reader	Exodus 12:1-8, 11-14 *or the story of the first Passover is told*

All sing

I see his blood upon the rose,
in the stars his glorious eyes.
His body gleams amid the snows.
His tears fall from the skies.

I see his face in every flower,
his voice in song of birds,
and, carved by his eternal power,
rocks are his written words.

All pathways by his feet are worn.
His heartbeat moves the sea.
His crown of thorns twines every thorn.
His cross is every tree.

Echoes words of Joseph Mary Plunkett

Reader	John 13:1-15

Intercession

*Prepared or spontaneous intercessions may be
offered for the unity of God's people and world*

Leader	God of the tears,
All	Give us tears for your people.
Leader	God who mothers us,
All	Draw us into your arms.
Leader	God who is One,
All	Make us one with you.

Night Prayer for Thursday of Holy Week

Leader   Tonight our hearts are heavy.
Our Christ has given love, given it exquisitely.
In his tiredness he has washed the tired feet
of his faithful friends.
In his generosity he has given bread to his betrayer.
In his prophetic provision he has,
with bread and wine,
bequeathed a sacrament that keeps him always
present to us.
In his prayers he has placed the Church of every
time in the divine heart.
In his bitter anguish in the garden he has fought
with demons and with doubt.
He has been led away captive
to be mocked and tried.
He will not sleep this night
and he calls to us watch and pray.

All   Lord, we will watch and pray.

Leader   Lord, have mercy upon us.
All   Christ, have mercy upon us.
Leader   Lord, have mercy upon us.

*There may be singing of a song or chant, such as
O Christe Domine Jesu*

Reader   Psalm 77:1-12

Leader   O Christ, you teach us by your example
to remain faithful in hard times.
May we never be ashamed of you.
You teach us to pray for our weaker brothers
and sisters.

All   We pray for your Church:
where it is weak, strengthen it;
where it is divided, reunite it;
where it has lost its first love,
draw it back to your love that loves
even to death.

Reader   Jesus said:
I give you a new command –
Love one another.
As I have loved you, so you must love
one another.
There is no greater love than laying down one's
life for another.

All   Jesus, we love you.
Have mercy on us for our faithless ways.
Restore us to our first love
that we may lay down our lives for one another.

Leader   Let us pray for our brothers and sisters
as Jesus prayed on the night before he died:
we pray that they may be one with you
and one with each other.

Anyone may mention persons or peoples
There may be singing

Leader   Father,
though you may seem distant,
we pray that you will keep us
and those for whom we have prayed
in your love this night,
in that love with which you loved your Son.
May you be in them and may they be in you.

Leader	Let us hold Christ's cross in our hearts through the darkness of this night.
All	The darkness is not dark with you, O Lord.
Leader	Watching or sleeping, Lord, may you be in us, and may we be in you.
All	Watching or sleeping, we will remain in you.

Good Friday

Good Friday marks the day Christ died. It is a day of abstinence from activity and food in order to be inwardly present with Jesus on the Cross. Some traditions forego Holy Communion on Good Friday, in order to experience with Jesus the apparent 'absence' of God.

Good Friday Morning Prayer

A wooden cross may be placed in view of everyone
Devotions such as the following may be used

Lament

Leader   Today we grieve, for the Son of the Living God
is led away to die on a cross.

Reader   At the cry of the first bird
they began to crucify you.
O cheek like a swan.
It was not right ever to cease lamenting.
It was like the parting of day from night.

Early Irish Poem

The imagined reproaches of the eternal Son of God to the people of the world

The 'refrain' in the following is sung to the tune
Glory be to Jesus by Thomas Ken

All   Lord, have mercy on us; cleanse us from our sins.
Lord, have mercy on us; turn our hearts again.

Reader   My people, what wrong have I done to you?
I am your Creator,
I have entrusted the land to you,
yet you have violated its laws
and misused my creatures.
What good have I not done to you?
Answer me.

All   Lord, have mercy on us; cleanse us from our sins.
Lord, have mercy on us; turn our hearts again.

Reader I entrusted the world to you,
yet you have polluted its air
and created the means to destroy it.
My people, what wrong have I done to you?
What good have I not done for you?
Answer me.

All Lord, have mercy on us; cleanse us from our sins.
Lord, have mercy on us; turn our hearts again.

Reader I made you in my likeness,
yet you have marred my image
and degraded body and spirit.
I made my children of one blood
to live in families rejoicing in one another,
but you have embittered the races
and divided the peoples.
My people, what wrong have I done to you?
What good have I not done for you?
Answer me.

All Lord, have mercy on us; cleanse us from our sins.
Lord, have mercy on us; turn our hearts again.

Reader I freed you from slavery,
yet you handed me over to death and jeered at me.
I opened the sea before you,
but you opened my side with a spear!
What good have I not done for you?
Answer me.

All Lord, have mercy on us; cleanse us from our sins.
Lord, have mercy on us; turn our hearts again.

Reader   I fed you in the desert,
guided you with cloud by day and night,
yet you led me to Pilate!
I struck down rulers who would have harmed you,
yet you struck me with a reed.
My people, what wrong have I done to you?
Answer me.

All   Lord, have mercy on us; cleanse us from our sins.
Lord, have mercy on us; turn our hearts again.

Reader   I gave you from the rock living waters
of salvation;
you gave me bitter drink,
you quenched my thirst with vinegar!
What good have I not done for you?
Answer me.

All   Lord, have mercy on us; cleanse us from our sins.
Lord, have mercy on us; turn our hearts again.

Reader   I put the sceptre into your hand
and made you a royal people,
but you crowned me with the crown of thorns!
I made you great by my boundless power,
yet you hanged me on the gallows of the cross!
My people, what wrong have I done to you?
What good have I not done for you?
Answer me.

All   Lord, have mercy on us; cleanse us from our sins.
Lord, have mercy on us; turn our hearts again.

Reader   I gave you my teachings,
but you have eschewed integrity.
I have come to you in this your land,
yet you have betrayed my sacrifice
and spurned my love!
What good have I not done for you?
Answer me.

All   Lord, have mercy on us; cleanse us from our sins.
Lord, have mercy on us; turn our hearts again.

There may be silence and singing

God's Word

*There may be readings from the gospel accounts of
Christ's last day on earth or these may be told as stories*

Intercession

There may be prepared intercessions

*The leader invites any who wish, to kneel by the
cross and touch it with their forehead or lips.*

*This may be accompanied by quiet, meditative music,
or singing in the Spirit, which may continue longer*

Leader   Hail! life-giving cross,
invincible banner of pure religion,
gate of paradise,
strength of believers,
defence of the Church.
By you the curse has been undone, destroyed,
the power of death devoured,
and we have been raised from earth to heaven.
Unbeatable weapon,
demonic powers' foe, martyrs' glory,
boast of holy monks, salvation's harbour,
from you the world receives great mercy.

When all creation saw you,
all things' Maker and Creator,
hang naked on the cross,
it was changed by fear, and wailed.
The sun's light failed and the earth quaked.
The rocks were rent and the temple's veil
was rent in two.
The dead were raised from their tombs,
and the powers of heaven cried out
in astonishment:
How amazing this is!
The Judge is judged,
he wills to suffer death,
to heal and renew the world.

From an Orthodox Vespers

There may be singing

Leader   May the Christ who walked on wounded feet
walk with you on the road.
May the Christ who serves with wounded hands
stretch out your hands to serve.
May the Christ who loves with wounded heart
open our hearts to love.

Good Friday Midday Prayer

*This service comprises various readings, which may form
part of extended meditations for up to three hours at the foot
of the cross, interspersed with silences and singing*

Reader The sun concealed its proper light;
it lamented its Lord.
A swift cloud went across the blue sky,
the great stormy sea roared.
The whole world became dark,
great trembling came on the earth;
at the death of noble Jesus great rocks burst open.
A fierce stream of blood boiled until the bark
of every tree was red.
It would have been fitting for God's elements –
the fair sea, the blue sky, the earth –
to have changed their appearance,
lamenting their calamity.
The body of Christ exposed to the spear-thrust
demanded harsh lamentation –
that they should have mourned more grievously
the Man by whom they were created.

Blathmac

Reader Wondrous was the tree of victory
and I was stained by sin, stricken by guilt.
I saw this glorious tree,
joyfully gleaming, adorned with garments,
decked in gold; the tree of the Ruler
was rightly adorned with rich stones;
yet through that gold I could see the agony
once suffered by wretches, for it had bled
down the right-hand side.
Then I was afflicted, frightened at this sight;

309

I saw that sign often change its clothing and its hue,
at times dewy with moisture,
yet I lay there for a long while
and gazed sadly at the Saviour's cross;
until I heard it utter words;
the finest of trees began to speak:

'I remember the morning a long time ago
that I was felled at the edge of the forest
and severed from my roots.
Strong enemies seized me,
bade me hold up their felons on high,
and made me a spectacle.
Men shifted me on their shoulders
and set me on a hill.
Many enemies fastened me there.
I saw the Lord of humankind
hasten with such courage to climb upon me.
I dared not bow or break there
against my Lord's wish, when I saw the surface
of the earth tremble.
I could have felled all my foes, yet I stood firm.
Then the young warrior, God Almighty,
stripped himself, firm and unflinching.
He climbed upon the cross, brave before many,
to redeem humankind . . .
They drove dark nails into me;
dire wounds are there to see,
the gaping gashes of malice;
I dared not injure them.
They insulted us both together;
I was drenched in the blood
that streamed from the Man's side
after he set his spirit free . . .

'I saw the God of hosts cruelly stretched out.
Darkness with its clouds
had covered the Lord's corpse,
the bright radiance.
A shadow went out forth,
dark beneath the clouds.
All creation wept,
lamented the King's death.
Christ was on the cross.

'There they lifted him from his heavy torment;
they took Almighty God away.
The warriors left me standing there,
stained with blood;
sorely was I wounded
by the sharpness of spear-shafts.
They laid him down, limb-weary;
they stood at the corpse's head,
they beheld there the Lord of Heaven;
and there he rested for a while,
worn out after battle.
And then they began to build a sepulchre;
under his slayer's eyes,
they carved it from the gleaming stone,
and laid therein the Lord of Victories.
Then, sorrowful at dusk
they sang a dirge before they went away, weary,
from their glorious Prince;
he rested in the grave alone.
But we still stood there, weeping blood,
long after the song of the warriors
had soared to heaven.
The corpse grew cold,
the fair human house of the soul.

'I have not many friends of influence upon earth;
they have journeyed on from the joys of this world
to find the King of Glory;
they live in heaven with the High Father,
they dwell in splendour.
Now I look day by day for that time
when the cross of the Lord,
which once I saw in a dream here on earth,
will fetch me away from this fleeting life
and lift me to the home of joy and happiness
where the people of God are seated
at the feast in eternal bliss,
and set me down where I may live
in glory unending
and share the joy of the saints.
May the Lord be a friend to me,
he who suffered once for the sins of all
here on earth on the gallows tree.
He has redeemed us; he has given life to us,
and a home in heaven.'

From The Dream of the Rood,
trans. Kevin Crossley-Holland

Reader O Son of God,
do a miracle for me and change my heart;
your having taken flesh to redeem me was more
difficult than to transform my wickedness.
It is you who, to help me, went to be scourged
by the Jews;
you, dear child of Mary,
are the refined molten metal of our forge.
It is you who made the sun bright,
together with the ice;
it is you who created the rivers and the salmon
all along the river . . .

Though the children of Eve ill-deserve
the bird flocks and the salmon,
it was the Immortal One on the cross
who made both salmon and birds.

Fifteenth century, Irish

Good Friday Evening Prayer

Leader	Crucified Christ, Son of the Father, conceived by the Holy Spirit, born of the Virgin Mary,
All	We adore you.
Leader	Crucified Christ, bearing contempt, forgiving your enemies, remaining always true,
All	We adore you.
Leader	Crucified Christ, Treasure-house of wisdom, champion of justice, fount of love,
All	We adore you.
Leader	Crucified Christ, faithful to the end, gatekeeper of paradise, eternal Friend,
All	We adore you.

God's Word

Reader	Isaiah 53:10-12

There may be silence or singing
The following words spoken by Jesus are read

First	All you who pass along the road, Look and see if any grief can be compared to mine.
Second	My God, my God, why have you abandoned me?
Third	It is finished.

Fourth   Father, into your hands I commit my spirit.

All   Jesus, remember me when you come into your kingdom.

Leader   The earth quaked, the curtain dividing the temple was torn in two.

All   Jesus, remember me when you come into your kingdom.

Leader   The rocks split, the graves opened, the bodies of many saints rose again.

All   Jesus, remember me when you come into your kingdom.

Reader   Hebrews 4:14-16; 5:7-9 *or* John 18:12-19:37

The Great Intercession

The form of this varies according to local custom. Themes should include the Christian Church throughout the world, the unity of Christians; Jews, Moslems and those of other faiths; those unable to believe; those who exercise power in the world.

Good Friday Night Prayer

Leader In the name of the Father I come to rest,
lying on my bed in your name, O noble King.
I place the tree upon which Christ was crucified
between me and the heavy-lying nightmare,
between me and each evil thing.

From County Cork, collected by Douglas Hyde

Reader O King of the Friday,
whose limbs were stretched on the cross;
O Lord who did suffer
the bruises, the wounds, the loss;
we stretch ourselves beneath the shield
of your might;
some fruit from the tree of your passion
fall on us this night!

Irish

First I lie in my bed as I would lie in the grave,
your arm beneath my neck,
O suffering Son of Mary.

Second Angels shall watch me as I lie in slumber.
Angels shall guard me in the sleep of the grave.

Third The Great Physician shall tend my frame.
The guardian angel shall shield my soul.
The Three shall keep me for ever.

Silent vigil or free prayer around lighted candles

Leader Now we go to our sleep;
may we awake in health.
All But if it should be the sleep of death,
may we awake on your right arm.

Leader   May our soul be in your hands,
O King of the heaven of heavens.

All   You bought us with your own life
that no harm should ever destroy us.

Leader   While the body dwells in sleep,
may the soul soar in the wings of heaven.

All   Early and late, day and night,
may our soul be meeting with you.

Leader   Power of powers, by whose sure guiding
we have emerged from the deep,
now, underneath your brooding wings of love,
grant us the boon of sleep.

Creative Activities
for Good Friday

1. A bare wooden cross may be laid in a central position, or placed in earth, like a bare tree.

2. Passion plays and walks of witness may be performed in public places.

3. Children may make Easter gardens on trays, using earth, moss, stones, twigs and flowers to create three crosses on a hill and a burial place beyond.

Easter Eve –
Saturday in Holy Week

In the Celtic Christian tradition it is important to stay with the body of a deceased person, to be with them as they pass over from one mode of existence to another; to focus intently on memories and to offer symbols of devotion such as anointing oils. This applies supremely to the remembrance of Christ's death. Therefore normal activities should be reduced as much as possible on this day following his death, in order to do these things.

As well as being the day Christ died, it is the day he visited the world of the dead in order to release spirits still in chains.

The visual focus might be two branches of a tree stripped of its leaves, shaped as a cross, or an icon of Christ descending into the world of the dead. Tokens of devotion might include flowers, incense or candles.

In the evening it is common to gather for a vigil in darkness or dimmed light. During this there may be biblical readings of dark moments in human history that were followed by the promise of God's covenant; these may be interspersed by silence, singing, prayers, poems and storytelling. The following biblical passages may be read or told as stories: Genesis 1:1-5, 26-end; Genesis 7:1-5, 10-18; Genesis 9:8-13; Genesis 22:1, 2, 9-13, 15-18; Exodus 14:15–15:1a; Ezekiel 37:1-14.

Baptismal vows may be renewed as part of a vigil or church service.

Following the Jewish idea of each day beginning at sunset, some traditions celebrate the passing over of Christ from the darkness of death to the light of resurrection as the climax of a vigil. People may gather around a fire outdoors. A large Easter candle, which represents the risen Christ, may be lit at the fire. The people sing chants or songs as they return to the place of worship. Each person may light a candle from the Easter candle.

A service of Holy Communion to celebrate the resurrection may follow at midnight or before and there may be singing, dancing or feasting. Alternatively, a rota of people may keep vigil through the night in the place of worship, and then gather at sunrise to welcome and celebrate Christ risen from death.

One of the following prayers of the heart may be repeated throughout the day.

> Lord Jesus Christ, truly God, truly human,
> have mercy on me, a sinner.

or

> Jesus we adore you, we stay with you,
> we offer you signs of our love.

Morning Prayer for Saturday in Holy Week

Leader Father, you grieve for your Son.
All Creation, you weep for your Maker.
Leader We will not desert him.
All We will bring our tears and tokens of our love.

There may be chanting or singing

Reader Psalm 53 *or* Psalm 60:1-5

Leader Today a grave holds him
who holds creation in his hand.
A gravestone covers him
who covers the heavens with glory.
Life sleeps.
Hell trembles.
The human race waits with bated breath.

All We have been buried with Christ
through baptism.
In faith we will journey with him
into dark and unknown places.

Leader He who holds all things together
was lifted up on the cross
and all creation lamented.
The sun hid its rays.
The stars withheld their light.
The earth shook in fear.
The seas fled and the rocks were split.
Tombs were opened.
The bodies of holy people were raised.
The netherworld groaned.

321

The authorities spread a false report
about Christ's resurrection.
All creation waits with bated breath.

All   We have been buried with Christ
through baptism.
In faith we will journey with him
into dark and unknown places.

God's Word

Reader   Job 14:1-14

I weep when I think upon death,
and behold our beauty,
fashioned after the image of God,
lying in the tomb –
disfigured,
dishonoured,
bereft of form.

Eternal remembrance. Eternal remembrance.
Saints.
Angels.
Eternal remembrance.
We who remain on earth. Eternal remembrance.

All   Amen.

Reader   Matthew 27:57-66

Leader   We bless Joseph who came to the Governor
by night
and asked for the Life of all
to be laid in his garden of graves.
We bless you for Mary who with sorrow wept
as she saw her son hanging on the tree,
her heart pierced with a sword,
as the prophet Simeon had foretold.

We bless you for the women
who went to the grave to watch, to weep
and to offer fragrant spices of devotion.

All We, too, will watch and weep and offer our
devotion.

*There may be silence or an act of devotion such as
the lighting of a candle, music, or the burning of
incense, followed by singing*

Reader What is this mystery that befalls us?
Why have we been given over to corruption?
Why have we been wedded to death?

In truth it is by the command of God.
O happy fault,
that through decay and death life may come,
more glorious than mere mortals can conceive.

Leader Lord, you go forth on your journey.
The mortal shall be clothed with the immortal.
The perishable shall be clothed
with the imperishable.
We shall be changed.
All flesh shall see it.
The spirits of the dead shall be raised.
Lord, go forth on your journey.

Intercession

Let us pray for this world,
which bears the marks of death and decay
and lies open before its Creator.

*There may be silent, free or prepared intercessions
followed by singing*

Leader Let us hope in God who will come to our aid.
Father who sought you,
Christ who bought you,
Spirit who taught you,
hold you in Trinity's clasp.

Midday Prayer for Saturday in Holy Week

Reader   Psalm 141

Lament

Leader   Let us recall what was said
about the One whom we mourn.

First   No one ever loved as he loved.

Second   Someone might lay down their life
for a person who did them good,
but he laid down his life
for those who did him only harm.

First   No one spoke as he spoke.
He spoke with authority.

Second   He knew what was within people.

First   We observed him, he was full of grace and truth.

Second   We were drawn to him because he alone
had the words of eternal life.

First   He was the voice of the poor,
of the dispossessed;
a voice saying, 'Come to me,
all you who are loaded with heavy burdens.'

Second   He cried over our city,
'How often I would have gathered you to me
as a hen gathers her chicks,
but you would not heed me.
Now it is too late.'

Leader   We mourn a life of such goodness,
cut down in its flower.
We mourn for a people who forfeited
the flowering of their destiny.

Leader	We mourn for a planet which rejected its Maker. We mourn for ourselves, who languish, alone and lost.
All	Lord, we offer you our tears, our memories, our tenderness, our faith.

There may be silence, candle-lighting or singing

Leader	Lord, for arrogance that pretends we are self-sufficient,
All	Forgive.
Leader	For pride and contempt towards others,
All	Forgive.
Leader	For resentment, and failure to mercy,
All	Forgive.
Leader	For building up walls of hostility,
All	Forgive.
Leader	For worship of money,
All	Forgive.
Reader	Blessed are they who mourn, for they shall be comforted. Blessed are the meek, for they shall inherit the earth.
Leader	O Christ, who declared the thief on the cross who cried to you, 'Remember me,' to be a citizen of paradise, make me, a sinner, worthy of the same. You who rule our souls and bodies, in whose hand is our breath,
All	Save us and help us we humbly beseech you, O Lord.

Leader   We pray for those who perish
and those who are lost,
in this world and the next.

All   Save them and help them
we humbly beseech you, O Lord.

Leader   O Christ, like the seed that falls into the ground
and yet bears fruit,
may we yet see the fruit of eternal life on earth.
O Christ, you are the new representative
of the human race.
Free the people in captivity,
in this world and the next.

O Christ, Son of the living God,
you alone have the words of eternal life.
Through baptism we have been buried with you
in death.
Raise us up to walk the earth in newness of life.

All   O Christ, you go through the grave
and the gates of death.
Open to us the gate of glory.

Evening and Night Prayer for Easter Eve

The following material may be used as part of a vigil or as separate acts of prayer. Many branches of the Church provide a full Easter Vigil order.

Reader Psalm 90

Leader Come, all peoples and worship Christ,
for he is our God who comes to free the world from deceit.
Today hell groans and cries out:
'My power has been destroyed.
I received a mortal as one of the dead,
but I am unable to keep him prisoner,
and with him I shall lose all my captives.
I held in my power the dead of all the ages,
but look, he is raising them all.'

All Glory to you, Lord,
who by your cross shall save us all.

Reader My heart faints within me,
yet I know that my Redeemer is alive
and that he will arise on earth at last.
When I awake he will set me beside him,
and in my flesh I shall see God.
I shall see no stranger, but I shall see him as he is.

Echoes Job 19:24-27

There may be singing

Leader O Christ,
you remembered those who forgot your words
about the sign of Jonah,
who after three days was delivered from the fish.

	Remember, too, those in our world who have lost hope.
All	Come to us, save and deliver us, O Lord.
Leader	O Christ, you remembered those who went to their tombs without knowing you.
All	Come to them, save and deliver them, O Lord.
Reader	1 Peter 3:18-22
Reader	(*or all sing, to the tune Gonfalon Royal*)

Now while the body, quiet and still,
lies wrapped in bands of linen fair,
the glow of life and warmth and power
flickers in hell's cold darkling air.

And while the myrrh and aloes' balm
perfume his feet and hands and head,
Christ's spreading light pierces the gloom
and lights the kingdom of the dead.

The doors of bronze burst at his cry
and all the sons of Adam wake;
he harrows hell and breaks death's bonds,
and all the powers of darkness shake.

Adam and Eve, that primal pair,
are led on high to liberty;
while patriarch and prophet stand
and sing the song of jubilee.

The dying thief beholds his Lord
fulfil the promise of the King;
while saints of that first covenant
join with angelic choirs and sing.

The breaking of the Easter dawn
reveals the body of the Lord
endued with life and love and power;
incarnate is the eternal Word.

All glory, Christ, our risen King,
who with the Father reigns above
within the Holy Spirit's bond –
eternal Life and Light and Love.

Christ harrows hell,
by Brother Ramon, SSF

Leader	Into our place of darkness,
	into our place of strife,
	into our fears and worries,
All	Come with eternal life.
Leader	Into those who are dying,
	into those weary of life,
	into those tired from exertions,
All	Come with eternal life.
Reader	I am the seed waiting to shoot up.
	I am the bud waiting to bloom.
	I am the life-force gathering power.
	I am the dawn-light breaking soon.
Leader	This is the night when you saved our forebears
	in the faith:
	you freed the people of Israel from their slavery
	and led them dry-shod through the sea.
	This is the night when the pillar of fire
	destroyed the darkness of sin.
	This is the night when Christ, the true Lamb,
	whose blood consecrates the homes
	of all believers, is slain.

Leader This is the night when Jesus Christ
broke the chains of sin and death
and rose triumphant from the grave.
What good would life have been to us
if Christ had not come as our Redeemer?
This is the night when Christians everywhere,
washed clean of sin and freed from all
that degrades them, are restored to grace
and grow together in holiness.

Lord Jesus Christ,
who at this hour lay in the tomb
and so hallowed the grave to be a bed of hope,
may we lie down in hope and rise up with you.

All May we lie down in hope and rise up with you.

Intercession

Reader God of all spirits,
who has trampled down death,
overthrown the Devil
and given life to your departed servants . . .

Names might be mentioned

. . . pardon every transgression
and bring them to a place of life, fulfilment
and rest.

You who love all people,
you who are the Resurrection and the Life,
establish yourself in the heart of that greater
family where all are royal souls.

The Light of Christ at Midnight

*If the resurrection is celebrated at or before midnight
a large Easter candle is lit*

Leader Christ is risen!
All   He is risen indeed! Alleluia!
Leader Christ is the light of the world,
All   Whose light will shine for ever. Alleluia!

*There may be dancing or songs such as the
following*

Christ as a light, illumine and guide me.
Christ as a shield, overshadow me.
Christ under me,
Christ over me,
Christ beside me on my left and my right.
This day be within and without me,
lonely and meek yet all-powerful.
Be in the mouth of each to whom I speak,
in the mouth of each who speaks to me.
Christ as a light, illumine and guide me.

*John Michael Talbot,
after St Patrick's Breastplate*

*Each may have a candle lit from the Easter
candle*

Leader Rejoice, O earth, in shining splendour,
radiant in the brightness of your King.
Christ has conquered!
Glory fills you!
Darkness vanishes for ever!
All   May the light of Christ, rising in glory,
banish all darkness from our lives.

Creative Activities for Holy Week

1. On the first (Palm) Sunday give everyone a cross made of palm leaves.

2. On this Sunday hold an open-air procession with a donkey.

3. Create and display a large diary of the last week in Christ's life.

4. Create a display of tools such as may have been used in Jesus' carpenter's shop, including nails, and hammer; write the 'Jesus, Master Carpenter of Nazareth' prayer (see Friday Midday Prayer) on a card.

5. On Thursday remove familiar objects from your place of worship (or strip the altar) and meditate on what it means to be stripped of everything, as was Jesus.

6. On Thursday place a container of water and a towel on a rug. Each person kneels in turn and touches the towel, or passes the bowl along so that each washes the feet of the person next to them.

7. On Thursday hold a Jewish Passover Meal.

8. On Friday gather with fellow Christians from other churches for a prayer and witness walk through the locality.

9. On Friday make a bare cross of rough wood and place it as the focus of the worship area.

10. On Friday each person places a pin in the upright wooden cross, to represent the nails that pierced Christ then or pierce him now.

11. On Friday evening drape a white winding sheet over the empty cross to symbolise the covering over the deceased Christ.

12. Make small Easter gardens on trays, which depict the hill of crucifixion with three crosses on it, and a garden cave for burial.

13. On Saturday follow up any vigil by inviting young people of all ages to bring sleeping bags and stay in the church or worship building all night, taking turns to watch and pray.

14. Decorate bare wooden crosses with flowers.

Easter

At the heart of Christianity is the belief that God raised from the dead the one whom the apostles had seen die on a cross. Referring to the Jewish custom of sacrificing a lamb to God, St Paul wrote, 'Our Paschal lamb has been sacrificed, therefore let us keep the feast.' From the beginning, the Christian Passover was at the heart of the Church of the new covenant as the Jewish Passover was at the heart of the 'church' of the old. The resurrection was preceded by the forty days of vigil. Those preparing for baptisms were clothed in white on Easter Day and immersed in the baptismal water, thus representing the burial of Christ (under the water) and the resurrection (coming up out of the water.) That is why it is traditional to renew baptismal promises at Easter.

No form of Easter Day liturgy is given here since several exist in official forms elsewhere, and the Morning, Midday, Evening and Night Prayers for Sunday are on the Easter theme.

In Celtic lands the fact that Easter coincides with Spring has led to much use of the imagery of new life in nature to illustrate the new life that Christ brings. On Easter Sunday, therefore, the decorating of crosses, homes and churches with flowers, candles, and signs of new life is to be encouraged.

The celebration of the resurrection, following the Saturday Easter vigil in the early hours of Sunday morning, is followed by an Easter Day Eucharist in which, sacramentally, we are reunited with our risen Lord.

Easter

Easter lasts for forty days from Easter Sunday until Ascension Day, which is always a Thursday. The worship patterns for Sundays may be used, preceded by one of the Easter candle-lightings below. The following prayer may be included.

Leader	Risen Christ,
	you burst from the grave.
All	Help us to burst into life.

Leader	You breathed on your disciples.
All	Breathe life into us.

Leader	In our baptism, O Lord Christ,
	our self-centred life is buried,
All	And we rise up with your new life in us.

Leader	Day by day, may we be buried.
All	Day by day, may we rise anew.

The First Easter Candle-lighting

The Easter candle is lit

Reader	The Lord is risen.
All	He is risen indeed. Alleluia!
Reader	Jesus Christ is the Light of the world.
All	A light no darkness can quench.
Reader	Jesus, rising in glory, scatter the darkness from our paths.
All	Alleluia!

Reader	Risen Lord, you revealed yourself to Mary in the garden at dawn.
	Reveal yourself to us in the dawnings of our lives.
All	Jesus, we worship you with joy.

Reader	Risen Lord, you revealed yourself to the fisherfolk as they toiled in vain at their work. Reveal yourself to us in the long hours of our toil.
All	Jesus, we worship you with joy.
Reader	Risen Lord, you revealed yourself to the walkers as they welcomed you into their home. Reveal yourself to us as we walk and make welcoming our homes.
All	Jesus, we worship you with joy.
Reader	Risen Lord, you revealed yourself to Thomas when he felt the scars in your body. Reveal yourself to us as we reach out to the scars of the world.
All	Jesus, we worship you with joy.
Reader	Jesus, you revealed yourself to many as they met beneath the skies. Reveal yourself to us in the spacious freedom of creation.
All	Jesus, we worship you with joy.

The Second Easter Candle-lighting

The Easter candle is lit

Leader	Christ is the first-fruit of a new creation.
All	Christ our King has risen. Alleluia!
Leader	Rejoice, heavenly powers! Sing, choirs of angels!
All	Christ our King has risen.
Leader	Exult, all creation around God's throne. Sound the trumpet of salvation!
All	Christ our King has risen.
Leader	Rejoice, O earth, in shining splendour, radiant in the brightness of your King!
All	Christ our King has risen.

Leader	Christ has conquered death! Glory fills you! Darkness vanishes for ever!
All	Christ our King has risen.
Leader	Rejoice, O Church! Exult in glory! The risen Saviour shines upon you!
All	Christ our King has risen.
Leader	Let this place resound with joy, echoing the mighty song of all God's people!
All	Christ our King has risen. Alleluia!
Leader	The Lord has passed over from death to life, from the perishable to the imperishable.
All	Christ our King has risen. Alleluia!
Leader	We too will pass over with him. Our perishable bodies shall be clothed with immortality.
All	Christ our King has risen. Alleluia!

The Third Easter Candle-lighting

The Easter candle is lit

Leader	Risen Christ, you turned Mary's tears into joy.
All	Turn our tears into joy.
Leader	Risen Christ, you turned the travellers' despair into hope.
All	Turn our despair into hope.
Leader	Risen Christ, you turned the disciples' fears into boldness.
All	Turn our fears into boldness.
Leader	Risen Christ, you turned an empty catch into fullness.
All	Turn our empty routines into fullness.
Leader	Risen Christ, you turned Thomas' unbelief into trust.
All	Turn our unbelief into trust.

Leader   Jesus Christ is the Light of the world:
All   A light that no darkness can quench.

Leader   The long reign of sin has ended,
             a new age has dawned,
             a broken world is being renewed,
             and we are once again made whole.
All   Alleluia!

Fourth Easter Candle-lighting

The Easter candle is lit

Reader   Jesus Christ is the light of the world. Alleluia!
All   A light no darkness can quench. Alleluia!

Reader   Risen Christ, you have entered into darkness,
             despair and death.
             Rising in glory, you accompany all
             who have to face these in turn.
             You fell to the ground and in weakness cried out
             to God.
             You come to us in our weakness and give us joy.
             You give the cup of life.
             You quench our every thirst.
             You showed yourself to the disciples.
             You turned hearts of stone into flesh.
             Now we see you, radiant Sun of suns.
             You clothe the peacemakers in raiment of light.
             You transform us into your likeness.
             First-born of the living,
             you will lead the festal procession of all who die
             in you.
All   Alleluia! Christ is risen indeed!

Creative Activities for Easter

1. On Easter Sunday, ashes from the Easter Eve bonfire may be placed in a container. Using the forefinger, the sign of the cross may be made with the ashes on the foreheads of all who wish it.

2. Decorate the wooden cross used on Good Friday with flowers.

3. Make Easter gardens.

4. At sunrise on Easter day go to a high place in silence to see the sun rise. Cast symbolic burdens over the edge (checking it is safe to do so first), using stones or biodegradable items.

5. Make Easter eggs.

Ascension

This begins on the Thursday ten days before Pentecost Sunday. It marks the last of the forty days that the physically resurrected Christ spent on earth, his farewell and his final commission.

As Christians have reflected upon this event, they have realised its significance for the human race. Christ, as the representative of the people of earth, has taken humanity back into God.

Jesus called his followers to spend the days following his physical disappearance waiting on God, in order to receive the Holy Spirit, or Power, which God would send them.

Morning Prayer for Ascension

Leader Christ is risen!
All He is risen indeed. Alleluia!
Leader Christ has ascended!
All Our High King – he shall reign for ever.
Leader In love of the King of Life, let us celebrate.
All Alleluia!

Proclamation

There may be singing

Reader Psalm 92; 104; 110; 117; 139; 147:1-12; 148; 149; *or* 150

The following Proclamation, or The song of Christ's glory (see Evening Prayer) may be said

Leader Trumpets of the earth proclaim:
Christ, who once in earth had lain,
goes in triumph now to reign.
All Alleluia!

Leader He sits with God upon his throne;
the Father's glory is his own;
he the eternal, radiant Son.
All Alleluia!

Leader All human life with him is raised.
The weakest ones by heaven are praised.
Now high and low on him have gazed.
All Alleluia!

On occasions when a confession is appropriate the following may be used

First	O Saviour of the human race,
	O true physician of every disease,
	O heart-pitier and assister in times of misery,
	O fount of true purity and true knowledge,
All	Forgive.

Second	O star-like sun,
	O guiding light,
	O home of the planets,
	O fiery-maned and marvellous one,
All	Forgive.

Third	O holy scholar of holy strength,
	O overflowing, loving, silent one,
	O generous and thunderous giver of gifts,
	O rock-like warrior of a hundred hosts,
All	Forgive.

Attributed to St Ciaran, adapted

God's Word

Reader	2 Kings 2:1-15 *or the Old Testament reading of the day*
Leader	High King,
All	You are crowned with glory.
Leader	Victor in the race,
All	You call us to follow you.
Leader	High Priest,
All	You understand our every need.
Leader	Eternal Giver,
All	You shower your gifts on every soul.
Leader	Head of the Church,
All	You wish no one to be separate from your Body.
Leader	Sender,
All	You promise us your Holy Spirit.

Reader   Luke 24:50-53; Acts 1:1-11; Matthew 28:16-20;
         or 1 Peter 2:4-10

         There may be a creed, silent meditation, teaching,
         creative activity or singing

Intercession

Leader   High King of the universe,
         a cloud hid you from sight,
         yet, in you, mortal humanity has been raised
         to life in God.
         We pray for those whose life is clouded:
All   Raise them to life in you;
Leader   For those clouded by fear:
All   Raise them to life in you;
Leader   For those clouded by anxiety:
All   Raise them to life in you;
Leader   For those clouded by hostility:
All   Raise them to life in you

         The leader may invite any to add requests, using
         the same format of words

Any   For those clouded by . . .
All   Raise them to life in you.

First   May tiny infants in the womb be raised to life
         in you.
Second   May the handicapped and ailing be raised to life
         in you.
Third   May bronzed and brave adventurers be raised
         to life in you.
Fourth   May thinkers and researchers be raised to life
         in you.
Fifth   May the battle-scarred and weary be raised
         to life in you.

Leader Ascended Lord,
you call those who follow you to a time
of waiting
that they may be able to receive
the empowering Spirit
and the gifts you delight to shower
on your Church.
Take from us obstinate refusals.
Give us receptive hearts.
Make us fertile ground.

There may be silence, free prayer or singing

Leader May the King of glory fill you with joy,
make you expectant,
keep you in unity,
and bring you the Strength from on high.
All Alleluia!

Midday Prayer for Ascension

Leader   Jesus, you embraced our humanity and took it
into the heart of God.

All   Alleluia!

Leader   You clothe human life in great dignity.

All   Alleluia!

Leader   Now we will revere you in all we do.
Help us to reverence you in all we do,
to discern you in every place
and to love you in each person we meet.

All   Alleluia!

Reader   He who descended into the world below
also ascended far above the heavens
in order that he might fill all things
and give gifts to his people . . .
that we might come to maturity,
to our full stature in Christ.

Ephesians 4:10-11

First   You came down

All   To lift us up.

Second   You descended to earth

All   That earth might ascend to heaven.

Third   You descended to the dead

All   That the dead might rise to life.

First   In the heat of the day,

All   Lift us up.

Second   In our fretting cares,

All   Lift us up.

Third   In our difficulties,

All   Lift us up.

First   In our tiredness,

All   Lift us up.

Second	In disappointment,
All	Lift us up.
Any	In . . .
All	Lift us up.

Reader	Lift us Lord, out of darkness into light, out of despair into hope.
	Lift us, Lord, out of sadness into joy, out of failure into trust.
	Lift us, Lord, out of anger into forgiveness, out of pride into freedom.
	Psalm 121

There may be silence or singing

Leader	O my Lord, you are very great. You are clothed with honour and majesty. You are wrapped in light as with a garment. You can do immeasurably more than we can ask or imagine by the power which is at work within us. We give glory to you through the ages of ages.
All	Amen.

Reader	Bless the Lord, O my soul. Praise the Lord!

Psalm 104:1, 2, 35.

Leader	Your kingdom come, your will be done, on earth as it is in heaven.

There may be free prayer as follows

Any Your kingdom come in . . . *(enter place names as appropriate)*

There may be singing

All Yours, Lord, is the greatness,
the power,
the glory,
the splendour and the majesty.
Everything in heaven and earth is yours.
All things come from you,
and of your own do we give you.

Leader May the Eternal Glory shine upon us.
May the Son of Mary stay beside us.
May the life-giving Spirit work within us.

All Amen.

Evening Prayer for Ascension

Leader Christ departs,

All But Love's fragrance ever lingers.

Leader Death is conquered,

All Fear has lost its power.

Leader A human heart now lives in God,

All The fullness we long for we shall now receive.

There may be singing

Reader Psalm 24; 93; 97; *or* 98

Leader Ascended Lord, you have made us living stones
of the temple you are to build.

All We offer all that we are and all that we have to you.

Leader King of Glory,

All Ennoble us.

Leader King of Grace,

All Cherish us.

Leader King of Life,

All Renew us.

Leader King of Promise,

All Surprise us.

God's Word

Reader Isaiah 52:7-12 *or the Old Testament reading
of the day*

The Song of Christ's glory

Leader Christ Jesus, though you were in the form of God
you did not cling to equality with God.

All You emptied yourself,
taking the form of a servant;
you were born in human likeness.

Leader	Being found in human form
	you humbled yourself and became obedient,
	even to death on a cross.
All	Therefore God has highly exalted you
	and given you a name above every other name:
Leader	That at the name of Jesus every knee should bow,
	in heaven and on earth and under the earth,
All	And every tongue confess
	that Jesus Christ is Lord,
	to the glory of God the Father.
	For ever and ever.
	Amen.

Philippians 2:6-11

*The following or another New Testament passage
may be read*

Reader	The eleven disciples went to Galilee,
	to the mountain to which Jesus
	had directed them.
	When they saw him they worshipped him;
	though some doubted.
	Jesus came to them and said:
	'All authority in heaven and earth
	has been given to me.
	Go therefore to all peoples,
	immersing them in the presence of the Father
	and of the Son
	and of the Holy Spirit,
	and teaching them to carry out everything
	that I have commanded you.
	And remember, I am with you always,
	to the end of the age.'

Matthew 28:16-20

There may be teaching, creative activity or singing

Intercession

Leader	We pray for the peoples of our world:
All	Immerse them in your life.
Leader	We pray for parched and hungry people:
All	Immerse them in your life.
Leader	We pray for torn and exiled people:
All	Immerse them in your life.
Leader	We pray for lonely and unloved people:
All	Immerse them in your life.
Leader	We pray for unjust and oppressive people:
All	Immerse them in your life.
Any	We pray for . . .
All	Immerse them in your life.

Leader   Ascended Lord,
you call those who follow you to a time of waiting,
that they may be able to receive the gifts
you delight to shower on your Church,
and to receive the empowering Spirit.
Take from us obstinate ways.
Give us receptive hearts.
Make us fertile ground.

All   Promised Spirit,
come as the dew in the night,
come as the rain on dry land,
come as the fire in hours of cold,
come as the light in the dark.
Holy Spirit,
come, renew our tired frames,
turn our deserts into pools of water,
renew in us your image of love.

There may be silence, singing or free prayer

All   The grace of our Lord Jesus Christ,
the love of God
and the fellowship of the Holy Spirit
be with us all, evermore.
Amen.

Night Prayer for Ascension

Leader   Christ departs, but Love's fragrance ever lingers.
All   Alleluia!
Leader   He was constrained but is now set free.
All   Alleluia!
    Death is conquered; fear has lost its power.
All   Alleluia!
Leader   A human heart now lives in God.
All   Alleluia!
Leader   The fullness we long for we shall now receive.
All   Alleluia!

Reader   Psalm 113

There may be singing or creative activity

Leader   The One who once was crowned with thorns
    is crowned with glory now.
    The One who descended to earth
    and the underworld now lifts us up,
    drawing all to himself.
All   Lord, lift us up.
Leader   We pray for the down-trodden and destitute:
All   Lord, lift them up.
Leader   We pray for the deserted and despairing:
All   Lord, lift them up.
Leader   We pray for our loved ones:
All   Lord, lift them up.
Leader   Let us pray, aloud or silently,
    for people on our hearts.

Names may be mentioned

Leader   Let us say together *The Song of Christ's Glory*

All   Christ Jesus was in the form of God,
    but did not grasp at equality with God.

He emptied himself, taking the form of a servant,
and became as human beings are.
Being in every way like a human being,
he was humbler yet,
even accepting death on a cross.
Therefore God has raised him high
and bestowed on him a name above every name:
that at the name of Jesus
all beings in heaven, on earth
and in the underworld
should bend the knee,
and every tongue acknowledge
that Jesus Christ is Lord,
to the glory of God the Father.

*A reader may instead, or also, read one of the
following passages:* John 16:28; Ephesians 4:7-13;
Hebrews 10:12-14; *or* 1 Peter 3:18-22

Leader   Prepare us to receive the Spirit of Christ,
All   The Spirit of strength and wisdom and joy.

There may be silence, spontaneous words or singing

Reader   Ancient legend says that before Christ left
              the earth he told his disciples:
              I have no hands but yours,
              I have no eyes but yours,
              I have no lips but yours,
              I have no feet but yours.

Leader   As we go to rest we offer ourselves to you, Lord.
All   May our hands be your hands.
              May our eyes be your eyes.
              May our lips be your lips.
              May our feet be your feet.

Leader   Great God, as the haze rises from mountaintops,
           raise our souls from the granite of death,
All   Before we go to sleep.

Leader   As we lay down our clothes,
           may we lay down our struggles,
All   Before we go to our sleep.

Leader   Lift from us our anguish,
           lift from us our malice,
           lift from us our empty pride,
All   Before we go to our sleep.

Leader   Great God, give us light,
           Great God, give us grace,
           Great God, give us joy,
All   Before we go to our sleep.

Leader   May the crowned King hold a crown over us,
           may the Eternal Glory shine glory upon us,
           may the Lord give us his peace,
All   As we sleep. Amen.

Creative Activities for Ascension

1. Early in the morning go to the highest point in your locality. Sing, pray and play musical instruments.

2. Go to a public place and let off balloons filled with helium, on which you have painted words of Jesus.

3. Those present raise their right arm to imitate Christ's final blessing and commissioning of his disciples.

4. Face the four corners of the earth in turn and repeat the words of Jesus in Matthew 28:18-20.

Pentecost

The forty days between Easter and Ascension are in contrast to the forty days of Lent. Pentecost is the climax of all, the festival of the Holy Spirit sent by the Father through Jesus into the Church. Pentecost also celebrates the fulfilment of Jewish prophecy, including Jesus' promise to his followers 'that the Power from on high will come upon you' (Acts 1:8).

In Celtic Christian tradition Pentecost is followed by a 'little Lent'. This was a forty-day period, with light fasting, to focus on living in the power of the Spirit.

Morning Prayer for Pentecost

Leader   Creator Spirit, come,
fresh as the morning dew.
Inflaming Spirit, come,
kindle our hearts anew.

There may be singing

God's Word

Reader   Psalm 36:5-9 *or* Psalm 139:7-12, 23-24

A Song of Ezekiel

I will gather you from the nations.
I will sprinkle pure water upon you
and cleanse you from all that defiles.

All   I will put a new spirit within you
and you shall be my people.

Reader   A new heart I will give you.
I will remove your heart of stone
and give you a heart of flesh.

All   I will put a new spirit within you
and you shall be my people.

Reader   You shall be my people and I shall be your God.

All   Glory to God, Creator, Redeemer
and ever-flowing Spirit.

Reader   Ezekiel 37:1-14; Jeremiah 31:31-34; Joel 2:28-29;
or the Old Testament reading of the day

Leader   Spirit of the quiet earth,
Spirit breathing hope to birth,
sustain in us the fire of love.

All   Spirit of God, rest on your people:
waken your song deep in the hearts of all.

Leader	Spirit blowing through creation,
	love that cannot be contained,
	bring forth for us the wonders you proclaim.
All	Spirit of God, rest on your people:
	waken your song deep in our hearts.
Leader	Spirit moving through our lives,
	working in our memories,
	heal, restore, and bring us into life.
All	Spirit of God, rest on your people:
	waken your song deep in our hearts.
Leader	Spirit breaking through our egos,
	Spirit tearing down our walls,
	be the voice that challenges and calls.
All	Spirit of God, rest on your people:
	waken your song deep in our hearts.
Reader	Acts 2:1-11; John 16:4b-15; Acts 4:23-31;
	or the New Testament reading of the day

Communing

Leader	When Pentecost came the disciples were together . . .
	and there came what looked like tongues of flame.
	These separated and rested on the head of each one individually.

Acts 2:1a, 3

Leader	Flame of love, reach into our inmost heart.
All	Come, flame of love.
Leader	Flame of truth, reach into our inmost mind.
All	Come, flame of truth.
Leader	Flame of seeing, reach into our inmost vision.
All	Come, flame of seeing.

359

*Creative activity, storytelling, teaching, sharing
or singing*

Leader   Come from the four winds, mighty Spirit of God,
and revive your weary people.
In our labour,
All   Be our Refreshment.
Leader   In our adversity,
All   Be our Strength.
Leader   In our distress,
All   Be our Comfort.

Leader   Strength-giver, may your fibre grow in us.
Fortifier, may your praises swell in us.
Indweller, may your presence dwell in us.

God of the call, God of the journey,
you have anointed your servants
from the Day of Pentecost until now.
Anoint us as you will for the ministries you will.

Here we wait, alert and open,
praying that you will come to us . . .

*There may be silence, music, open ministry, laying
on of hands, singing in the Spirit or another
creative activity*

The following or another song may be sung

Come, Holy Spirit, our souls inspire
and lighten with eternal fire.
Implant in us your grace from above.
Enter our minds and hearts with love.

O come, anointing Spirit of peace,
well-spring of life and gentleness.
Past ages called you the Paraclete.
Your gifts you bring to make us complete.

You are the Power of God's right hand,
Promise of God to a waiting land.
Life-giving words of human tongue
illumine now our hearts again.

Into our souls come pour your love.
Refresh our weak frames with life from above.
Give grace and courage to endure.
Cast far away the evil power.

Grant us your peace throughout our days;
with you as Guide in all our ways
no power on earth can cause us harm,
and we shall know as we are known.

Lead us to perfect communion
with Father, Son and Spirit, One:
the Three in One and One in Three,
now and for ever, eternally.

Adapted from Veni, Creator Spiritus,
ascribed to Rabanus Maurus,
a ninth-century Solitary in Gaul

Intercession

Leader   O Spirit be free in me.
Let me not bind you through fear
of where your disturbing power will lead.
Burst through this brittle shell,
shake me to the foundations,
strip me to the core,
which is my essence and your love.

There may be silence or chanting
Each of the following intercessions may be extended

Leader   Spirit of God,
among the wheels of industry,

All   Renew the face of the earth;

Leader	Among the computers of commerce,
All	Renew the face of the earth;
Leader	Among crime-infested neighbourhoods,
All	Renew the face of the earth;
Leader	Among tired and broken families,
All	Renew the face of the earth;
Leader	Among the lonely and the sick,
All	Renew the face of the earth;
Leader	Among the drugged and disillusioned,
All	Renew the face of the earth;
Any	Among . . .
All	Renew the face of the earth.

There may be singing

Leader	The blessing of the perfect Spirit be yours.
	The blessing of the triune God pour upon you,
	graciously and generously,
	hour by hour.

Pentecost Midday Prayer

Reader   In the beginning, O God,
your Spirit swept over the chaos of the cosmos
like a wild wind,
and creation was born.
In the deep and unsettled waters of our lives
and our lands today
let there be new birthings of your almighty Spirit.

Jesus said: If any one is thirsty,
let them come to me and drink.
From the heart of the person who believes in me
shall flow rivers of living water.
He said this about the Spirit, which those who
believed in him were to receive.

John 7:37b-39a

Leader   Spirit of the living God,
anoint my creativity, ideas and energy
so that even the smallest tasks
may bring you honour.
When I am confused,
All   Guide me.
Leader   When I am weary,
All   Energise me.
Leader   When I am burned out,
All   Infuse me.

Leader   Release in us the power of your Spirit
that our souls may be free to roam
your boundless stretches of space.
All   May we soar high like the eagle,
see horizons as yet undreamed of,
glow with fires of compassion,
flow with streams of creativity.

First	Breath of God, blow away all that is unclean.
All	Rain of God, revive our withered lives.
Second	Wind of God, blow us where you will.
All	Breeze of God, refresh our tired frames.
Reader	River of God, flow through us and heal our land.
All	River of God, flow through us and heal our land.

Silent or free prayer or singing

Reader	Psalm 46

Leader	Be with us Lord, now, in the middle of the day.
All	Filled with your Spirit, may we journey on with you.

Leader	Great Spirit, Wild Goose of the Almighty, be our eye in the dark places, be our flight in the trapped places, be our host in the wild places, be our brood in the barren places, be our formation in the lost places.

Evening Prayer for Pentecost

Leader	You led your people by a cloud;
All	Lead us by your Spirit now.
Leader	You lit your people by a fire;
All	Light us by your Spirit now.

There may be singing

Leader	Flame of love,
All	Light us up.
Leader	Flame of beauty,
All	Light us up.
Leader	Flame of wisdom,
All	Light us up.
Leader	Flame of peace,
All	Light us up.

Reader	Psalm 150; 104:25-35 *or another psalm*

Leader	Spirit of God,
All	The breath of creation is yours.
Leader	Spirit of God,
All	The groans of the world are yours.
Leader	Spirit of God,
All	The wonder of communion is yours.
Leader	And we are filled.
All	And we are filled.

God's Word

Reader	Exodus 31:1-11; 33:7-11; 1 Samuel 10:1-7; *or the Old Testament reading of the day*

Reader   O King of the Tree of life,
the blossoms on the branches are your people,
the singing birds are your angels,
the whispering breeze is your Spirit.

All   O King of the Tree of Life,
may the blossoms bring forth the sweetest fruit,
may the birds sing out the highest praise,
may your Spirit cover all with her gentle breath.

Reader   Romans 8:22-27; 1 Corinthians 12:4-11; *or
the New Testament reading of the day*

*This may be followed by a creed, teaching, sharing
or a creative activity*

There may be singing

Intercession

Reader   Holy Spirit, fulfil in us the work begun by Jesus.
Make fruitful the prayer we make on behalf
of the world.
Speed the hour when each of us will achieve
a deep interior life.
Invigorate our work,
subdue our natural presumption,
raise us to humility, wonder and generous courage.

May no vain attachment hinder our vocation.
May no selfish interest cause us to shrink
from the demands of justice.
May no personal scheming reduce our love
to petty dimensions.
May all be noble in us:
the search and the reverence for truth,
the willingness to sacrifice even to death.

Reader   May all be accomplished according to the spirit
of your Son's last prayer for his Church
and through the Spirit of love
which you send to her,
to each soul
and to every people.

Echoes a prayer of Pope John XXIII

God, whose breath gives energy for struggle,
set us free to grow as your children.
Open our ears that we may hear the weeping
of the world.
Open our mouths that we may be a voice
for the voiceless.
Open our eyes that we may discern
your just and gentle ways.
Open our hearts that we may bring courage
and faith to life.

There may be singing

Reader   Come Holy Spirit, from heaven shine forth
with your glorious light!
Most kindly, warming Light,
enter the inmost depths of our hearts.
Thaw that which is frozen, kindle our apathy,
illumine our path.

All   Come like fire, and kindle love in our hearts.
Come like the wind, and breathe fresh life
into our frames.
Come like the tides, and immerse us
in your presence.
Come from the earth; sustain and nourish
our being.

Night Prayer for Pentecost

Night-lights are lit

Leader   When Pentecost came the disciples
were together . . .
and there came what looked like tongues of flame.
These separated and rested on the head
of each one individually.

Acts 2:1a, 3

Leader   Flame of love, reach into our inmost heart.
All   Come, flame of love.
Leader   Flame of truth, reach into our inmost mind.
All   Come, flame of truth.
Leader   Flame of seeing, reach into our inmost vision.
All   Come, flame of seeing.

There may be singing

Reader   Psalm 139:1-12

Leader   Holy Spirit,
All   Come to us with wisdom.
Leader   Holy Spirit,
Come to us with cleansing.
Leader   Holy Spirit,
All   Come to us with peace.

There may be a pause

Leader   For your Spirit permeating every atom of creation,
All   We praise you with wonder in our being.
Leader   For your creativity planted deep in every soul,
All   We praise you with wonder in our being.

Leader	As the sun sets,
All	Renew the face of the earth.
Leader	Where there are tired and broken people,
All	Renew the face of the earth.
Leader	Where night life breeds disillusion,
All	Renew the face of the earth.
Leader	Where those we care for dwell,
All	Renew the face of the earth.

Names of loved ones may be mentioned

Leader	As we wait on you now,
All	Fill us anew.
Leader	May the Spirit of the Lord rest upon you; the spirit of wisdom and understanding.

Isaiah 11:2

In silence people kneel or sit with hands open to receive.

This may be followed by prepared, silent or informal intercessions, sharing, laying on of hands or singing in the Spirit

Leader	The Lord shall give us beauty instead of ashes
All	And take the frowning from our brows.
Leader	Sleep soundly, sleep in peace. May the Spirit pour upon you as you sleep, work in you as you dream, and refresh you for the morning.

Prayers and Preparations before or after Pentecost

Jesus asked his closest followers to stay together until the Spirit, promised by the Father, came above them (Acts 1:4-5). About 120 of them devoted themselves to prayer during the nine days between Jesus' Ascension and their experience of God's power on the Day of Pentecost (Acts 1:14-15).

In the Celtic tradition the forty days following Pentecost are observed as a Lent. The focus is less on strict abstinence and more on waiting on God and walking in the power of the Spirit.

A Nine-day Vigil

Those wishing to dedicate the nine days before Pentecost to prayerful preparation may use the following as a framework for prayer. It may also be used after Pentecost. These prayers are most effectively made while focusing on slow, rhythmical breathing.

Day 1

Leader   Come, O Spirit of Love
that goes to any lengths,
that breaks through a lifetime's crippling habits,
that wells up from the depths.

All   Come, O Spirit of Love.

Day 2

Leader   Come, O Spirit of Joy
that brings a song into haggard lives,

a serenity into our being
and a sparkle into our eyes.

All   Come, O Spirit of Joy.

Day 3

Leader   Come, O Spirit of Peace
that heals mistrust
and brings us into harmony with the still centre
of the universe.

All   Come, O Spirit of Peace.

Day 4

Leader   Come, O Spirit of Kindness
that delights to sweeten the lives of others
and to do beautiful things for God.

All   Come, O Spirit of Kindness.

Day 5

Leader   Come, O Spirit of Goodness
that opens the heart to Christ in friend
and stranger.

All   Come, O Spirit of Goodness.

Day 6

Leader   Come, O Spirit of Gentleness
that bears all things without harshness
or hardness.

All   Come, O Spirit of Gentleness.

Day 7

Leader   Come, O Spirit of Fire
that burns away lust and double-minded ways.

All   Come, O Spirit of Fire.

Day 8

Leader Come, O Spirit of Wisdom
that teaches us to see into the nature of things
in order to know, speak and do what is right.

All Come, O Spirit of Wisdom.

Day 9

Leader Come, O Spirit of Power
that snaps the chains of fear
and casts out the demons of hell and
hopelessness.

All Come, O Spirit of Power.

Prayers before meals for forty days after Pentecost

Holy Spirit of God,
you are the source of all that lives,
of all that grows,
of all that provides us with food.
May we know your presence with us
as we share this meal.

On your last days on earth you promised
to leave us the Holy Spirit.
As we eat,
may your Spirit come like blood into our veins
so that we will be driven entirely by your will.
Blow over the wealthy people
so that they will be humble.
Blow over the poor people
so that they will receive their true worth.

Echoes a prayer from Ghana

Creative Activities for Pentecost

1. Those who wish, stand or kneel while an agreed person lays hands on their head and prays the following or other words:

   Come, Holy Spirit, your soul inspire
   and lighten with eternal fire.
   Implant in you the grace from above.
   Enter your mind and heart with love.

2. Place a bowl of water on a table and, as the following words are spoken, invite people to splash the parts of the body indicated in italics below.

   We refresh ourselves in the waters of life:
   a drop of light on the *eyes*,
   a drop of grace on the *tongue*,
   a drop of life on the *head*,
   a drop of love on the *heart*.

3. A bowl of water is placed on a table and each person splashes some over their face and hands, praying words such as 'Spirit, wash me and make me new, flow out through me to others'.

4. A living flame burns throughout the time of worship in the form of a fire or burning lamp. Before the closing prayer, each person is given a candle which they light from this fire.

5. A crafted or cut-out Wild Goose (a Celtic symbol of the Holy Spirit) is displayed or placed on the meal table.

Trinity

In the Celtic tradition the Trinity is not simply allotted a season in the Church's year but is recognised as the very fabric of its life and worship at all times. It was only in the West, as late as the fourteenth century, that Trinity Sunday was introduced on the week following Pentecost.

Since in the Celtic tradition the forty days following Pentecost are a third Lent – an opportunity to seek God in solitude, but often, in the Western hemisphere, in the open air – we begin this section with a Vigil Prayer on the Trinity for use as a basis for reflection during the Third Lent.

The fourfold patterns of worship on the Trinity are included here for convenience; each may be used at any time.

Vigil on the Trinity for use in the Third Lent

O God, almighty Father of love,
Creator of the elements;
O God of flaming fire and rushing wind;
O God of waves from ocean's bed;
O God of solid earth
and spinning constellations;
O God eternal, without corruption;
O God who once ruled hell and all its rabble;
O God who governs the myriad beings of light;
O God to whom all must give account;
O God who is, and was, and shall be –
have mercy on us.

O God, almighty Saviour, Jesus Christ,
eternally born of God, Son of the Father,
beginning of all things,
likeness of the Father,
Arm of God,
Hand of God who reaches out to us,
Light of light,
Sun of suns;
Morning Star,
Bough of Creation,
Fount of everlasting life,
born of the Virgin Mary;
Son of David, Son of Abraham, Son of Humanity,
Mediator and Shepherd of the flock;
prophet, teacher, priest;
O Gate of Life;
O fiery-maned Lion;

O Gentle Lamb;
O Champion of tests;
O Crucified Friend –
have mercy on us.

O God, almighty Spirit,
supreme among all spirits,
Finger of God,
protector of believers,
comforter of the sorrowing;
O Spirit who shapes the flux of the cosmos
and brings order to chaos,
Breath of God,
Enabler of speech,
Bringer of Wisdom,
Inspirer of holy Scriptures;
O Spirit of counsel;
O Spirit of love;
O Spirit of joy;
O Spirit of peace;
O Spirit of prophecy;
O Spirit who brings truth to light;
O Spirit who burns up guilt;
O Spirit who washes us from sin;
O Spirit who inflames our hearts –
have mercy on us.
All glory to you, Father, Saviour and Spirit holy.

Echoes tenth-century Irish Litanies

Morning Prayer for Trinity

Leader   God who is One,
All   You create us in diversity.
Leader   God who is Three,
All   You draw us into unity.

Leader   We come to the Three who are love.
All   We come to the Three who are here.

There may be singing

Lament

Leader   We grieve that we who are made
to reflect your threefold love
have violated our nature and yours.
All   Holy God, holy and immortal,
have mercy upon us.
Leader   We have not reflected the mercy
of your Father's heart.
We have not reflected the mothering
of your Saviour's heart.
We have not reflected the outgoing
of your Spirit's heart.
All   Holy God, holy and immortal,
have mercy upon us.

Forgiveness of sins may be declared or there may be music or silence

Reader   Psalm 8 *or the psalm of the day*

I arise today in a mighty strength:
the God who is one;
the God who is Three,
All   Creating all through love.

Reader	I arise today in the might of the Father,
	in the strength of the Son,
	in the gentleness of the Spirit,
All	Affirming all through love.

God's Word

Reader	Exodus 3:1-6, 13-15 *or the Old Testament reading of the day*
	We bless you for the sun:
All	Its source of fire,
	its beams of light,
	its rays of warmth.
Reader	We bless you for water:
All	When it is ice,
	when it is steam,
	when it is flowing free.
Reader	We bless you for a human being:
	the thinking being,
	the doing being,
	the feeling being.
	We bless you for the Triune God:
All	The Triune who creates,
	the Triune who takes flesh,
	the Triune who empowers.
Reader	John 16:5-15 *or the New Testament reading of the day*
All	Glory to the Father,
	glory to the Son,
	glory to the Spirit,
	ever Three in One.

There may be teaching, sharing, silence or singing
Any of the following prayers may be used

Thanksgiving

Leader	Power of powers,
All	We worship you.
Leader	Light of lights,
All	We worship you.
Leader	Life of lives,
All	We worship you.
Leader	Source of life,
All	We turn to you.
Leader	Saviour of life,
All	We turn to you.
Leader	Sustainer of life,
All	We turn to you.
Leader	Love before time,
All	We adore you.
Leader	Love in darkest time,
All	We adore you.
Leader	Love in this time,
All	We adore you.

Intercession

Reader Father, you bring worlds to birth.
You bring us to birth and you affirm us.
We bring to you unaffirmed aspects of ourselves
and unaffirmed people in the world.

People, or aspects of ourselves, may be offered

Reader Father affirm them.
All Father, affirm them.

Reader Saviour, you reach into our brokenness
and make us whole.
You reach out to those who are alienated
and bring them home.
We pray for broken and alienated people.

Names may be mentioned

Reader Saviour, bring them home.
All Saviour, bring them home.

Reader Spirit, you permeate all creation and renew
the springs of life.
We pray for those who are parched.

Names may be mentioned

Reader Spirit, renew them.
All Spirit, renew them.

Leader Eternal God and Father,
you create us by your power
and redeem us by your love:
guide and strengthen us by your Spirit,
that we may give ourselves in love and service
to one another and to you.
Through Jesus Christ our Lord.
All Amen.

There may be free prayer and singing

Leader Into the Sacred Three I immerse you.
Into their power and peace I place you.
May their breath be yours to live.
May their love be yours to give.

Midday Prayer for Trinity

Leader   Open our eyes to see you reflected all around us:
in the sun that is fire, light and warmth;
in the water that is stream, ice and drink;
in parents who make love and conceive;
in our work and rest and care.

Reader   God said:
Let us make human beings in our likeness.

Genesis 1:26a

Leader   Thank you for the little trinities that reflect to us
your nature:

Females   For love-making, conceiving and nurturing;

Males   For young and old, male and female
enjoying life together;

All   For the fellowship of nationalities, airwaves,
and sport.

*There may be shared or silent reflection or the
litany for use in a personal vigil may be used*

Reader   Glory to the Birther,
glory to the Son,
glory to the Spirit.

Leader   In our journeying this day,
keep us, Father, in your way.
In our play and in our work,
guide us, Saviour, by your word.
In our thoughts and in our talk,
may we, Spirit, with you walk.
In our friendships let us be
in the Blessed Trinity.

There may be free prayer or singing

Leader   The blessing of the Source be yours.
The blessing of the Saviour be yours.
The blessing of the Spirit be yours.
The blessing of the Three of limitless love
pour upon you,
mildly and generously,
hour by hour.

Evening Prayer for Trinity

Leader	The Three who are over my head;
All	The Three who are under my tread;
Leader	The Three who are over me here;
All	The Three who are over me there;
Leader	The Three who in heaven do dwell;
All	The Three in the great ocean swell;
Leader	Pervading Three, Oh be with me.
All	Pervading Three, Oh be with me.

There may be singing

Reader	Psalm 85; 90; 113; 115; 146; *or* 147
Leader	For my shield this day I call: a mighty power, the Holy Trinity.
All	Faith in the Three, trust in the One, creating all through love.
Leader	In faith I trust in the Father of all:
All	He's my refuge, a very strong tower.
Leader	For my shield this day I call:
All	Christ's power in his coming, Christ's power in his dying, Christ's power in his rising.
Leader	For my shield this day I call: the mighty Spirit who breathes through all.
All	Faith in the Three, trust in the One, making all through love.
Reader	Isaiah 59:15b-21 *or the Old Testament reading of the day*

Leader The Father is always present.
The Son is always self-giving.
The Spirit is always outgoing.
Forgive us for failing to reflect their likeness.

*A silence, a declaration of forgiveness,
mime or music may follow*

Reader Mark 1:1-11 (on Trinity Sunday) *or the New
Testament reading of the day*

*There may be recital of a creed, teaching,
sharing, creative activity or singing*

Leader Glory to you, Birther, glory to you.
Glory to you, Saviour, glory to you.
Glory to you, Spirit, glory to you.

Birther, who brought worlds into being,
bring to birth what you purpose for us.

*If there is guided or free prayer, pray for
good things to be brought to birth*

Saviour, who reconnected an estranged world
to its Source,
reconnect us to the Source of our being.

*If there is guided or free prayer, pray for
estranged facets of God's world to be reconnected*

Spirit, who breathes through everything that lives,
breathe fullness of life into us.

*If there is guided or free prayer, pray for withered
people and places to be restored to fullness of life*

Triune God, who delights to bring diversity
in unity,
bring unity to our diversity.

If there is guided or free prayer, pray for groups and peoples to reflect God's unity in diversity

Leader We give you thanks for the little trinities
that reflect your nature to us in community:
for the man and wife who make love and conceive;
for different ages and races at one in recreation.

Triune, you call us to reflect your unity
in diversity.
We pray for places where community
has been destroyed;
may people turn to you,
and community grow again.

May the love of the Three give birth
to new community.
May the life of the Three give birth
to new creativity.
May the oneness of the Three give birth
to a new unity.

There may be free prayer and singing

May you bear the marks of the friendship
of God.
May the Three of limitless love animate you
and each one you shall meet.

All Sacred Three, may your Friendship be encircling
home and family.

Trinity Night Prayer

*A chant, such as Gloria, gloria, in excelsis Deo
may be sung between sentences*

Reader   I light this candle in the name of the Creator
who birthed the world and breathed life into me.

Chant

First   I light this candle in the name of the Saviour
who entered the world and stretched out his
hand to me.

Chant

Second   I light this candle in the name of the Spirit
who pervades the world and fills me.

Chant

Third
All   We light three lights for the Trinity of love:
God above us,
God beside us,
God beneath us.

Fourth   Father, cherish me,
Son, cherish me,
Spirit, cherish me,
Three all-kindly.

Fifth   God make me holy,
Christ make me holy,
Spirit make me holy,
Three all-holy.

Sixth   Three aid my hope,
Three aid my love,
Three aid my eye,
Three all-knowing.

There may be singing

Reader *The following or another psalm may be read*

Answer me when I call, O God,
for you are the God of justice.
You set me free when I was hard-pressed:
be gracious to me now and hear my prayer.

Prayers may be offered by whoever wishes

Many are asking: 'Who can make us content?'
The light of your countenance has gone from us,
O God.

Yet you have given my heart more gladness
than those whose corn and wine increase.
I lie down in peace, and sleep comes at once,
for in you alone, O Lord, do I dwell unafraid.

From Psalm 104 – version by Jim Cotter

Leader Our dear ones bless, O God,
in every place where they are,
especially . . .

Names may be mentioned

The grace of our Lord Jesus Christ,
the love of God,
and the fellowship of the Holy Spirit
be with us all.

There may be free prayer or singing

Leader Day has ended;
All Father, guard us sleeping.
Leader Night has come;
All Saviour, guard us sleeping.
Leader Our minds need calm;
All Spirit, guard us sleeping.

Leader	Look on us, Lord;
All	Father, guard us sleeping.
Leader	Warm us, Lord;
All	Saviour guard us sleeping.
Leader	We rest in you, Lord;
All	Spirit, guard us sleeping.

Reader As I enter into sleep,
keep my soul, O Father, keep.
As I enter into rest,
renew my frame, O Saviour blessed.
When I wake with work to do,
Holy Spirit, see me through.
Holy Three, my shield, my wall,
be my rest, my joy, my all.

Leader May the blessing of the Son
help you do what must be done.
May the Spirit stroke your brow
as weary down to sleep you go.
May the Father mark your rest,
empower you for tomorrow's test.

Ramon Beeching

All We will lie down this night in the fellowship
of the glorious Father.
We will lie down this night in the fellowship
of Mary's Son.
We will lie down this night in the fellowship
of the aiding Spirit.
We will lie down this night with the Three of love.

Creative Activities for Trinity

1. Read through the intercessions in Morning Prayer; then walk around the streets and make a list of everything that reflects the Trinity.

2. Prepare prayers, role-play or pictures that reflect what you have observed.

3. Display a clover leaf or shamrock (which St Patrick is thought to have used to illustrate the Trinity) cut out of ribbon. Give each person one to pin to his or her clothing.

4. Find a leaf of a tree that has three points (for example, the maple leaf) and make a display.

5. Light three candles in a circle.

6. A bowl of water is placed where all can see. A leader dips a hand into the water and makes the sign of the cross over another person, using the words below. As people queue at the bowl that person does the same for the next person and so on. More than one bowl may be used if necessary.

May the Creator come into your head that you, too, may create.

The person's forehead is signed with water

May the Saviour come into your heart, that you, too, may serve.

The person's heart is signed with water, lightly with the tip of a finger, where appropriate

May the Spirit come into your lips that you, too, may converse.

The person's lips are signed with water

When the signing with water is completed the leader says:

May God give you all:
love to create,
love to serve
and love to converse,
so that you may reflect the Trinity on earth
and commune with the Trinity in eternity.

Remembrance of Saints, Ancestors and War Dead

This season begins with All Hallow's Eve (31 October), All Saints (1 November) and All Souls (2 November), and continues until Remembrance Sunday, the second Sunday in November. This is generally the Sunday nearest to 11 November, the day the First World War ended. Remembrance of Ancestors is appropriate any time during this season, especially on 31 October or 2 November.

A Candle-lighting

For use between All Hallow's Eve (31 October) and Remembrance (11 November)

First   In the darkness of this passing age
your saints proclaim the glory of your kingdom.
Chosen as lights in the world, they beckon us on
as we journey towards the greater light of Christ.

A large candle is lit

Second   The Lord is our light and salvation.
Whom then, shall we fear?
All   In your light we shall see light.
Second   In your light even the darkness is not dark.
Whom then shall we fear?
All   In your light we shall see light.
Second   The light shines for ever.
Whom then shall we fear?
All   In your light we shall see light.

A smaller candle is lit

Third   I light this in remembrance of our ancestors.
All   Gatherer of souls, may we, with them,
commune with you.

Pause
A smaller candle is lit

Fourth   I light this in remembrance of the great souls
of the world.
All   Ennobler of souls, may we, with them,
reflect your glory in the world.

Pause
A smaller candle is lit

Fifth   I light this in memory of those who have fallen
             in war or violent acts.

All   Comforter of souls, may their desires and ours
             be fulfilled in you.

Pause

First   We bless you our great God.
             You have raised up for us a mighty Saviour.
             You promised through your prophets
             to show mercy on our ancestors,
             and to remember your holy covenant.
             In your tender mercy the dawn from on high
             shall break upon us
             to shine on those who dwell in darkness
             and the shadow of death
             and to guide our feet into the way of peace.

                    Selected from Luke 1:68-79

All   Bring us with your saints to glory everlasting.

All Hallow's Eve

The Eve of All Hallows (or All Saints' Day) has passed into popular usage as Halloween and has developed a dynamic in twenty-first-century culture that deserves adequate matching Christian liturgy.

'Nights of Light' take the form of vigils followed by Eucharists or veneration of the Blessed Sacrament. At 'Angels' parties', people may dress up as particular angels or as historical saints. At household or church meals, stories of natural or spiritual ancestors are recounted.

This material is designed for the northern hemisphere, where Halloween coincides with the coming of dark nights. We recommend that in the southern hemisphere this is used at a similar period.

Morning Prayer
for All Hallow's Eve

Proclamation

Leader   We come into the presence of the Creator of lights.
We come into the presence of the Saviour from ills.
We come into the presence of the Spirit of power.

Reader   We arise today in the power of God
who flings stars into space.
We arise today in the strength of Christ
who scatters the dark.
We arise today in the strength of the Spirit
who sustains us all.

All   We arise today in the soaring of angels,
the victory of saints and the hope of life eternal.

There may be singing

Reader   Psalm 97

Forgiveness

Leader   Light-creator, evil cannot make its home
where you are welcomed in.

All   Forgive us for the places where your light
has been shut out.

Leader   Light-giver, fear and fault-finding have no place
where your love is invited in.

All   Forgive us for the places where your love
has been shut out.

Leader   Light-conductor,
loneliness and self-sufficiency have no place
where your saints are entertained.

All   Forgive us for the places where your saints
have been shut out.

God's Word

Reader	1 Samuel 16:14-23
Leader	God of time, God of the saints:
All	You are stronger than the elements, stronger than the shadows, stronger than the fears, stronger than the spirits and phantoms that assail us.
Reader	Luke 10:17-24

There may be teaching, meditation or creative activity

Proclamation

Leader	With Christ, to whom the spirits were subject,
All	We claim the victory of the Lord.
Leader	With the desert Christians from whom the demons fled,
All	We claim the victory of the Lord.
Leader	With hermits who made wild places safe with prayer,
All	We claim the victory of the Lord.
Leader	With martyrs who vaulted over death,
All	We claim the victory of the Lord.
Leader	With prayer warriors who overthrew the giants of hell,
All	We claim the victory of the Lord.
Leader	With Patrick who freed his land of serpent powers,
All	We claim the victory of the Lord.
Leader	With Columba who rebuked the powers of darkness,
All	We claim the victory of the Lord.

Leader	With Brigid who turned strongholds into havens of peace,
All	We claim the victory of the Lord.
Leader	With Cuthbert, healer and conqueror of the dark places,
All	We claim the victory of the Lord.
Leader	With the saints of this place,
All	We claim the victory of the Lord.

Intercession

Leader   Circle the places that will become disused in the coming season of darkness.

Any may name places

Leader   Circle the places where dark or distracting forces now gather.

Any may name places

Leader   Circle the groups in thrall to phantoms and ghouls.

There may be free prayer and singing

Leader
All   May fears diminish and peace increase,
for yours is the kingdom,
the power and the glory,
for ever and ever.
Amen.

Leader   The shield of Christ be over us:
the shield of the powers to guard us;
the shield of the saints to hearten us.

Midday Prayer
for All Hallow's Eve

Leader For our shield today we call to us
All Strong powers of the angels obeying,
shining presence of the holy and risen ones,
prevailing prayers of godly fathers and mothers.

Leader For our shield today we call to us
All The truths of apostles,
the visions of prophets,
the victories of martyrs.

Leader For our shield today we call to us
All The vigils of hermits,
the innocence of virgins,
the deeds of heroes.

Leader Around us today we gather these forces
to save our soul and body
All From dark powers that assail us,
from false devisings,
from evils within and without.

Reader Psalm 18:1-3

Leader Compassionate God of heaven's powers,
All Screen us from people with evil intentions.
Leader Compassionate God of freedom,
All Free us from curses and spells.
Leader Compassionate God of eternity,
All Free this place from bad influences of the past.

Leader	Circle us, Lord.
All	Keep darkness out,
	keep light within.
	Keep falsehood out,
	keep truth within.
Leader	Circle us, Lord.
All	Keep evil out,
	keep good within.
	keep fears without,
	keep trust within.

Anyone may repeat the circling prayer for various places, such as

Circle this city/village, Lord . . .
Circle our . . . (*building*), Lord . . .
Circle our schools, Lord . . .
Circle our homes, Lord . . .
Circle . . .

Reader At the name of Jesus, every knee shall bow,
in heaven, on earth and under the earth,
and every tongue shall confess
that Jesus Christ is Lord.

Philippians 2:10-11a

There may be singing or silent prayer

The Lord's Prayer

Leader Be with us now, Lord, in the middle of the day.
Keep us in the presence, the power and the peace
of God.

All May the saints and the angels watch over us.

Evening Prayer
for All Hallow's Eve

Leader	God of time,
	God of eternity,
	God of the saints,
All	You are stronger than the elements,
	stronger than the shadows,
	stronger than the fears.

There may be singing

God's Word

Reader	Psalm 11
Leader	Christ Jesus, though you were in the form of God
	you did not cling to equality with God.
All	You emptied yourself,
	taking the form of a servant;
	you were born in human likeness.
Leader	Being found in human form
	you humbled yourself
	and became obedient, even to death on a cross.
All	Therefore God has highly exalted you
	and given you a name above every other name:
Leader	That at the name of Jesus every knee should bow,
	in heaven and on earth and under the earth,
All	And every tongue confess
	that Jesus Christ is Lord,
	to the glory of God the Father.
	For ever and ever.
	Amen.

Philippians 2:6-11

Reader	Isaiah 43:1-10
Leader	With Christ, to whom the spirits were subject,
All	We claim the victory of the Lord.
Leader	With the desert Christians from whom the demons fled,
All	We claim the victory of the Lord.
Leader	With hermits who made wild places safe with prayer,
All	We claim the victory of the Lord.
Leader	With martyrs who vaulted over death,
All	We claim the victory of the Lord.
Leader	With prayer-warriors who overthrew hell's great might,
All	We claim the victory of the Lord.
Leader	With Patrick who freed his land of serpent powers,
All	We claim the victory of the Lord.
Leader	With Columba who rebuked the powers of darkness,
All	We claim the victory of the Lord.
Leader	With Brigid who turned strongholds into havens of peace,
All	We claim the victory of the Lord.
Leader	With Cuthbert, healer and conqueror of the dark places,
All	We claim the victory of the Lord.
Leader	With the saints of this place,
All	We claim the victory of the Lord.
Leader	We place into your hands the places that will be little used in the season of darkness and cold.
Reader	Revelation 21:1-8

Thanksgiving

All   Glory and honour and power are yours by right,
O Lord our God,
for you created all things and by your will
they have their being.
Glory and honour and power are yours,
O Lamb who was slain,
for by your death you set folk free for God
from every language, tribe and people,
to make them a kingdom of priests
to stand and serve our God.
To God who sits on the throne, and to the Lamb,
be praise and honour, glory and power,
for ever and ever.
Amen.

Echoes Revelation 5

*There may be creative activity, teaching, meditation
or singing*

Intercession

Leader   We place into your hands the season we leave
behind.

Any may name activities

We place into your hands winter's patterns,
which you call us now to live.

There may be a pause

May fears diminish and peace increase
in the people and places we now name.

*Names of people and places may be spoken
spontaneously or in prayers prepared earlier*

Leader   May fears diminish and peace increase
in the places and people we have named,

All   For yours is the kingdom, the power and the glory,
for ever and ever.
Amen.

Leader   The shield of Christ be over us,
the shield of the angels to guard us,
the shield of the saints to hearten us,
the shield of life eternal.

All   The God of life go with us
to protect us from ill,
to keep our hearts still,
to strengthen our will.

Night Prayer for All Hallow's Eve

Leader   The shield of God be with us this night:
the strong powers of the angels obeying,
the glorious company of the holy and risen ones,
the prayers of the fathers and mothers,
the visions of prophets,
the deeds of steadfast believers.

All   From dark powers that assail us,
from false words that ensnare us,
from fears that invade us,
the shield of Heaven protect us.

There may be singing

Reader   Psalm 16

First   O Christ, Son of the living God,
may your holy angels guard our sleep.
May they watch over us as we rest
and hover around our beds.

Second   Let them reveal to us in our dreams
visions of your glorious truth,
O High Prince of heaven,
O High Priest of the holy ones.

Third   May no dreams disturb our rest
and no nightmares darken our dreams.
May no fears or worries delay our willing,
prompt repose.

Reader   Hebrews 12:1-2, 22-24; Revelation 7:9-17;
Matthew 5:1-10; *or* 1 John 3:1-3

There may be praise enthroning Christ and
displacing all that does not bow the knee to him.
This may be interspersed with arrow prayers, words
or other scriptures, or the following may be sung

Before the ending of the day,
Creator of the world, we pray
that you, with steadfast love, would keep
your watch around us while we sleep.

From evil dreams defend our sight,
from fears and terror of the night.
Tread underfoot our deadly foe
that we no sinful thought may know.

O Father, this we ask be done
through Jesus Christ, your only Son,
and Holy Spirit, by whose breath
our souls are raised to life from death.
Amen.

Leader	God of strength, God of eternity, God of the saints,
All	You are stronger than the shadows, stronger than the spirits, stronger than human ill-will.
Leader	With John the loved disciple who soars like an eagle,
All	We rest in life eternal.
Leader	With Ninian of the shining Household of Faith,
All	We rest in life eternal.
Leader	With Brigid, midwife of faith to the people,
All	We rest in life eternal.
Leader	With Aidan, gentle shepherd and apostle of England,
All	We rest in life eternal.

Leader   With Hilda, bright jewel of the Church,
gatherer of the faithful,

All   We rest in life eternal.

Leader   With Cuthbert, healer and conqueror
of the dark places,

All   We rest in life eternal.

*This may be followed by music or by silence during
which other words from God may be spoken
spontaneously . . .*

Leader   Circle the places where the dark forces gather.

Places may be named

Circle places of fear.

Places may be named

Circle our dear ones, O God, and keep them
in every place where they are.

People may be named

All   May the great and strong heavenly army
encircle them all with their outstretched arms,
to protect them from the hostile powers,
to put balm into their dreams,
to give them contented, sweet repose.

Leader   We make the sign of the cross of Christ *(make
sign)*.
O Christ of the dying and of the victorious
rising,

All   Your cross between us and all things fearful,
your cross between us and all things
coming darkly towards us,
your cross be our sure way from earth to heaven.

Leader   May your cloud of witnesses who shine so brightly enfold us as we sleep.

All   The saints of God to will us,
the peace of God to still us,
the love of God to fill us,
tonight and for ever.
Amen.

Creative Activities
for All Hallow's Eve

1. Organise a procession, holding banners or intercession sticks, to walk round the building and its precincts, claiming protection from and the victory of Christ over all powers of evil.

2. Form a circle and use the circling prayers.

3. Hold an angel party, in which people dress up as, or tell stories of, great Christian witnesses or tell of angel experiences.

4. Hold a vigil or keep a candle burning throughout the night to represent the light of Christ and the prayers of the saints in glory.

5. Display photographs or mementos of ancestors.

6. Display the icon of Christ descending into hell to release the trapped spirits.

7. Hold a prayer walk holding hollowed figures of saints made from large vegetables or other materials with lights inside them.

8. Hold a 'Reverse Trick or Treat'. Knock on doors offering residents a treat – this could be a biscuit, cake, artefact or greetings card in the shape of a saint.

All Saints

For use at any time, particularly the week following Pentecost, 13 May or 1 November.

In the Celtic tradition, and generally in the early Church, a Christian who had influenced many others to live holy lives was declared to be a saint at his or her funeral, and was commemorated on the anniversary of their birth into heaven; that is, on the day of their death.

It was soon realised that there is great value in celebrating from time to time the whole community of these holy people, and including in their number those about whom not enough is known to warrant a commemoration day of their own. St Ephrem of Syria (d. 373) encouraged this. By the time of St Chrysostom (d. 407) this celebration was assigned to the first Sunday after Pentecost, and the Eastern Orthodox Church retains this day still. In the West, in the time of the Celtic Mission it was celebrated on 13 May but in the eighth century it was transferred to 1 November.

Morning Prayer for All Saints

Leader We call on the Creator of lights.
    We call on the Shaper of saints.

Leader We arise today
All   In the glorious company
    of the holy and risen ones,
    in the prayers of the fathers and mothers,
    in the truths of apostles.

Leader We arise today
All   In the visions of prophets,
    in the victory of martyrs,
    in the vigils of hermits.

Leader We arise today
All   In the innocence of virgins,
    in the courage of heroes,
    in the friendship of those
    in love with the King of life.

God's Word

Reader Psalm 112:1-9

Leader Light-creator,
    evil cannot make its home
    where you are welcomed in.
All   Forgive us for the places where your light
    has been shut out.
Leader Light-giver,
    fear and fault-finding have no place
    where your love is invited in.
All   Forgive us for the places where your love
    has been shut out.

Leader	Light-conductor, loneliness and self-sufficiency have no place where your saints are entertained.
All	Forgive us for the places where we have shut them out.

There may be silence or an assurance of forgiveness

Reader	Wisdom 5:14-16 *or* Jeremiah 31:31-34

Proclamation

Leader	With John the loved disciple who soars like an eagle,
All	We claim the victory of the Lord.
Leader	With the desert fathers who were weaned from selfishness,
All	We claim the victory of the Lord.
Leader	With Ninian of the shining Household of Faith,
All	We claim the victory of the Lord.
Leader	With Illtyd, holy and learned sage,
All	We claim the victory of the Lord.
Leader	With David, flame and faith-builder of Wales,
All	We claim the victory of the Lord.
Leader	With Patrick, slave of Christ and apostle of the Irish,
All	We claim the victory of the Lord.
Leader	With Brigid, midwife of faith to the people,
All	We claim the victory of the Lord.
Leader	With Mungo, faithful pilgrim and founder of communities,
All	We claim the victory of the Lord.
Leader	With Columba, Christ's giant of the Isles,
All	We claim the victory of the Lord.
Leader	With Aidan, gentle shepherd and apostle of England,
All	We claim the victory of the Lord.

Leader	With Hilda, bright jewel of the Church, gatherer of the faithful,
All	We claim the victory of the Lord.
Leader	With Cuthbert, healer and conqueror of the dark places,
All	We claim the victory of the Lord.
Leader	With the saints of this place,
All	We claim the victory of the Lord.
Leader	*Names of local or other saints may be added*
All	We claim the victory of the Lord.

Reader Therefore,
with all this host of witnesses encircling us,
we must strip off every handicap,
strip off sin with its clinging folds
to run our appointed course with steadfastness,
our eyes fixed upon Jesus as the pioneer
and perfection of faith.

Hebrews 12:1-2a

There may be teaching, creative activity or singing

Thanksgiving

Reader We thank you that in your saints of yesterday
and today
we see the many-splendoured facets
of human life flowing in its fullness.
We thank you for those who give their all
in the service of others,
for those who overcome heroic odds
with nobility of spirit,
for those who are gracious in defeat
and magnanimous in triumph,
for those who are content with the little things,
for those who show us how to truly love.

Intercession

Spurred on by them we offer you our talents,
our temperaments,
our tasks,
our trials,
our triumphs.

There may be silence, free prayer and singing

Leader Keep us worthy of our calling
that we may come with your saints to glory
everlasting.

Midday Prayer for All Saints

First   On this day of the saints of life,
send the dew that makes faith grow strong;
establish in our beings the law of eternal love.

Second   On this day of the saints of power,
quell the wrath of the squalls that break;
be with us in the eye of the storm,
your compass in our hearts.

Third   On this day of the saints of virtue,
be with us in our tasks;
heaven's company sharing our work,
bringing us mercy and peace.

Reader   Psalm 33:1-5

Leader   The victorious ones are with us;
All   We shall overcome.
Leader   They are with us when dark clouds assail;
All   We shall overcome.
Leader   They are with us when the world goes grey;
All   We shall overcome.
Leader   They are with us when the flowers all fade;
All   We shall overcome.
Leader   They are with us when the birds cease to sing;
All   We shall overcome.
Leader   They are with us when the people lie in dust;
All   We shall overcome.
Leader   They are with us now in the heat of the day;
All   We shall overcome.

There may be a song such as We shall overcome

Reader   Luke 6:20-22 *or* Luke 6:20-31

There may be silence or free prayer

Reader   Give to us in our need
the smile of God to cheer us,
the trust of God to lift us,
so we may do in this world you have made
as saints and angels do in heaven.

Evening Prayer for All Saints

Leader   In the darkness of this passing age
                your saints declare your presence
                and bring to us your glory.

All   Glory to God for ever.

Reader   Psalm 52, 112 *or* 117

Leader   Each day and each night that we attune
                to the saints of light,

All   We shall not be downtrodden,
                we shall not be corroded,
                we shall not be enslaved,
                we shall not be abandoned,
                we shall not be left in the dark.

Alleluias or other words may be sung

God's Word

Reader   Zephaniah 3:9-23

Any or all of the following may be said or sung

Leader   We give you thanks for our saints
All   Who shine in the world and light up our way.
Leader   We give you thanks for the midwives
                of the Faith
All   Who shine in the world and light up our way.
Leader   We give you thanks for the martyrs for Christ's
                love
All   Who shine in the world and light up our way.
Leader   We give you thanks for those who fight for
                equality of regard
All   Who shine in the world and light up our way.

Leader	We give you thanks for those who seek the dignity of life and labour
All	Who shine in the world and light up our way.
Leader	We give you thanks for those who foster appreciation of diverse cultures
All	Who shine in the world and light up our way.
Leader	We give you thanks for those who hand on the fire of faith
All	Who shine in the world and light up our way.
Leader	We give you thanks for those who are true shepherds of their people
All	Who shine in the world and light up our way.
Leader	We give you thanks for those who follow holy callings
All	Who shine in the world and light up our way.
Leader	We give you thanks for . . .
All	Who shine in the world and light up our way.
Leader	In union with the angelic beings who sing the eternal song of victory:
All	Holy, holy, holy, is the One who was, and is, and is to come.

Reader	Revelation 7:9-12

Thanksgiving

Leader	Blessed are those who are invited to the feast at the throne of God, who shout out in wonder and praise:
All	Honour and wisdom and power are yours by right, O King of the ages. Glory, thanksgiving and praise belong to you for ever.

There may be singing, meditation, teaching or creative activity

Intercession

Leader God of the watching ones,
who shine so brightly
and beckon us so eagerly:

All Make us strong and holy like them
that we may live more boldly
and glimpse the eternal kingdom.

Leader God of the waiting ones,
as the saints do in heaven
may we do on earth:

All In using our gifts,
in caring for others,
in holy dying.

There may be free or prepared intercessions

Leader Great God of the saints,
we join our prayers with theirs.
Knit us together with those
you have already called.
Hasten the day when we shall be one.

All As they shine,
may we shine;
as they do in heaven,
may we do on earth.

Leader May we walk in their steps
and join them in glory everlasting.

Night Prayer for All Saints

Leader   The shield of God be with us this night:
the glorious company of the holy and risen ones,
the prayers of the fathers and mothers,
the visions of prophets,
the deeds of steadfast believers.

All   From dark powers that assail us,
from false words that ensnare us,
from fears that invade us,
the saints in heaven protect us.

Reader   O Christ, Son of the living God,
may your holy saints guard our sleep.
May they watch over us as we rest
and hover around our beds.

Reader   Let them reveal to us in our dreams
visions of your glorious truth.
May no fears or worries delay
our willing, prompt repose.

Reader   Hebrews 12:1-2, 22-4; Matthew 5:1-10;
1 John 3:1-3; *or* Philippians 2:5-15

There may be singing

Leader   With John the loved disciple who soars
like an eagle,
All   We rest in life eternal.
Leader   With Ninian of the shining Household of Faith,
All   We rest in life eternal.
Leader   With David, flame and faith-builder of Wales,
All   We rest in life eternal.
Leader   With Patrick, slave of Christ and apostle
of the Irish,
All   We rest in life eternal.

Leader	With Brigid, midwife of faith to the people,
All	We rest in life eternal.
Leader	With Columba, Christ's giant of the Isles,
All	We rest in life eternal.
Leader	With Aidan, gentle shepherd and apostle of England,
All	We rest in life eternal.
Leader	With Hilda, bright jewel of the Church, gatherer of the faithful,
All	We rest in life eternal.
Leader	With Cuthbert, healer and conqueror of the dark places,
All	We rest in life eternal.

This may be followed by music or by silence during which anyone may give thanks for a saintly person whose memory they value

Leader May the saints and the Saviour watch over our
loved ones this night,
in every place where they are,
especially . . .

Anyone may mention names

All May the great and strong heavenly army
encircle them all with their outstretched arms,
to protect them from the hostile powers,
to put balm into their dreams,
to give them contented, sweet repose.

Leader	I lie down this night with the Three of Love,
All	And they will lie down with me.
Leader	I lie down this night with the holy and risen ones,
All	And they will lie down with me.
Leader	I lie down this night with the whole company of heaven,
All	And they will lie down with me –

Leader   God, the saints and the angels,
All   Lying down with me.

Leader   With the saints in glory we make the sign
               of the cross of Christ *(make sign)*.

All   May your cross be between us and all things
               harmful;
               your cross light up for us the company of heaven.

Leader   May your cloud of witnesses who shine so brightly
               enfold us as we sleep.

All   The saints of God to will us,
               the peace of God to still us,
               the love of God to fill us,
               tonight and for ever.
               Amen.

Creative Activities for All Saints

1. Display or project a picture or icon of each saint mentioned.

2. Any person may mention a Christian, past or present, whose life or writings have given them inspiration.

3. All light a candle to represent a saint of God who has inspired them.

4. Hold a party at which each person wears the mask of a saint.

Remembrance of Ancestors and All Souls

These patters are for use at any time, but especially in the season of encroaching darkness and on 2 November, All Souls' Day.

In the Celtic tradition the dead are habitually remembered. The later practice in the Western Church, initiated by the Benedictines, of allocating remembrance of dead loved ones to one day, 2 November, was an innovation.

Morning Prayer for Remembrance of Ancestors and All Souls

Leader I arise today
in the presence of a great company;
their Maker shielding them,
their Saviour lighting them,
the Spirit drawing them.

All Blessed are you, Creator and lover of souls:
you uphold us in life and sustain us in death –
one God who mothers us all.

There may be singing

Reader Psalm 42 *or* 43

Leader Father, have mercy on us and forgive us our sins.
All Have mercy upon us.
Leader Saviour, have mercy on those we love
but see no longer.
All Have mercy upon us.
Leader Spirit, have mercy on the souls of all times
and places.
All Have mercy upon us.

Kyrie eleison or other pleas for mercy may be sung

God's Word

Reader Isaiah 25:6-9

Leader Blessed be you, Guardian and God of all
peoples:
you have raised up for us a mighty Saviour.

All   You have come to set your people free.

Leader   The Dawn from on high shall break upon us,
to shine on those who dwell in darkness
and the shadow of death.

All   You have come to set your people free.

Reader   Luke 14:15-24

*This may be followed by sharing, teaching, silence,
singing or creative activity*

Thanksgiving

Leader   We give you thanks for those who,
through their presence or their deeds of love,
have enriched the world by their lives;
especially for our fathers and mothers,
and their parents before them,
for our loved ones,
and those who are our spiritual kin.

Intercession

Leader   On behalf of each ancestor let us pray.

Reader   May the King of seas and stars hear me.
May the Honour of Paradise admit me.
May love never fail.
May God's friendship be with me for ever.

*Echoes Meilyr ap Gwalchmai,
twelfth-century Welsh bard*

Leader   Give rest to your children,
where sin and separation are no more
but light and life everlasting.
You only are immortal, Creator and Maker of all.
We are mortal, formed of earth.

From you we come;
to you we return.
We will give glory to you through ages of ages.
Amen.

All   Your peace be upon us,
one family, knit together in your love.

Leader   Fill us with grateful and loving memories,
and now let us behave gently,
that we may die peacefully,
that our children may stretch out their hands
upon us
as we are laid to rest.

Echoes a prayer from Nigeria

Midday Prayer for Remembrance of Ancestors and All Souls

Leader Remind me, Lord, in the midst of the day
that without my forebears I would not be here.

Calm me, Lord, in the midst of the day,
that I may remember those who have gone before.

Renew me, Lord, in the midst of the day,
with gratitude for those from whom I come.

All Praise Yahweh, all nations.
Extol God, all peoples,
whose faithful love is strong,
whose faithfulness is never ending.

Psalm 117

First Moon, you gave light to our ancestors.
Second Air, you gave breath to our ancestors.
Third Earth, you gave food to our ancestors.
Fourth Water, you gave life to our ancestors.
All Creator of moon and air, earth and water,
it was you who gave our ancestors their being.
From you they came; to you they returned.
Glory to you.

First *(may face east)*
Great Spirit,
as the sun rises in the east,
so our ancestors arose out of your love.

Second *(may face north)*
Great Spirit,
as you shine like the bright North Star,
so our ancestors steered their course by you.

Third   *(may face west)*
Great Spirit,
in the dimness of memory this alone we know:
that as the sun goes to its rest in the west,
so our ancestors went to their rest in you.

Fourth   *(may face south)*
Great Spirit,
our gene pool is yours.
As the sun completes its circle,
so our ancestors who are near to us in time,
and those who are distant,
are all encompassed in your love.

Leader   Jesus said: Blessed are those who mourn;
they shall be comforted.
God of eternity,
from you we come;
to you we go.
Have mercy on those who have gone.
Give peace to we who remain.

Let us keep silence and recollect our ancestors
and those people who, though now dead,
have loved or influenced us.
Let us savour their lives,
complete our farewells
and commend them to God.

Silence or music

High king of the holy angels,
take possession of the beloved soul
and guide it home to the Three of limitless love;
yes, to the Three of limitless love.

Carmina Gadelica, adapted

All   They are yours, O Lord, you lover of souls.

Wisdom 11:26b

Evening Prayer for Remembrance of Ancestors and All Souls' Day

Leader   Keeper of kindreds,
encompass our forebears and our family
in your reconciling arms,
in your strong arms of love.

Reader   Psalm 23 *or* 139:1-18

Reader   Almighty God, Father, Son, and Holy Spirit,
to me the least of saints,
to me allow that I may keep a door in Paradise;
that I may keep even the small door
that is least used,
the stiffest door.
If it be in your house, O God,
that I can see the glory even afar,
and hear your voice,
and know that I am with you, O God.

Columba

There may be singing

God's Word

Reader   The souls of the upright are in God's hands
and no torment can touch them.
The unenlightened regarded their departure
as disaster,
their leaving us as annihilation,
but they are at peace.
If, as it seemed to us, they suffered punishment,
their hope was rich with immortality;
slight was their correction,
great will their blessings be.

God was putting them to the test
and has proved them worthy to be with him.
He has tested them like gold in a furnace
and accepted them as a perfect offering.
They will shine like sparks
that run through the stubble.
They will guide nations, lead peoples
and the Lord will be their King for ever.
Those who trust in God will understand the truth,
those who are faithful will live with him in love,
for grace and mercy await his holy ones,
and he intervenes on behalf of his chosen.

Wisdom 3:1-9

There may be singing or music

Thanksgiving

Leader Eternal God who mothers us all,
sinners find mercy in you and saints find joy.
You hold all souls in life;
the dead as well as the living are in your care.
Thank you for the wonder and variety
of human lives.
We remember in your presence and give you
praise for:

One reader or several may read the following

Reader(s) Wise souls in our land;
those who brought wit, invention or music;
those whose work or care enriched others;
the frail and those frustrated in their hopes;
those who disappointed even themselves;
the quiet and faithful ones;
those who showed courage in triumph or trial;
forgotten souls remembered now by you alone.

Remembrance

Leader   Now we remember loved ones who have passed
on in recent years.

*Names from the Book of Remembrance of the local
faith community or parish may be read; each may
light a candle in memory of a loved one and place
it on a stand or altar.*

*Each or any deceased person may be named and
quiet requiem music may be played or sung. After
each name or group of names a choir or everyone
may sing or say:*

Now, Lord God, receive your servant

and at the end of the naming:

Now, Lord God, receive your servants for whom
you gave your blood.

Leader   May these your servants, shedding those things
that held them back on earth,
now be clothed in eternal beauty.

Reader   Since it was you, O Christ,
who bought each soul –
at the time it gave up its life,
at the time of returning to clay,
at the time of the shedding of blood,
at the time of its last breath.
at the time you delivered judgement –
may your peace be on your ingathering of souls.
Jesus Christ, Son of gentle Mary,
your peace be upon your own ingathering.

*There may be readings, poems or sharing of
memories and singing*

God's Word

Reader   1 Corinthians 15:42-49

There may be singing

Leader   May you be as free as the wind,
as soft as sheep's wool,
as straight as an arrow,
that you may journey into the heart of God.

Night Prayer for Remembrance of Ancestors and All Souls

Leader When shadows lengthen and the departed
return to our thoughts,

All Lord of the dark night of death, be with us yet.

Leader We are mortal, formed from the earth,
returning to dust.

All You alone are immortal, the Creator and Saviour
of all.

Leader As we linger with the shades of memory,

All Heaven's praises pierce graveside tears.

Leader Recall us to your Presence,
touch us with your hope,

All And charge us with your glory.

There may be singing

Reader O being of brightness, friend of light
from the blessed realms of grace
gently encircle me, sweetly enclosing me
guarding my soul-shrine from harm this day.
Keep me from anguish.
Keep me from danger.
Encircle my voyage over the seas.
A light will you lend me
to keep and defend me,
O beautiful Being, O guardian this night.
Be a guiding star above me.
Illuminate each rock and tide.
Guide my ship across the waters
to the waveless harbour side.

Collected by Caitlin Matthews

Reader Wisdom 3:1-5

Leader	The beauty of human life is reduced to dust and we grow sad.
All	Our beginning and our end are by your command, O God.
Leader	Before mortals were born they were known and loved by you.
All	They have their worth eternally in you.
Leader	We remember before you, Immortal God: our fathers and mothers, and their parents in turn; those we were closely bound to, and those more distant who touched us through their lives; friends and relations; those who served you faithfully in their life; those who hurt or harmed us; those who suffered an untimely death; those whose faith is known to you alone; brothers and sisters in Christ; those who inspire us through their lives, their writings, their deeds of love; holy and healing souls.

Any may name deceased loved ones or light a candle in their memory

All	Jesus, Mediator between earth and heaven, through you we share with these our love.
Leader	We entrust them to you because you alone are trustworthy; your compassion knows no end.

All may sing or say

Glory, glory, glory to the Lord,
glory to the Lord God almighty, *(repeat)*
who was, and is, and is to come;
glory, glory, glory to the Lord.

Reader   Jesus said:
This is the will of the One who sent me,
that I should lose none of those
that he has given me.
And I will raise them up at the last day.

John 6:39

Leader   Christ has risen.
Courage you dead!
Death has lost its hold.
The world of the dead is stripped of its power.

All   He will raise us up imperishable.
He will give us resurrection.
We shall know as we are known by you.
Light eternal will shine upon us.

*There may be singing, silence, requiem music or
sharing of thoughts*

Leader   Hear us, merciful Father,
as we remember in love those
whom we have placed in your hands.
Acknowledge the sheep of your own fold,
sinners of your own redeeming.

All   Enfold them in your arms of mercy,
and in the company of the beings of light.

Leader   Tender angels, draw them into your Presence.
Singing angels, lift them into your Presence.

There may be singing

Leader   Enfold them and us in the sleep of all sleep:
the sleep of peace without doubt,
the sleep of true being,
the sleep of life eternal.

All   Amen.

Creative Activities
for Remembrance of Ancestors
and All Souls

1. Display photographs or drawings of ancestors. Their names may be written down and read out.

2. Make notches in a stick to represent different ancestors.

3. Tell stories of ancestors.

4. Make a wreath of rosemary (for remembrance) and ivy (symbol of eternal life).

5. Place a white flower of remembrance upon this wreath or before a cross.

6. Recall a story or memory of an ancestor or of a loved one who has passed away in the past year.

7. Celebrate with fireworks souls who have lit up the local landscape.

National Remembrance of War Dead

In the Celtic Christian tradition remembrance of the dead is encouraged, as is solidarity with the community among whom we live, past and present.

These services focus on those who were killed in war or by other acts of violence. They are for use on any appropriate local or national occasion, such as, in many countries, 11 November and the Sunday following; Anzac Day (25 April) in Australia and New Zealand.

Morning Prayer for the Remembrance of War Dead

Leader   Creator God, who brings one day to a close
and a new day to dawn,
we remember those who gave their lives today
that we might have a tomorrow.

The following may be said or sung

All   O God, our help in ages past,
our hope for years to come,
our shelter from the stormy blast,
and our eternal home.

Under the shadow of your throne
your saints have dwelt secure;
sufficient is your arm alone,
and our defence is sure.

Before the hills in order stood,
or earth received her frame,
from everlasting you are God,
to endless years the same.

A thousand ages in your sight
are like an evening gone;
short as the watch that ends the night
before the rising sun.

Time, like an ever-rolling stream,
bears all its sons away;
they fly, forgotten as a dream
dies with the opening day.

O God, our help in ages past,
our hope for years to come,
be our defence while life shall last,
and our eternal home.

Isaac Watts, based on Psalm 90

Leader Eternal God,
we thank you for the wondrous gift of life
and for the awesome gift of choice.
We honour the immense gift of possibility,
for good or ill,
which you have given to your human family.

Remembrance

Leader Today, in your presence, we remember:
when the lights went out in two world wars
and in many lesser conflicts;
when millions died in foul trenches
or mass genocide;
when six million died in gas chambers;
when thousands died from acts of terror or revenge.

Other tragedies may be mentioned

We mourn for the goodness and wisdom
that died with them;
for the skill and wit that perished;
the learning, the laughter and the leadership
that were lost.
The world has become a poorer place
and our hearts become cold as we think
of the splendour that might have been.

All Lord God of every age, have mercy on us.

If there is a local roll call, the following may be used

Reader   Guardian of all people,
we remember and entrust to your keeping
the following who gave their lives:

Names are read out; photographs, mementos, wreaths, cards
or flowers may be placed before a cross or memorial; poems
or prayers may be read, and children may hold large poppies
or peace banners. These may be blazoned with particular
qualities of fallen heroes that they wish to pass on.

All stand as the following or other words are spoken:

Reader   They shall not grow old,
as we that are left grow old:
Age shall not weary them, nor the years condemn.
At the going down of the sun
and in the morning
we will remember them.

All   We will remember them.

*Silence is kept, music may sound, after which there
may be singing*

God's Word

Reader   2 Samuel 23:13-17; Isaiah 2:1-5; 25:1-9; 26:1-4;
Micah 4:1-5; *or* Wisdom 3:1-9

Leader   War is the price we pay
for the selfishness of peoples;
for greed, pride, and hatreds unattended to.
Let us confess our share in what is wrong
and our failure to build peace based upon good
relationships and just dealings.
Christ, victim of hostility,

All   Have mercy on us.

Leader	Christ, vanquisher of barriers,
All	Have mercy on us.
Leader	Christ, linking us across the shores of treachery and time,
All	Have mercy on us.
Leader	This world is home to one vast human family:
All	We sleep beneath one roof, the starry sky; we warm ourselves before one hearth, the blazing sun.
Leader	Upon one floor of soil we stand, and breathe one air and drink one water, and walk the night beneath one luminescent moon.
All	The children of one God, we are brothers and sisters of one blood, and members in one worldwide family of God.

From the Book of Remembrance,
Cathedral of St Paul the Apostle, Los Angeles

Reader   Luke 23:27-43; Romans 8:31-39; Ephesians 4:25-5:2 *or* Revelation 21:1-7

Thanksgiving

Let us bless God, who has made us and all creation, who in Christ has triumphed over evil and death, whose Spirit is with us to guide and inspire.

All   Thanks be to God.

There may be singing

Leader   For those who endured captivity, torture or death that others might be free; for liberation of many from cruelty of occupation and oppression; let us bless the Lord.

All   Thanks be to God.

445

Leader	For the heroism of those who served
	in armed services or on the home front
	to provide relief, medical care or supplies,
	let us bless the Lord.
All	Thanks be to God.

Leader	For the patient suffering of the inhabitants
	through the time of scarring;
	for the dedication of those who kept alight
	the torch of freedom
	and sustained hope in others.
	Let us bless the Lord.
All	Thanks be to God.

Leader	For the reconstruction of communities
	and the reconciliation
	of peoples of different nationality and creed
	following the years of destruction,
	Let us bless the Lord.
All	Thanks be to God.

There may be singing

Intercession

Reader We pray for an end to the injustices
that become breeding grounds of war.
We pray for the restoration of fellowship
and the building of integrity.
We pray for commitment to the unending
struggle against selfish ways
and the violation of others' dignity.
We pray for that peace which is the fullness
and blossoming of life.

All share together in the Lord's Prayer

Leader Your kingdom come through the growth of
friendship and trust,

All For yours is the kingdom, the power and the glory,
for ever and ever.
Amen.

*There may be singing, a procession to a war
memorial, or creative activity, or the Peace may
be given, as follows:*

Leader The peace of the Lord be always with you.
All And also with you.

Leader Let us give one another a sign of peace.

*All give a customary sign of peace such as a
handshake, kiss or hug, using words such as*

Peace be with you.

There may be singing

Leader Let us go in the Spirit of Christ,
to honour the dead,
to serve the living,
and to build the common good.

Midday Prayer for the Remembrance of War Dead

Leader   Still us, Lord.
In the middle of the day we will remember.

First   We remember the waste of life and wit
and learning.

Second   We remember the love that was never shared.

Third   We remember the torture of body and mind.

Fourth   We remember those who died
without understanding or valour.

Fifth   We remember those who have no grave
to mark their sacrifice.

A candle may be lit and there may be silence

Reader   Lord, you have had mercy on your land;
you have forgiven your people's sins.
Restore us, O God our Saviour.
Make us strong again.
Show us your unfailing love.
Surely you are ready to save those who honour you
and your saving presence will remain in our land?
Love and faithfulness will meet;
justice and peace will come together;
human loyalty will reach up from the earth
and divine righteousness will look down
from heaven.

Verses from Psalm 85

There may be singing

Leader   We give thanks for those who put duty before life.
We give thanks for the loyalty and fortitude
of those who kept the home fires burning
during dark times.

All   We dedicate ourselves
to give our best in service to others,
to use our talents to the full,
to reach out to those who differ from us.

*There may be meditation or sharing. Poppies may
be placed in a bowl or white peace ribbons may be
fixed to clothing*

Reader   Jesus says:
Happy are you who are peacemakers;
you will be called God's children.
My peace I give to you,
not as the world gives do I give to you.

All   Lead us from fear to trust.
Lead us from despair to hope.
Lead us from hate to love.
Lead us from war to peace.
Deep peace of the Son of peace,
fill our hearts, our workplace, our world.

All share together in the Lord's Prayer

The grace of our Lord Jesus Christ,
the love of God
and the fellowship of the Holy Spirit
be with us all, evermore.
Amen.

Evening Prayer for the Remembrance of War Dead

Leader Like candles in the night, they shone
and flickered out.
Lord God be with us yet, lest we forget.

There may be singing

The world has travailed long;
the scars of conflict remain deep within our being:
so many hopes blighted;
so many lives cut down in their flower;
so many attitudes soured and unhealed.

All We confess we have turned our backs on wisdom;
that through our indifference we allow injustice
and resentment to grow in others,
which become the breeding ground of war.

Leader Lord Jesus Christ,
who gave your life that all might live,

All Have mercy on us; Lord, have mercy.

A song asking for mercy may be sung

Reader Psalm 100

Remembrance

Leader Tonight we remember the ravages of war
and violence;
we remember when evil ruled,
intent to destroy the freedom to vote,
to think, to live;
we remember those we know who died
as a result of war or tragedy.

Any may mention names

Leader   We remember too, those whose very names
are lost.

There may be silence, sharing or singing

God's Word

Reader   The whole country was covered with darkness
for three hours. At about three o'clock
Jesus cried with a loud voice,
'My God, my God, why have you forsaken me?' . . .
Jesus again gave a loud cry and breathed his last.
Then the curtain in the Temple was torn in two
from top to bottom. The earth shook,
the rocks split apart, the graves broke open,
and many of God's people who had died
were raised to life.

Selected from Matthew 27:45-52

The sun concealed its proper light;
it lamented its Lord.
A swift cloud went across the blue sky;
the great stormy sea roared.
The whole world became dark,
great trembling came on the earth;
at the death of noble Jesus great rocks burst open.
A fierce stream of blood boiled
until the bark of every tree was red.
It would have been fitting for God's elements –
the fair sea, the blue sky, the earth –
to have changed their appearance,
lamenting their calamity.
The body of Christ exposed to the spear-thrust
demanded harsh lamentation –
that they should have mourned more grievously
the Man by whom they were created.

Blathmac

Intercession

Leader   Still stands your ancient sacrifice.
Lord God of hosts be with them yet.
Receive your children
for whom you shed your blood.
Their destiny on earth was cut short;
grant them eternal fruit in your kingdom.

There may be meditative music, teaching or singing

Still stands your ancient sacrifice:
A humble and a contrite heart.
Lord God of hosts be with us yet,
lest we forget.

All   Lest we forget.

Each of the following may be illustrated by symbols or actions. Each may be read by one reader or several

First   Heal the ancient wound that festers
in humanity's heart.

Second   Salvage hope from the wrecks of time.

Third   May compassion grow in places
where much blood has been shed.

Fourth   Come to those who suffer pain and injustice.

Fifth   Heal those who can barely live
with their memories of injury or loss.

Leader   The communion of the living,

All   Salute the community of the dead.

Leader   Give us wisdom,
give us courage for the living of our lives.
Spur us onwards;
lift us upwards to build a worthy heritage.

There may be teaching and singing

Leader   God of compassion, you have never deserted
your people.
Cover with the shield of your Presence
those who were struck down.
Bind their souls and ours into one communion.

May they and we feel the warmth of being God's
loved ones.
May the saints and the Saviour watch over them
and us.
May God's peace be with us all for ever.

Night Prayer for the Remembrance of War Dead

Leader   As leaves fall to the ground,
we recall the fallen in war.

All   In the barrenness of trees without leaf,
we turn to God immortal.

There may be singing

Reader   Arise, cry out in the dark
as the watches of the night begin;
pour out your heart like water
in the presence of the Lord.

Lamentations 2:19a

Leader   We remember the slain, the forgotten
and the forlorn.
Let us name them now, in silence or aloud.

Any may mention names

On those who were snatched from earth
by violent death,

All   Holy Jesus, grant rest eternal.

Leader   On those whose sleep is stolen by the ravages
of memory,

All   Holy Jesus, grant rest eternal.

There may be a pause or meditative music

Leader   We lie down this night surrounded by the
guardian angels of those who have died.

All   May their angels and ours encircle us all.

Reader   We lay down this night our selfishness and pride,

All   And any ill-will
towards those who have caused us grief.

Reader   Revelation 21:1-7 *or another reading*

Leader   As the sun sets upon us,
All   It rises on our kin beneath an eastern sky.
Leader   All humankind are one vast family;
All   This world our home.
Leader   Christ, linking us across the shores of treachery and time,
    give us your peace this night:

All   Peace between victor and vanquished;
    peace between rich and poor;
    peace between children and old folk;
    peace to the one at the door.

Leader   In each hidden thought our minds start to weave,
All   Be our canvas and our weaver.
Leader   In each wounded memory to which we cleave,
All   Be our counsel and our healer.
Leader   We lie down this night
    with the Three of Forgiving Love.
    The fragments of our lives we lay now
    at their feet.
All   May the saints and the Saviour watch over us.
    May we sleep in deepest peace.

Creative Activities for the Remembrance of War Dead

1. Wear a red poppy as a reminder of those who shed blood in war. (The disturbance caused to the soil by war activities often causes poppies, which are a symbol of Remembrance throughout the Commonwealth, to flower and proliferate.)

2. Create a cross made of wood and invite any person who wishes to attach a poppy to it.

3. Wear a white ribbon as a sign that the best memorial to those who died is a commitment to build peace.

4. Keep two minutes silence.

5. Play 'The Last Post' on a trumpet, organ or recorded disc.

6. Display pictures or project footage of tragedies in time of war or peace.

7. Visit a local war memorial.

8. In the southern hemisphere, hold a dawn service.

APPENDIX

Music

There is such a diversity of music available for hymns, songs, chants and dance that we do not include more than a few suggestions in the text as indicated in the following index:

Some Psalms

Psalm 1

First   Happy are those who heed neither the words
nor the ways of the godless,
whose delight is in God's law
on which they meditate day and night.

Second   They are like trees planted by streams,
which yield their fruit every season.
Their leaves do not wither;
they flourish in all they do.

First   The godless are not so.
They are like refuse blown about by the wind.
They are like wrongdoers who fail
to fool a court of justice
Even if they sidle in with those who do right,
they are exposed for what they are.

Second   The way of the godless will come to nothing,
but God looks after the path of those
who do right.

Psalm 16:9-12

Leader   I keep the Lord always before me;
All   Because you are at my right hand,
I shall not be moved.

Leader   I keep the Lord always before me;
All   Therefore my heart is glad, and my soul rejoices;
my body also rests secure.

Leader   I keep the Lord always before me;
All   For you do not give me up to destruction
or let your faithful ones see the Pit.

Leader   I keep the Lord always before me;
All   You show me the path of life. In your presence
there is fullness of joy.

| Leader | I keep the Lord always before me; |
| All | In your right hand are pleasures for evermore. |

Psalm 23

First	God is my shepherd,
	who refreshes me in green pastures,
	restores me by quiet waters,
	and leads me to the right ways.
Second	With God I lack nothing I truly need.
First	Even though I walk through the valley
	of the shadow of death,
	I will fear no evil, for you are with me,
	your protecting staff comforts me.
Second	With God I lack nothing I truly need.
First	You prepare a feast for me
	even when hostile people surround me.
	You anoint me with oil and my life overflows.
Second	With God I lack nothing I truly need.
All	Surely goodness and mercy shall follow me
	all the days of my life,
	and I will dwell in your presence for ever.

Psalm 24

Leader	The earth belongs to God,
	as do all things and people who live on it.
	Out of the fluid cosmos God created
	its firmness.
First	Who may ascend to the high dwelling of God?
Second	Whoever is clean of heart
	and whoever does not cling to what is false
	will receive the Almighty's blessing
	and the Saviour's embrace.

	Such are those who seek the face of our forebears' God.
All	Open up the gates that the King of glory may come in.
First	Who is the King of glory?
Second	The Immortal God, mighty and strong, is the King of glory.
All	Open up the gates that the King of glory may come in.
First	Who is the King of glory?
All	The Eternal One of all power is the King of glory.

Psalm 63

First	O God, I long for you from early morning; my whole being desires you. Like a dry, worn-out and waterless land my soul is thirsty for you.
Second	Let me see you in the place of prayer; let me see how glorious you are. Your constant love is better than life itself, and so I will praise you. I will give thanks as long as I live.
First	I will raise my hands to you in prayer. My soul will feast and be satisfied, and I will sing glad songs of praise to you.

Psalm 65

All	All praise to you, O God. We give honour to you who answers our prayer.
Reader(s)	When corruption threatens to destroy us, you forgive our failings. You are the hope of the earth and the farthest seas.

By your strength you established the mountains.
You are clothed with might.
You silence the roaring of waves and sea.
You silence the tumult of the peoples.
Those who live at earth's furthest bounds
are awed by your signs.
You make the gateways of the morning
and evening shout for joy.
You visit the earth and water it,
you greatly enrich it.
The river of God is full of water.
You provide the people with grain
you have prepared.
You soften the earth with showers
and bless its growth.
You crown the year with your goodness;
your ways overflow with richness:
the desert pastures overflow,
the meadows gird themselves with flocks,
the valleys deck themselves with grain –
they shout and sing together for joy.

All   All praise to you, O God.
We give honour to you who answers our prayer.

Psalm 67

First   God be gracious to us and bless us.
May your face shine upon us.

Second   Make known your ways on earth;
your saving health among all nations.

All   May all the peoples praise you, O God;
may all the peoples praise you.

First   May the nations be glad and sing for joy;

Second   For you rule the peoples justly
and guide the nations upon earth.

All	May all the peoples praise you, O God;
	may all the peoples praise you.
First	Then the land will yield its produce
	and our God will bless us.
Second	You will bless us
	and the ends of the earth will honour you.

From Psalm 84

First	You forgave the sins of your people
	and restored your land, O God.
Second	Restore us, also, O God our Saviour.
	Show us your unfailing love:
	revive us again that we may rejoice in you.
First	I will listen to what the Eternal God,
	who promises us divine peace, will say.
Second	Your salvation is near those who reverence you
	so that your glory may dwell in our land.
First	Love and faithfulness meet together;
	justice and peace embrace.
Second	Faithfulness springs forth from the earth;
	righteousness looks down from heaven.
First	The Eternal God will give us a harvest
	of goodness.
Second	Righteousness prepares the way for you
	to move among us.

From Psalm 104

First	Creator God, how great you are!
	You clothe yourself in light.
	You stretch out the skies like a tent.
Second	Winds are your messengers.
	Flames are your servants.
First	You water the earth.
	You bring food for us from the earth.

Second	How abundant are your works, O God:
	in wisdom have you made them all –
	the creatures teeming the earth.
First	There is the sea, vast and wide;
	innumerable things, small and great,
	live within it.
Second	All these look to you for their food
	in due season.
	When you send forth your Spirit
	they are created
	and you renew the face of the earth.
First	May your glory last for ever.
	May you always have joy
	in what you have created.
Second	May our thoughts always give you pleasure.
	May we always rejoice in you.

From Psalm 144

Men	May our sons be like plants that grow up strong.
All	Happy the people whose God is the Eternal Source.
Women	May our daughters be like pillars which grace a palace.
All	Happy the people whose God is the Eternal Source.
Leader	May our stores be filled with worthy goods.
All	Happy the people whose God is the Eternal Source.
Leader	May creatures and crops grow into well-being.
All	Happy the people whose God is the Eternal Source.
Leader	May our streets be free from clamour and crime.
All	Happy the people whose God is the Eternal Source.

Some Proclamations

A Benediction

Leader	Bless the Lord, all created things;
All	To the Lord be praise and glory for ever!
Leader	Bless the Lord, you uncreated beings;
All	To the Lord be praise and glory for ever!
Leader	Bless the Lord, sun and moon.
All	Bless the Lord, clouds and sky.
Leader	Bless the Lord rain and wind.
All	To the Lord be glory and praise for ever!
Leader	Bless the Lord, cold and heat.
	Bless the Lord, winter and summer.
	Bless the Lord, earth and sea.
All	To the Lord be glory and praise for ever!
Leader	Bless the Lord, all that grows in the ground.
	Bless the Lord, all that swims in the waters.
	Bless the Lord, all that flies in the air.
All	To the Lord be glory and praise for ever!
Leader	Bless the Lord all people on earth.
	Bless the Lord all beings in heaven.
	Bless the Father, Son and Holy Spirit.
All	To the Lord be glory and praise for ever!

From the Septuagint version, book of Daniel

Christ was Revealed in Human Form

All	Christ was revealed in human form,
	shown to be right by the Spirit,
	contemplated by angels,
	proclaimed among the nations,
	believed in throughout the world,
	taken up into heaven.

A very early creed – 1 Timothy 3:18

Christ's Baptism

Leader	The Immortal who bowed the heavens bows his head before a mortal.
All	Glory!
Leader	The Uncreated enters the stream of created life.
All	Glory!
Leader	God becomes one with us, and we are made one with God.
All	Glory!
Leader	Our lost innocence is restored and the world is charged with the grandeur of God.
All	Glory!
Leader	Father-love cascades over the Son; the Spirit pours upon him; God in Trinity is revealed.
All	Glory! Glory, ever and everywhere!

Creed

All   Out of nothing you brought all things into being.
From the four elements you form creation
and crown the year's cycle with seasons.
The spiritual powers tremble before you.
The sun salutes you.
The water-springs serve you.
We thirst for you.

You pour forth the air for breathing.
You establish the earth for sustaining.
You create our souls and give us eternal worth.
You send Jesus for our healing.

The Cross, We Shall Take It

Leader	The cross –
All	We shall take it.
Leader	The Bread –
All	We shall break it.
Leader	The pain –
All	We shall bear it.
Leader	The joy –
All	We shall share it.
Leader	The Gospel –
All	We shall live it.
Leader	The Love –
All	We shall give it.
Leader	The Light –
All	We shall cherish it.
Leader	The dark –
All	God shall perish it.

John Bell

The Drama of Creation

Leader	In the beginning, God made the world:
Women	Made it and mothered it,
Men	Shaped it and fathered it;
Women	Filled it with seed and the signs of fertility;
Men	Filled it with life and with song and variety.

An Easter Anthem

The plague that struck Egypt
passed by the followers of God.
They escaped the tyrant's grip
and passed through the river to freedom.
Christ, the People's Champion, passed through
a death and hell to be yeast of truth and love.

Easter Festival

Leader   Rejoice, heavenly powers!
            Sing, choirs of angels!

All   Christ our King has risen. Alleluia!

Leader   Exult, all creation, around God's throne:
            sound the trumpet of salvation!

All   Christ our King has risen. Alleluia!

Leader   Rejoice, O earth, in shining splendour,
            radiant in the brightness of your King!

All   Christ our King has risen. Alleluia!

Leader   Christ has conquered death!
            Glory fills you!
            Darkness vanishes for ever!

All   Christ our King has risen. Alleluia!

Leader   Rejoice, O Church!
            Exult in glory!
            The risen Saviour shines upon you!
            Let this place resound with joy,
            echoing the mighty song of all God's people!

All   Alleluia!

The Exordium

All praise belongs to God, Lord of Creation,
the Compassionate, the Merciful,
Ruler of Judgement Day!
You alone we worship;
to you we pray for help.
Guide us to the straight path:
the path of those you have graced;
not of those who have incurred your anger,
nor of those who have gone astray.

Glory and Honour

All   Glory and honour and power are yours by right,
O Lord our God,
for you created all things and by your will
they have their being.
Glory and honour and power are yours,
O Lamb who was slain,
for by your death you set people free for God
from every language, tribe and people,
to make them a kingdom of priests
to stand and serve our God.
To God who sits on the throne, and to the Lamb,
be praise and honour, glory and power,
for ever and ever.
Amen.

Echoes Revelation 5

Jesus, Saviour of the World

Leader   Jesus, Saviour of the world, come to us
in your mercy.
All   We look to you to save and help us.
Leader   By your Cross and your life laid down,
you set your people free.
All   We look to you to save and help us.
Leader   When they were ready to perish,
you saved your disciples.
All   We look to you to save and help us.
Leader   In the greatness of your mercy,
free us from our chains.
All   Forgive the sins of all your people.
Leader   Make yourself known as our Saviour
and mighty deliverer.
All   Save us and help us that we may praise you.

Leader	Come now and dwell with us, Lord Christ Jesus.
All	Hear our prayer and be with us always.
Leader	And when you come in your glory,
All	May we be one with you
	and share the life of your kingdom.

Ninian's Catechism

Leader	Happy you who are poor in heart;
All	Yours is the kingdom of God.
Leader	Happy the clear in heart;
All	You will see God.
Leader	Happy you who are gentle;
All	The future belongs to you.
Leader	Happy you who hunger for justice;
All	You will be filled.
Leader	Happy you who weep for the world;
All	You will laugh.
Leader	Happy you peacemakers;
All	You will be called God's children.
Leader	Happy are you when you are defamed or excluded;
All	Leap for joy, your reward in heaven is great.

Out of Nothing

Leader	Out of nothing you created a cosmos.
All	Saviour God, we bless you.
Leader	Out of chaos, you created order.
All	Saviour God, we bless you.
Leader	Out of eternity you created me.
All	Saviour God, we bless you.
Leader	Out of wasteland you created a garden.
All	Saviour God, we bless you.
Leader	Out of a barren womb you brought forth
	a people.
All	Saviour God, we bless you.

Patrick's Creed

Leader We believe, O God of all gods,
    that you are the eternal Maker of life.
    We believe, O God of all gods,
    that you are the eternal Maker of love.

All   We believe, O Lord and God of all people
    that you are the Creator of the high heavens,
    that you are the Creator of the skies above,
    that you are the Creator of the oceans below.

Leader We believe, O Lord and God of all people,
    that you are the One who created our souls
    and set their course,
    that you are the One who created our bodies
    from earth,
    that you gave to our bodies their breath
    and to our souls their possession.

All   God, bless to us our bodies.
    God, bless to us our souls.
    God, bless to us our living.
    God, bless to us our goals.

Simeon's Song

Faithful vigil ended,
watching, waiting, cease:
Master, grant your servant
his discharge in peace.

All your Spirit promised,
all the Father willed,
now these eyes behold it
perfectly fulfilled.

This your great deliverance
sets your people free;
Christ their light uplifted
all the nations see.

Christ, your people's glory!
Watching, doubting cease;
grant to us your servants
our discharge in peace.

Timothy Dudley Smith

The Song of Christ's Glory

Leader   Christ Jesus, though you were in the form of God
you did not cling to equality with God.

All   You emptied yourself, taking the form of a servant;
you were born in human likeness.

Leader   Being found in human form
you humbled yourself
and became obedient, even to death on a Cross.

All   Therefore God has highly exalted you
and given you a name above every other name:

Leader   That at the name of Jesus every knee should bow,
in heaven and on earth and under the earth,

All   And every tongue confess that Jesus Christ
is Lord,
to the glory of God the Father.
For ever and ever.
Amen.

Philippians 2:6-11

A Song of the Wilderness

The wilderness and the dry land shall rejoice,
the desert shall blossom and burst into song.

They shall see the glory of the Lord,
the majesty of our God.

Strengthen the weary hands,
and make firm the feeble knees.

Say to the anxious, 'Be strong, fear not,
your God is coming with judgement,
coming with judgement to save you.'

Then shall the eyes of the blind be opened
and the ears of the deaf be unstopped.

Then shall the lame leap like a hart,
and the tongue of the dumb sing for joy.

For waters shall break forth in the wilderness
and streams in the desert.

The ransomed of the Lord shall return
with singing,
with everlasting joy upon their heads.

Joy and gladness shall be theirs,
and sorrow and sighing shall flee away.

Isaiah 35:1, 2b-4a, 4c-6, 10

Glory to the Father and to the Son
and to the Holy Spirit;
as it was in the beginning, is now
and shall be for ever. Amen.

The Song of Zechariah

Reader We bless you, Lord God of Israel,
coming to ransom your people;

All Raising up saving power
in the family of your servant David,
as you said by the mouth of your prophets
in days of old.

Reader You set us free from oppression,
free from the hands of our foes.
This is your bond of love with our forebears,
your covenant binding for ever;

All Your oath to our father, Abraham,
assuring us that, freed from fear,
delivered from all oppression,
we will serve you in goodness and love
to the end of our days.

Reader This child will be called your prophet.
He will walk in your presence
and prepare the way you will come,
announcing your people's salvation
with pardon for all their sins.

All Through the love in the heart of our God
the Rising Sun will come to us,
shining on those in the dark
who lie in the shadow of death,
and guiding our steps into peace.

or

Leader Blessed are you, Lord, the God of Israel.
You have come to your people and set them free.

All You have raised up for us a mighty Saviour,
born of the house of your servant, David.

Leader	Through your holy prophets, you promised of old to save us from our enemies, from the hands of all who hate us;
All	To show mercy to our forebears and to remember your holy covenant.
Leader	This was the oath God swore to our father, Abraham, to set us free from the hands of our enemies;
All	Free to worship you without fear, holy and righteous before you, all the days of our life.
Leader	And you, child, shall be called the prophet of the Most High, for you will go before the Lord to prepare the way,
All	To give God's people knowledge of salvation by the forgiveness of their sins.
Leader	In the tender compassion of our God the dawn from on high shall break upon us,
All	To shine on those who dwell in darkness and the shadow of death, and to guide our feet into the way of peace.

Te Deum Laudamus

We praise you, O God:
we acclaim you as the Lord;
all creation worships you:
the Father everlasting.
To you all angels, all the powers of heaven:
the cherubim and seraphim,
sing in endless praise,

Holy, holy, holy Lord,
God of power and might:
heaven and earth are full of your glory.

The glorious company of apostles praise you:
the noble fellowship of prophets praise you.
The white-robed army of martyrs praise you:
throughout the world,
the holy Church acclaims you.
Father, of majesty unbounded:
your true and only Son, worthy of all praise,
the Holy Spirit, advocate and guide.
You, Christ, are the King of glory:
the eternal Son of the Father.
When you took our flesh to set us free:
you humbly chose the Virgin's womb.
You overcame the sting of death:
and opened the kingdom of heaven
to all believers.
You are seated at God's right hand in glory:
we believe that you will come to be our judge.
Come then, Lord, and help your people,
bought with the price of your own blood:
and bring us with your saints to glory
everlasting.

Thanksgiving

Glory to the Supreme God,
the Maker, the Saviour, and the Spirit,
who pour out their life for us,
always and for ever.

Unity

In Christ there is no longer Jew and foreigner,
there is no longer slave or free,
there is no longer male or female;
all are one in Jesus Christ.

Sources

Acta Publications, *A Contemporary Celtic Prayer Book* (Chicago: Acta Publications).

Adam, David, *The Rhythm of Life: Celtic Daily Prayer* (SPCK Triangle, 1996).

Carmichael, Alexander (compiler), *The Carmina Gadelica* (Floris Books, 1994).

Church of Scotland, *The Book of Common Order of the Church of Scotland* (St Andrew Press, 1994).

Columba Press, *The Glenstal Book of Prayer* (The Columba Press, 2001).

Costley, Sarah and Charles Kightly, *A Celtic Book of Days* (Thames and Hudson, 1998).

Crowley, Vivianne, *Celtic Wisdom: Seasonal Rituals and Festivals* (Thorsons HarperCollins, 1998).

Curran, Michael, *The Antiphonary of Bangor and the Early Irish Monastic Liturgy* (Irish Academic Press, 1984).

Davies, Oliver, trans., *Celtic Spirituality* (New York: Paulist Press, 1999).

Duncan, Geoffrey, *A World of Blessing: Benedictions from Every Continent and Many Cultures* (Canterbury Press, 2000).

Earle, Mary C. and Sylvia Maddox, *Praying with the Celtic Saints* (Minnesota: St Mary's Press, 2000).

Foster, Raymond, *Called To Be Saints: Readings for Holy Days* (Church in Wales Publications, 1987).

Harling, Per, (ed.), *Worshipping Ecumenically* (World Council of Churches Publications, Geneva).

Hierarchies of Australia, England and Wales, and Ireland, *The Divine Office*, c. 1974, (Collins, 1987).

Matthews, Caitlin, *Celtic Devotional* (Godsfield Press, 1996).

Mowbray, *Celebrating Common Prayer: A Version of the Daily Office, SSF* (Mowbray, 1992).

Northumbria Community, *Celtic Daily Prayer from the Northumbria Community* (HarperCollins, 2000).

O'Leary, De Lacey, *The Daily Office and Theotokia of the Coptic Church* (London: Simpkin, Marshall, Kent & Co, Ltd, 1911).

O'Malley, Brendan (ed.), *A Celtic Primer* (Canterbury Press, 2002).

Perham, Michael (compiler), *Enriching the Christian Year* (SPCK/Alcuin Club, 1993).

Philip Newell, J., *Celtic Benediction: Morning and Night Prayer* (Canterbury Press, 2000).

Plummer, Charles (ed. and trans.), *Irish Litanies* (The Boydell Press, 1962).

Reform Synagogues of Great Britain, *Forms of Prayer for Jewish Worship* (The Reform Synagogues of Great Britain, 1977).

Robson, Pat, *A Celtic Liturgy* (HarperCollins, 2000).

Scott, David, *An Anglo-Saxon Passion* (SPCK, 1999).

Simpson, Ray, *Celtic Daily Light* (Hodder & Stoughton, 1977).

Simpson, Ray, *Celtic Worship Through the Year* (Hodder & Stoughton, 1997).

SPCK, *A Manual of Eastern Orthodox Prayers* (SPCK, 1983).

Taizé Community, *Praise in All Our Days: Common Prayer at Taizé* (Mowbray, 1981).

The *Revised Common Lectionary* was published by the Consultation on Common Texts (a body representative of all major branches of the church in USA and Canada) in 1992. It was adopted by the English Language Liturgical Consultation (ELLC) whose members come from ecumenical associations in English-speaking countries and continents. The Roman Catholic Church, the Anglican Church and most other churches have adopted it, in some cases with minor adaptations. The *Revised Common Lectionary* is truly therefore the lectionary of the world Church.

Ward, Hannah and Jennifer Wild (compilers) *Human Rites* (Mowbray, 1995).

Wild Goose Publications, *A Wee Worship Book: Fourth Incarnation* (Wild Goose Publications, 1999).

Wild Goose Publications, *The Iona Community Worship Book* (Wild Goose Publications, 1992).

Wybrew, Hugh, *Orthodox Feasts of Christ and Mary: Liturgical Texts with Commentary* (SPCK, 1997).

Wybrew, Hugh, *Orthodox Lent, Holy Week and Easter: Liturgical Texts and Commentary* (SPCK, 1995).

Acknowledgements

The publishers wish to express their gratitude to the following for permission to include copyright material in this book:

Andrew Dick, for 'We draw aside . . .', p. 111 © Andrew Dick

Bishop Timothy Dudley-Smith for permission to quote his hymn 'Faithful vigil ended'. Text © Timothy Dudley-Smith in Europe (including UK and Ireland) and in all territories not controlled by Hope Publishing Company.

Michael Mitton, for permission to quote his prayer 'Homemaker God' on p. 198. © Michael Mitton.

The Church of Scotland, for permission to reproduce the prayer 'God of all seasons' on p. 265, *The Book of Common Order of The Church of Scotland* © Panel on Worship, The Church of Scotland.

Boydell & Brewer Ltd, PO Box 9, Woodbridge, Suffolk, IP12 3DF, for permission to reproduce the extract from 'The Dream of the Rood' in *The Anglo-Saxon World* by Kevin Crossley-Holland. © 1994 Boydell & Brewer Ltd.

The Guardian of the Friary, The Society of Saint Francis, Hilfield Friary, Dorchester, Dorset DT2 7BE, for permission to reproduce the words to 'Now while the body, quiet and still' by Brother Ramon SSF. © The Society of Saint Francis.

The Iona Community, for permission to quote the prayer 'The Cross – we take it' by John Bell, from *A Wee Worship Book*. © 1999 Wild Goose Publications, Iona Community, Savoy House, 140 Sauchiehall Street, Glasgow G2 3DH, Scotland.

Copycare Ltd, for permission to reproduce the words on p. 332 to 'Christ as a light' by John Michael Talbot. © Birdwing Music/EMI Christian Music Publishing, Administered by CopyCare, PO Box 77, Hailsham BN27 3EF, UK. E-mail: music@copycare.com.

The Church of England Archbishops' Council, for permission to reproduce the canticle 'A Song of the Wilderness', p. 473. Extracts from *Common Worship: Services and Prayers for the Church of England* are copyright © The Archbishops' Council, 2000, and are reproduced by permission.

The version of the 'Te Deum Laudamus' on p. 475 is copyright © 1988 English Language Liturgical Consultation.

Every effort has been made to trace the owners of copyright material and it is hoped that no copyright has been infringed. Pardon is sought and apology made if the contrary be the case and a correction will be made in any reprint of this book.